Saving Israel

The Unknown Story of Smuggling Weapons
and Winning a Nation's Independence

Boaz Dvir

STACKPOLE
BOOKS

Guilford, Connecticut

Published by Stackpole Books
An imprint of The Rowman & Littlefield Publishing Group, Inc.
4501 Forbes Blvd., Ste. 200
Lanham, MD 20706
www.rowman.com
Distributed by NATIONAL BOOK NETWORK
800-462-6420

British Library Cataloguing in Publication Information available

Library of Congress Cataloging-in-Publication Data available
Names: Dvir, Boaz, author.
Title: Saving Israel : the unknown story of smuggling weapons and winning a nation's independence / Boaz Dvir.
Description: Lanham, MD : Stackpole Books, an imprint of the Rowman & Littlefield Publishing Group, Inc., 2019. | Includes bibliographical references. | Summary: "At the opening of Israel's war for independence in 1948, numerous Americans risked their lives, freedom, and citizenship to prevent what they viewed as a possible second Holocaust; their story is one of a covert operation involving smuggling, evading the FBI and State Department, connections to underground Jewish intelligence and military groups, and acts of personal bravery in purchasing weapons, ferrying them across thousands of miles, and taking them into combat"— Provided by publisher.
Identifiers: LCCN 2019038374 (print) | LCCN 2019038375 (ebook) | ISBN 9780811737265 (cloth) | ISBN 9780811766883 (epub)
Subjects: LCSH: Military assistance. | Israel—History, Military—20th century. | Israel—Armed Forces—History—20th century. | Israel—Defenses.
Classification: LCC UA853.I8 D85 2019 (print) | LCC UA853.I8 (ebook) | DDC 956.04/28—dc23
LC record available at https://lccn.loc.gov/2019038374
LC ebook record available at https://lccn.loc.gov/2019038375

♾️ The paper used in this publication meets the minimum requirements of American National Standard for Information Sciences—Permanence of Paper for Printed Library Materials.

Dedicated to my grandparents, Ozer and Rivka Grundman,
and my brother, Sha'ron Dvir, of blessed memory.

Contents

Preface

THIS BOOK TELLS THE LITTLE-KNOWN STORY OF OPERATION ZEBRA, A secret and illegal 1947–1949 mission to save newborn Israel. But there's a catch: There was no Operation Zebra. At least not officially. That is to say, no such title ever was issued. Instead, ten parts of an American-led effort to prevent the Jewish state's destruction earned individual titles, including:

- Operation Yakum Purkan, September 1947–March 30, 1948: The overseas creation of the Palestinian Jewish community's air transport command
- Operation Balak (also known as the Milk Run), March 31–August 12, 1948: The airlift of Czech arms to the Jewish state
- Operation Hassida, April 1–2, 1948: The first delivery of the Czech weapons
- Operation Duverne Izrael (Czech for "Confidential Israel"), May 1–August 12, 1948: The training of Israeli pilots, aircrews, mechanics, and paratroopers in Czechoslovakia
- Operation Pleshet (a combined air-ground effort), May 29–June 3, 1948: The effort to block the Egyptian advance on the heart of Israel, Tel Aviv
- Operation Navot, June 15–July 15, 1948: The delivery of three B-17 bombers to Israel via Czechoslovakia
- Operation Velvetta I, September 24–October 3, 1948: The attempt to deliver the first six Spitfire fighter planes to Israel from Czechoslovakia
- Operation Avak (Hebrew for "dust"), August 15–October 22, 1948: The airborne supply of besieged Israel Defense Forces (IDF) troops

in the Negev Desert and the aerial support for the IDF push to reclaim this territory

- Operation Velvetta II, December 15–26, 1948: The attempt to deliver twenty-five Czech Spitfires to Israel
- Operation Horev (an air-supported ground effort), December 22, 1948–January 7, 1949: The attempt to besiege the Egyptians in Gaza

After researching these operations for more than a decade, I realized that they made up one overarching effort. They all belonged to an umbrella mission henceforth referred to in this book, and perhaps beyond, as Operation Zebra (OZ).

OZ included several other operations, such as the recruitment, training, and deployment of fighter pilots. But those never received specific titles. They were nameless.

No more. Now they are all OZ.

Why Zebra? Mainly because that was the operation members' code name for Žatec, a Czech town that served as their mission's nerve center. During the most vital part of the operation, all flight routes led to and from Žatec. Zebra.

In addition, the African equid's stripes represented the mind-set of many operation members, particularly the leaders. To them, the creation of a Jewish state in Palestine—an extremely controversial concept at the time and, for many, today—was a black-and-white issue. As far as they were concerned, they were fighting for the purest of causes: providing a haven for Holocaust survivors and protecting the lives of 600,000 Palestinian Jews.

Of course, the Arab-Israeli conflict is far too complex to be black and white. It's relatively easy—once emotions are checked—to spot all the grey in the clash over Palestine during the first half of the twentieth century. The Arabs had valid points:

- In 1947, the United Nations (UN) allocated more than half of Palestine to the Jews despite the fact that they made up only one-third of the population. The other two-thirds—Muslim and Christian Palestinian Arabs—received less than half of the land on which many of them had deep roots.
- Countries such as the United States expected Palestine to do its refugee-settlement work by taking in the majority of the more than

250,000 Jews who survived the Holocaust. President Harry S. Truman failed to convince the British, who controlled Palestine at the time, to let in 150,000 Holocaust survivors.

- It was the Holocaust that drove the world to allow Israel's creation on land the Arabs considered theirs; yet it was the Germans (often with the cooperation of other Europeans), not the Arabs, who murdered two-thirds of their Jewish neighbors.
- The Arabs never inflicted anything like the Holocaust—or the Spanish Inquisition or Russian pogroms—on their Jewish neighbors. This showed that the Jews could live peacefully under an Arab rule in Palestine. There was no need for a Jewish state—and the war that came with it.

OZ members, however, saw it differently. They fought to prevent what they viewed as an imminent second Holocaust. Thus, they considered any moral equivalency between Arab and Jewish positions a matter of diplomatic acrobatics, brazen propaganda, or veiled antisemitism. Mostly tuning out the noise of the international debate, they kept their eyes on their prize: securing a permanent home for the Jewish refugees who had nowhere else to go. These World War II aviators put their lives and freedom on the line to achieve this goal.

Every aspect of their efforts—from the acquisition of arms to the repair of decommissioned US World War II planes to the airlift of Czech weapons to the creation of the Israeli Air Force—deserved its own operational title. However, these diverse efforts made up a singular puzzle: a puzzle that, when completed, showed humanity what a group of young people can do when they put everything on the line.

Why did the OZ members neglect to name their overall mission? This operation had countless moving parts. It lasted nearly two years. Its participants could not have anticipated all the different functions they would undertake. For instance, when they launched Operation Yakum Purkan to create an apparatus for smuggling weapons to the Yishuv (Palestine's Jewish community), they had no idea which or if any country would be willing to break an international embargo against selling arms to the Middle East.

At that point, none of the OZ members could have predicted Operation Balak—during which they brought in guns, ammunition, and fighter planes to newborn Israel from behind the Iron Curtain—much less Operation Zebra as a whole.

At that time, all they could hope was that the Jewish state would be born—and that it would avoid SIDS (sudden infant death syndrome). They went day by day, operation by operation.

Only in retrospect did they participate in Operation Zebra. And yet they did so from Day One.

Introduction

WHEN MY CZECH GRANDMOTHER, WHOM WE CALLED SAVTA, DIED IN HER early fifties at the same Israeli hospital in which I was born eleven years earlier, she took to the grave everything we should have learned about her side of the family.

All we know about Rivka Schindler Grundman is that she was the only member of her family to survive the Holocaust. For instance, we have no idea how many siblings she had and how they died.

We never asked, and she never told us.

We believe she arrived at Auschwitz, like most of the 88,000 Czech Jews sent to the Nazis' largest death camp, in 1944. We know Russian soldiers set her free on January 27, 1945. But we have no details about the months she spent there. Was she forced into sex labor in the camp's brothel? Was she experimented on by Horst Schumann and Carl Clauberg? These SS doctors, who left the twin experimentations to Josef Mengele, tested ways to eliminate Jews before they were born. If they tried to sterilize my Savta—a war crime they committed against hundreds of women by zapping their reproductive organs with X-ray machines—they failed. In 1946, my Savta gave birth to healthy twins, one of whom is my mother.

If my Savta, who never regained her health after Auschwitz II–Birkenau, was going to open up to anyone, it would've been to my younger brother, Sha'ron, and me. A depressed diabetic who tended to be reserved around adults, she let go a little around us. While her husband delivered household goods to grocery stores in the ultra-Orthodox Central-Israel city of Bnei Brak, she joined us in raiding his hidden candy stash, quizzed us about our social life, and smoked forbidden cigarettes. But the Holocaust never crossed her lips.

Our eyes raced from the smoke rings she blew to the Auschwitz serial-number tattoo on her left arm. We were too young to realize that we should have demanded to hear her life story. Instead, we just asked for leftover *cholent*, a potato-beef-bean-and-barley stew drained of any nutritional value by simmering overnight.

My Savta died of diabetic complications on the thirtieth anniversary of Israel's independence. My grandfather, Ozer Grundman, whom we called Saba, took over the *cholent* cooking and found a new hiding place for his Arcor Vienna suckers, which he handed out to kids at his Hasidic synagogue. But he, too, kept mum about his past. We knew that he was raised in Poland by German Jewish immigrants. Moreover, we knew several members of his side of the family escaped the Holocaust because they were our living, breathing uncles and aunts. However, the majority of the facts remained locked away like his candy.

In the late 1980s, when I became a journalist, I made it my top priority to convince my Saba to share his story. Although he had retired by then and had plenty of free time, he refused to be interviewed. I had to resort to a journalistic practice often derided by the public but valued by editors: aggressive reporting. On the first day of my 1991 vacation—a Sunday, which is Israel's Monday—I showed up at his doorstep. With a ready-to-be-clicked pen in one hand and a ready-to-be-filled reporter's notebook in the other, I wore a businesslike expression.

My Saba was unimpressed. He wanted to talk about my marriage/child-rearing prospects.

"Nu," he said, half-asking, half-prodding.

"Nu, you," I said. "Don't you want your future great-grandkids to know how their great-grandfather survived the Holocaust?"

"That," he said, "they should ask God."

My Saba thought I'd be gone after a few hours. I stayed the whole week, shadowing him everywhere he went. We walked to and from his synagogue, where he prayed, studied Talmud, and prompted his fellow congregants to inquire about my marriage/child-rearing prospects. We spent late afternoons in his neighborhood park, where he read me headlines from *Yedioth Ahronoth*, Israel's largest daily paper. It was the only time I ever enjoyed hearing bad news.

During the next evening's Talmud lesson, my Saba and his study-mates explored the possible reasons why the Kabbalistic rabbi Shimon bar-Yochai and his son failed to adjust to the material world after spending twelve years in a Galilee cave engaged in mystical practice.

My Saba suggested that the bar-Yochais' post-cave struggle stemmed from possessing only spiritual knowhow at that point. Their "real-life" skills had faded.

On our way home, I asked my Saba whether his experience was somewhat similar: Did what he learned during the Holocaust apply only to that realm? Did he also have to revive his "real-life" skills after liberation?

My Saba arched his eyebrows.

I doubled down. He admitted that, after the Holocaust, he went through a long, painful readjustment.

When I noted that Savta never fully made the transition, he nodded.

This was the crack I was praying for. He finally saw my hand reaching out across the divide that separates many trauma victims from their loved ones.

During dinner that evening, my Saba started recounting his life story in the kind of suspenseful chronological order that made me forget I knew the ending.

Over the next several days, he described growing up in the picturesque Polish province of Świdnica, imploring his father in the mid-1930s to send him to a religious boarding school in Warsaw, feeling homesick and running away from the Hasidic yeshiva to visit his family, and working during the summer at his parents' grocery store. He talked about serving German customers at the start of World War II, being sent to a labor camp a few months later, repeatedly escaping the Nazis, repeatedly getting caught by the SS, surviving on icicles during a ten-day train ride to Buchenwald in Germany, and weighing about seventy pounds when the US Army liberated him in April 1945. He recalled joining other released skeletons in trying to lift an American soldier in celebratory gratitude, meeting and marrying Savta at a displaced-persons (DP) camp, and relocating with their blonde, blue-eyed babies to a DP camp in Rome.

Although they had the good fortune to avoid living in one of the repurposed former Nazi camps in which the Allies housed many Holocaust survivors, my grandparents floundered after the war. My Saba heard his calling on November 29, 1947, when the United Nations voted to split Palestine between the Arabs and Jews. Viewing it as a directive from God, Saba aimed to join the fight for the creation of a Jewish state.

Savta wondered whether her husband had lost his mind. She had heard that the Arabs rejected the UN plan and vowed to capture the Holy Land in its entirety after Great Britain ended its mandate in May 1948. Along with most of the world, she believed they'd succeed. Although far from military juggernauts, they had so much more firepower than Palestine's 600,000 Jews that they could, as Arab League Secretary-General Abd Al-Rahman Azzam Pasha asserted, "sweep them into the sea."

That's exactly why Saba wanted to go to Palestine: to help the Jews defend themselves. Savta countered that she hadn't survived one Holocaust to sign up for another. When he suggested she was being melodramatic, she quoted a series of clear-intention-of-annihilation comments by Middle Eastern leaders. For instance, the Arab Higher Committee's Jamal Al-Husayni declared, "The Arabs have taken into their own hands the Final Solution of the Jewish problem." He was referring to the Nazi plan to murder every Jewish man, woman, and child.

Al-Husayni and Pasha's confidence stemmed from the glaring arms disparity between the Arabs and Jews. The Jordanians, Egyptians, and Iraqis received the latest in combat equipment—including Spitfire fighters, Mosquito reconnaissance planes, and Matilda tanks—from the British. The Yishuv possessed limited supplies and few weapons: only enough rifles for one out of about three soldiers, bullets for just a few days of fighting, a couple of tanks, few machine guns, paltry artillery, and no air force.

Yet Saba persisted. The German version of the Latin phrase *unicuique suum* plastered across the Buchenwald gate—*jedem das seine*—echoed in his mind. He sought to flip it on its head. "To each his own." No, he told his wife. They must work for the common good and help establish a home for all Holocaust survivors. Besides, he said, she should trust his judgment. He listed several examples of his conscientious decision making, such as refraining from overeating upon his liberation. Several of his bunkmates became violently ill from devouring K-ration meatloaf and chocolate. Two of them never recovered from the ensuing brutal bout of diarrhea that depleted their bodies of the bare minimum on which they had survived. Saba, however, heeded the American doctors' warning.

Any chance Saba had of convincing his wife to move to Palestine evaporated on December 5, 1947, when the United States imposed an arms embargo on the region. This State Department–initiated move, which never stopped the United Kingdom from continuing to arm its Middle Eastern protectorates, threatened to suffocate the Jewish state before it could take its first breath.

The embargo forced the leaders of Palestine's Jewish community—and Saba—to take drastic measures. He "agreed" to go to America. Unaware that they needed visas, Savta assumed the ship they boarded in Italy in May 1948 was bound for New York. She became suspicious when, upon hearing her shipmates cheer at the sight of their destination, she spotted no sign of the Statue of Liberty or the Empire State Building. Disembarking in the Port of Haifa, she prepared to unleash the mother of all tongue lashings on her husband. But she had to shelve her grievances to bid an abrupt farewell to him as a camouflaged lorry whisked him and several other able-bodied men off to war.

Arriving at a Negev Desert outpost, Saba discovered that his platoon of thirty men—several, Holocaust survivors like himself—had only ten guns. They were getting by for the time being because the Egyptians bypassed some Israeli positions as they advanced toward Tel Aviv. Anticipating that the enemy would show up soon enough, my Saba thought his days as an escape artist were coming to an end. He prayed for guns. Any guns.

God, who had ignored so many of Saba's other prayers, answered this one. On a blistering day, a truck delivered crates of rifles and rounds of ammunition.

Gripping his gun, Saba finally felt in control of his destiny. His eyes gravitated to a small engraving on the gun. Could it be? He rubbed his eyes. He pressed his nose against the rifle to examine the insignia.

Yes. It sure was. A German eagle. In its talons, it clutched a pair of swastikas.

Swastikas? I thought. To me, the notion of Israeli troops fighting with Nazi weapons seemed ripped from *National Inquirer* headlines. My Saba assured me that his memory was as sharp as ever. That gun was the only non-religious material possession he ever deeply valued.

"Did it bother you at first?" I asked.

Saba shook his head. He and his fellow soldiers would have been happy with any guns. They were just relieved to have a way to protect themselves, their families, and their new country.

After a rare pause in his storytelling, my Saba turned to me to ask, "Do you know how we got them?"

I had no idea. But, as a journalist, I knew how to find people who would know the answer. I figured it'd take me a couple of days.

The only thing I established on the first day of my inquiry was that the whole Israeli military, not just my Saba's platoon, used Mausers and other Nazi-surplus weapons. But to come up with a complete answer, I had to conduct a great deal more research.

My first break came in 1995 when I wrote an article about WWII veterans to coincide with the fiftieth anniversary of the end of that war. During one of the interviews I conducted, a former US Air Transport Command (ATC) pilot, Leo Gardner, mentioned that after the war, he flew cargo planes for Israel.

"What did you transport?" I asked.

"Weapons," Leo said.

"Were these by any chance Nazi-surplus weapons?"

Leo's eyes sparkled.

In the following years, I spent as much time as I could with Leo. As a retiree, he was more serious about golfing than flying, but he occasionally took a light plane for a spin. Through him, I met another former OZ member living in South Florida. By the time I interviewed former fighter pilot Gideon "Giddy" Lichtman in his Pembroke Pines house, I had become a filmmaker and was making a documentary about the subject, titled *A Wing and a Prayer*, for Public Broadcasting Service.

One interview led to the next. Giddy introduced me to another former OZ fighter pilot, Leon Frankel. I flew to Minneapolis to document his story. One name that kept coming up was Adolph "Al" Schwimmer, who launched and ran OZ. When I called his home in Tel Aviv, his Israeli wife, Rina, answered. She refused to let me speak with him. I had to go through her, she said. I was asking a lot, she noted: to be the first—and, considering he was in his nineties, most likely the last—to film the operation leader talking about it.

Her answer was no. Al had hardly ever spoken about OZ. She saw no reason for that to change.

For the next eighteen months, I kept calling. I had long conversations in Hebrew with Rina, mostly about her life, family, friends, ideas, interests, and opinions. Sometimes we talked about the former OZ members with whom she and Al kept in touch. They included Leon, who had put in a good word for me.

"Yeah," Rina said, "I think he may have mentioned your name."

I avoided nudging Rina about interviewing Al. But when I started planning a trip to Israel to film material for *A Wing and a Prayer*, I knew I had to bring it up. At the time, Al was ninety-three.

"Can I interview him?"

"Why are you asking me?" Rina said. "Ask him."

She handed him the phone.

Within five minutes, Al said yes.

During my ten-day stay in Tel Aviv, I videotaped three interviews with Al and spoke with him off-camera for many hours.

Returning from Israel, I had enough footage and interviews for the film. But I still had more questions and wanted to verify every piece of information I had collected. So I conducted research for several more years.

By the time I finished, I had interviewed nearly thirty aviators, their family members, and experts around the world. I read every book, academic study, court record, FBI report, and document related to the subject. I spoke with Al and other OZ members on the phone quite often. I visited several of them as much as I could. And I triple checked every part of the story.

The information I gathered—much of it through exclusive interviews—made it possible for me to answer my Saba's question fully.

I've answered it in different ways, the latest of which is this book. This medium is the first to allow me to tell the complete story. I could fit only so much into the hour-long *A Wing and a Prayer*.

Yet this book utilizes a tried-and-true documentary tradition: reenactments. I felt compelled to re-create some of the OZ members' key interactions in order to properly portray their multilayered stories and larger-than-life personalities. As I conducted deep and detailed primary research, I gathered the building blocks I needed to construct scenes and dialogue that capture the spirit as well as the facts of their singular journey.

However, writing a book and making a documentary were not on my mind when I first fully answered my grandfather's question. In the summer of 2003, I received a call that Saba was fighting pancreatic cancer. I flew from South Florida to Israel to spend as much time as possible with him.

I waited for the right opportunity to bring up the Mausers. It came in the middle of my six-week stay. As we did almost daily, we spent the afternoon at a small urban park near his home. It was quiet. He had finished reading the newspaper but was not sleepy. He wanted to talk. I told him everything I knew at that point about OZ.

"A group of American aviators—Jews and non-Jews—risked their lives and freedom to bring you the only weapons they could get," I said.

His eyes lit up.

"Those boys," my Saba said, "gave us more than they could've ever imagined."

Auschwitz

When I completed a decade of research about Operation Zebra, I felt something was missing. So, I revisited my task list:

- Interview every available living OZ member? Done.
- Follow up several times with each interviewee to get more information and verify key points? Done.
- Study every court and FBI document? Done.
- Read every article, book, and academic paper related to this topic? Done.
- Converse with external reviewers, advisors, and experts? Done.

Nonetheless, my sense of omission lingered until I joined a couple of Penn State professors in leading a group of film students on a production tour of Poland. When I looked over our itinerary, I found the missing piece of my OZ research: Auschwitz.

The majority of the OZ members never set foot in Auschwitz, so why did I need to go there? Because practically all of my interviewees mentioned it. Although only some listed it as their reason for joining the illegal operation, it symbolized their collective guiding principle: preventing a second Holocaust.

Whether the 600,000 Jews living in Palestine in 1948 faced a second Holocaust is up for debate. Here's what we know: The Arabs carried out their threat of invasion. Beyond that, it's a guessing game. Had they won, would they have also fulfilled their vow to "sweep [the Jews] into the sea"? Would the expected killing, raping, and looting have reached a genocidal level? It's hard to tell. But even if the OZ members' fear was overblown, they were nonetheless driven by it.

In 1947–1949, when Operation Zebra took place, the world had just started learning about and grasping the magnitude of the Holocaust. In fact, it would be several years before people started using the term. Like most at the time, OZ members referred to the systematic murder of six million Jews as the Destruction or the Catastrophe. They believed a similar end awaited the Yishuv. (It is interesting to note that the Arabs came up with an analogous phrase—the *Nakba*, Arabic for "Catastrophe"—to describe the exile of more than 700,000 Palestinians during the 1948 war.)

Thus, going to Auschwitz, I believed, would help sharpen my understanding of the OZ members' mind-sets.

At 5:30 a.m. on our first full day in Poland, I hopped on a van that picked us up by the Hotel Klezmer Hois in Krakow's Jewish Quarter. If Auschwitz represents what the Nazis did to the Jews, then Kazimierz—the birthplace of klezmer music and the pre-WWII home of half a dozen vibrant synagogues, numerous kosher restaurants, and 64,000 residents—represents what European Jewry lost.

The van was quiet. Some of the students slept. Others, bleary eyed and jet lagged, glared out their windows at the dawn of a dreary day. Puncturing the silence, the baby-faced driver chatted with one of my colleagues. In awkward-yet-somehow-easy-to-follow English, he said the Poles hate two people: the Russians and "the Jewish."

Why do they hate "the Jewish"? Because the Jews, he said, unfairly blame the Poles for the Holocaust.

This generalized statement, by its tone born more of hate than observation, contained a grain of truth. Many Jews do believe that, based on the historical record, plenty of Poles helped the Nazis in their pursuit of the Final Solution. Moreover, some Jews and non-Jews, such as President Barack Obama, have used a term that understandably offends the Poles: "Polish death camps."

They were Nazi camps.

The term "Polish death camps" has so offended the Poles that they outlawed it as part of taking legal measures to deflect blame for any part of the Holocaust.

The only ones to blame, the Poles argue, are the Nazis. The Poles, they insist, did nothing wrong and, in countless cases, helped the Jews.

"My grandmother hid Jewish," the driver said.

It upsets him that, when he takes Jews to Auschwitz, they rarely ask for his opinion.

Perhaps that's because he offers it anyway.

It was then that I noticed it: a little doll—a sort of a small, stiff bobblehead—of a big-schnozed, yarmulke-capped, cash-sign-wearing Jew begging for money.

We asked the driver about it.

"A rabbi gave it to me," he said.

"It offends me," my colleague said.

"Why?"

"Because I'm Jewish."

"You don't look Jewish."

"What do Jews look like?"

"They all look the same," he said. To back up his claim, he noted that two Hasidic sisters he drove to Auschwitz bore a striking resemblance to each other. And neither looked like my colleague. So there.

"Do you know Barbra Streisand?" she asked.

He nodded.

"Some people think I look like her," my colleague says. "She's Jewish, too." In that case, the driver said, "She's not my type."

After a six-hour tour of Auschwitz I, which has been turned into a museum, and Auschwitz II, which has remained a bit more raw, the driver joined us for lunch at the cafeteria. (Yes, Auschwitz has a cafeteria. I recommend the potato pierogis.)

Over fish and chips, the driver expressed his satisfaction with the Polish economy's "weakness." It has prevented African and Middle Eastern immigrants from trying to come in, he noted, saving Poland from the fate of stronger European economies such as Germany and France, which have been overrun by immigrants.

You may wonder how the interaction with the van driver informed my work about OZ. It gave me a firsthand glimpse into antisemitism, something many of the operation members experienced as children. It was their confrontations with Jew haters that spurred several of them to become pilots.

I have rarely encountered antisemitism on such a personal level.

Until I visited Auschwitz, all I could think of were reasons that should have kept these aviators from joining OZ:

- They had paid their dues several times over during World War II.
- They were building their postwar lives (to join, some left such universities as Harvard and Columbia; some declined acceptance into medical school; and others had wives and babies or young kids).
- They were asked to risk their lives for another country.
- They were asked to risk their US citizenship.

It's the last two points, in particular, that had stumped me for years. It's one thing to risk your life for your country; it's another to risk your life for another country while breaking your own country's laws. But after visiting Auschwitz, I realize that for the OZ members, World War II did not conclude on September 2, 1945.

Walking through Auschwitz in the cold rain, I was struck by how menacing it still felt. The evil that fueled it still roams the earth. Just look at Rwanda and Syria. In 1947–1949, the OZ members wanted to keep fighting this evil, which, to them, was carried forward by the British, who placed thousands of Jewish refugees in former Nazi camps.

As I got on the van to ride back to Krakow with the antisemitic, xenophobic driver, I felt I had finally completed my OZ research.

After a day in Auschwitz, I finally understood.

Acknowledgments

I RECEIVED SO MUCH WONDERFUL ASSISTANCE ON THIS PROJECT THROUGH the years that I had a hard time choosing whom to thank first. Should I thank my Saba, who set me off on this journey? Operation Zebra transport pilot Leo Gardner, who introduced me to the mission? OZ fighter pilot Gideon "Giddy" Lichtman, the first to sit down for an on-camera interview? Ralph Lowenstein, my dear friend who archived the Americans and Canadians' contributions, including his own, to Israel's fight for independence and served as a historical consultant on *A Wing and a Prayer*? OZ leader Al Schwimmer, who gave me his only on-camera interview about the mission?

The three interviews I conducted with Al offer viewers and readers the only opportunity to hear directly from him about OZ.

Here are several more people to whom I'm eternally grateful, in alphabetical order:

- Sandra Brown, daughter of OZ chief pilot Sam Lewis, who preserved his stories on videos and audiotapes
- OZ transport pilot Sheldon "Ike" Eichel, who gave me all the time in the world
- OZ fighter pilot Leon Frankel, who put in a good word for me with Al Schwimmer
- Ralph Goldman, who worked at the secret North America headquarters of the Haganah, the Palestinian Jewish underground
- OZ transport and fighter pilot Collie Goldstein
- Benny Gshur, who wrote his Hebrew University doctoral dissertation about the IDF's foreign volunteers in the 1948 war

- David Harman, a Harvard PhD and Hebrew University professor who became friends with several OZ members, including Al Schwimmer
- Zdeněk Klima, a Czech archivist who's chronicled his country's sale of arms to Israel
- OZ transport and fighter pilot Lou Lenart, who took two years to convince to give me an interview
- OZ radio operator Harold Livingston, who always answered my calls and promptly replied to my emails
- OZ transport pilot Phil Marmelstein
- OZ C-46 and B-17 pilot Bill Novick
- David and Lawrence Ribakoff, sons of OZ transport pilot Martin Ribakoff, who have been helpful through the years
- Rina Schwimmer, Al's wife
- Danny Shapiro, an Israeli fighter pilot
- Lee Silverman, an American volunteer who served in Israeli Air Force (IAF) intelligence
- Fanya Soll, wife of OZ shop-chief Ray Selk
- OZ radio operator Eddie Styrak
- Israeli first lady Reuma Weizman, wife of OZ fighter pilot and later Israeli president Ezer Weizman

I want to thank my editor, Dave Reisch, and his assistant, Stephanie Otto; Penn State University Donald P. Bellisario College of Communications Dean Marie Hardin and Associate Dean Ford Risley; Retro Report's Kyra Darnton, Karen Sughrue, Barbara Dury, Joseph Hogan, Victor Couto, and Cullen Golden, with whom I co-produced a short documentary about this topic; film-producing partner Matthew Einstein; and University of Florida professors Gayle Zachmann, Sergio Vega, and Robert Mueller.

Thank you, also, to my wife, Rachel Wolkenhauer; parents, Dan and Eti Dvir; sister, Norit Dvir; my late brother, Sha'ron Dvir; and my twin boys, Aden and Ethan Dvir.

Main Characters

Modi Alon: Israeli fighter pilot. Born in the mystical mountain town of Safed, he served as a Royal Air Force (RAF) radio operator during World War II. Toward the end of the war, he enrolled in pilot training and flew British Spitfires in Italy. After the war, he majored in architecture at the Technion in Haifa.

Yehuda Arazi: Operation Zebra's point person in the United States for the Haganah, the Palestinian Jewish underground. Before World War II, he helped the British police squelch communism in Jerusalem. During the war, he joined British intelligence. After the war, among other responsibilities around the world, he headed the Jews' arms procurement in America. A master of disguises, he often assumed one of a dozen identities he created, including a rabbi and a businessman. The only thing he could never change was his limp.

Hal Auerbach: OZ all-purpose pilot. After graduating from UCLA, he worked for the Douglas Aircraft Company. During World War II, he flew reconnaissance for the US Navy in Pearl Harbor and Australia.

Nahum Bernstein: OZ's financial point person. A successful New York attorney, he grew up in a Russian Jewish home in Brighton Beach, Brooklyn. During World War II, he served as a wiretapper for the Office of Strategic Services (OSS), the predecessor to the Central Intelligence Agency (CIA).

George Frederick "Buzz" Beurling: OZ test pilot. "Canada's most famous WWII hero," he shot down more than thirty German and Italian planes, including several Messerschmitt Bf 109s, which were similar to the fighter planes Operation Zebra would bring to Israel in 1948.

Sheldon "Ike" Eichel: OZ fighter pilot. Growing up in New York, he faced little antisemitism and had only a marginal connection to his heritage. During World War II, he served as a B-24 bomber pilot in Europe. After learning about the Holocaust, he vowed to join the Jews "if they ever decide to fight."

Leon Frankel: OZ fighter pilot. He was bullied growing up in Minneapolis primarily because of his religion, about which he had little knowledge. During World War II, he served as a torpedo pilot in the Pacific. He received a Navy Cross for sinking a Japanese cruiser. After the war, he studied law at the University of Minnesota and co-owned a used-car dealership in Minot, North Dakota.

Leo Gardner: OZ deputy chief pilot. He served as a US Army Air Forces (USAAF) flight instructor and a US Air Transport Command (ATC) pilot during World War II. He was best friends with the operation's chief pilot, Sam Lewis. Before joining, he flew for TWA.

Bill Gershon: OZ transport pilot. Born in Denmark, he grew up in a religious Zionist home in New York. During World War II, he flew ATC cargo missions in Europe. Older and more serious than most of the other operation members, he became a mentor to several of them.

Coleman "Collie" Goldstein: OZ transport and fighter pilot. As a B-17 pilot in Europe during World War II, he saved the lives of his crew members when they were hit by German anti-aircraft flak and had to crash land in Nazi-occupied France. He did it so expertly that none of the ten men suffered more than minor injuries. He then joined the French resistance.

Chalmers "Slick" Goodlin: OZ fighter pilot. An American, he flew Spitfires for the Royal Canadian Air Force during World War II. Afterward, he worked as a test pilot for the Bell Aircraft Corporation, where he would've been the first to break the sound barrier had he not resigned over the US Air Force's refusal to guarantee his $150,000 ($1.73 million today) bonus.

Hank Greenspun: OZ weapons and supplies smuggler. He grew up in a traditional Jewish home in Brooklyn. During World War II, he served in General George Patton's Third Army in France and Germany and received a *Croix de Guerre* medal. After the war, he became Bugsy Siegel's press agent, helping the notorious mobster reopen the Flamingo Casino in Las Vegas.

Ernest Glen "Bud" King: OZ mechanic. The devout Christian served as a US Army Air Forces flight engineer during World War II and worked as a Consolidated Vultee mechanic in San Diego after the war.

Lou Lenart: OZ transport and fighter pilot. Born and raised on a livestock farm in Hungary, his only taste of Judaism was the blood on his lips during fistfights with antisemites. In the early 1930s, his family moved to a farm in Pennsylvania. As a teenager, he aimed to become a soldier so he could fight the Nazis. His wish remained a fantasy. Becoming a Marine fighter pilot, he served in the Pacific. His bitterness intensified when he learned that his extended family, including his grandparents, perished in the gas chambers.

Gordon Levett: Non-Jewish OZ transport and fighter pilot. He grew up in the slums of London. A technical mistake terminated his dream of shooting down Nazi planes during World War II. After the war, he worked at a laundromat, where he overheard the Jewish owners deplore their government's inhumane treatment of Holocaust survivors. He decided to join the Palestinian Jews' fight.

Sam Lewis: OZ chief pilot. He grew up in an upper-middle-class household in Venice Beach, California. He inherited his quirky personality from his father (a furrier) and mother (a poet who swam in the ocean every morning). The blue-eyed, high-cheek-boned ladies' man practiced yoga and rode a Harley. As an ATC pilot during World War II, he built a reputation as an ace aviator who could fly any transport plane under any condition.

Gideon "Giddy" Lichtman: OZ fighter pilot. He grew up in a crime-ridden neighborhood in Newark, New Jersey, during the Great Depression. His socialist parents scraped by teaching Hebrew school; yet they instilled a deep sense of charity in him, stationing him at street corners to collect coins for the Palestinian Jews. In the Pacific during World War II, he became known as a hotheaded, underutilized fighter pilot with exceptional skills.

Harold Livingston: OZ radio operator. He grew up in Haverhill, Massachusetts. During World War II, he served as an ATC radio operator in Europe, North Africa, and the Middle East. After the war, he served an ATC communications chief in Tripoli, Libya; Dhahran, Saudi Arabia; and Cairo, Egypt.

Phil Marmelstein: OZ transport pilot. He was an ATC pilot during World War II. He possessed sharp logistical skills.

John Frederick McElroy: OZ fighter pilot. A Canadian ace, he shot down a baker's dozen of German and Italian planes during World War II.

Bill Novick: OZ transport pilot. During World War II, he flew B-17 bombing missions in Europe. After the war, he prepared for and got accepted to medical school. He gave up his spot to join the mission.

Shmuel "Sam" Pomerance: OZ transport and fighter pilot. A resourceful aviator, he earned an aeronautical engineering degree from NYU, served as a USAAF flight engineer during World War II, and worked as a manager at Ranger Aircraft Company before joining the operation.

Bernarr McFadden "Pat" Ptacek: FBI agent. Besides exposing Operation Zebra, his claim to fame was his anti-communist work. He provided the key information President Harry S. Truman used to craft the 1947 Loyalty of Government Employees Act, generated a Red Scare in the film industry, and helped imprison the Hollywood Ten.

Shlomo Rabinovitch (later Shlomo Shamir): The Haganah's US representative. Arazi's predecessor. Born in Russia, he grew up in Palestine. A licensed pilot, he served in the British army's Jewish Infantry Brigade during World War II. After the war, he helped run Aliyah Bet, the push to settle Holocaust survivors in Palestine.

Martin "Marty" Ribakoff: OZ transport pilot. As a US Army Ferry Command pilot during World War II, he flew Curtiss-Wright C-46 Commandos over the Hump in China and received the Distinguished Flying Cross. He was one of Operation Zebra's most experienced transport pilots.

Milton "Milt" Rubenfeld: OZ fighter pilot. As a stunt pilot during World War II, he trained US and RAF air combatants in aerobatics. He was one of Israel's first fighter pilots.

Irvin "Swifty" Schindler: OZ transport pilot. Born and raised in Florida, he became a Zionist in Miami and a Gator at the University of Florida in Gainesville, where, besides majoring in business, he learned to fly.

Irwin "Steve" Schwartz: OZ chief recruiter. He grew up in a Zionist household in Brooklyn. He served as an ATC navigator during World War II. After the war, he joined the Haganah (the Palestinian Jewish underground) while continuing to work for the US ATC around the Middle East.

Adolph "Al" Schwimmer: OZ mastermind and leader. He grew up in a lower-middle-class household in Bridgeport, Connecticut. Physically abused by his alcoholic father, he spent his teenage years on a USAAF base as part of a Great Depression program. A football injury left one of his legs shorter than the other but never stunted his growth. As an ATC flight engineer during World War II, he earned a reputation as composed under pressure, practical, organized, and disciplined.

Reynold "Ray" Selk: OZ chief logistics officer. Born and raised in an Orthodox home, he stopped practicing Judaism as a young adult but remained loyal to his heritage. As an ATC mechanic during World War II, he became known as a strong project manager.

Boris Senior: OZ fighter pilot. He flew combat missions for the South African air force during World War II. Before joining Operation Zebra, he attended London University and belonged to the Irgun. He was a versatile pilot and logistical leader.

Lee Silverman: A UCLA basketball walk-on who volunteered for the new Jewish state in the 1948 war. He served in Israeli Air Force (IAF) intelligence and became friends with some of the OZ members.

Fanya Soll: Ray Selk's wife. She was seventeen when OZ and the Haganah raised funds and stored illicit weapons in her family's Beverly Hills home. She married Ray a few days after her high school prom. She liked to snoop around and ask questions.

William "Willie" Sosnow: Chief OZ mechanic. Raised in a Russian Jewish home in New York, he served as a US ATC mechanic during World War II.

Ernie Stehlik: OZ mechanic. Born in Czechoslovakia, he served as a US ATC mechanic during World War II, when he met Al Schwimmer.

Eddie Styrak: Non-Jewish OZ radio operator. He was born and raised in Detroit by Polish immigrants. During World War II, he liberated a Nazi concentration camp in Germany. After the war, he participated in Aliyah Bet. A gentle giant, he towered over most of the OZ members.

Ezer Weizman: Israeli fighter pilot. He served as a Royal Air Force (RAF) fighter pilot during World War II. He flew mostly in Egypt. After the war, he attended London University and belonged to the Irgun. He was one of a handful of pilots who founded the Haganah's Shrut Avir (Air Service), which consisted of two dozen light planes.

Charles "Charlie" Thompson Winters: OZ B-17 bombers supplier. He grew up in an Irish household in Brookline, Massachusetts. Polio left him with a limp that kept him out of the military during World War II. After the war, he owned and ran a produce export/import business in Miami and the Caribbean.

I

1947

I

March

It's a turbulent morning above the Pacific Ocean. On a Los Angeles–bound TWA (Trans World Airlines) Lockheed Constellation, flight engineer Adolph "Al" Schwimmer, twenty-nine, formerly with the US Air Transport Command (ATC), keeps to himself. He disappears into his corner when the captain and the co-pilot get into a heated exchange.

The co-pilot—Samuel Lewis, thirty, a high-cheek-boned California health nut and ATC veteran—jumps to his feet, waving his arms like a gorilla. Al exits the cockpit to reassure the alarmed flight attendants. Shutting the door behind him in a futile attempt to muffle the commotion, he smiles apologetically at the nervous passengers.

Hearing a thud, he rushes back into the cockpit to find the captain knocked out and the co-pilot towering over him, ready to land another punch. Al grabs Sam's arm in mid-air and drags him back to his seat.

Al checks on the captain. His upper lip busted, he's out cold. Al motions to Sam to help him place the captain's limp body on the flight engineer's seat.

Smirking like a teenager who just swiped his dad's car keys, Sam settles into the captain's seat.

"Do you know how to fly?" Sam asks Al, who takes the co-pilot seat.

"Thanks to you," Al says, "we're about to find out."

"Do you?" Sam repeats.

"I can handle the basics in an emergency," Al says.

"You should get more training and become a pilot," Sam says.

"Nah," Al says, glancing at the captain's bloodied mouth. "I like to eat solid food."

Sam shows Al the controls and reviews key protocols.

"Don't you want to know why I punched him?" Sam asks.

Al shakes his head no.

"You wouldn't understand, anyway," Sam says.

Al arches his eyebrows.

"He said TWA will never promote 'my kind,'" Sam says.

Al refuses to take the bait.

"Tell me, Al," Sam says, "how'd you get into aviation?"

Al could tell Sam that he fell in love with airplanes at the Vermont Army Air Forces base where he spent his teenage years as part of a Great Depression program; that aviation represented the "Great Escape to the Timeless Beyond" during his rough childhood; and/or that he:

- excelled in the courses he took at Curtiss–Wright Aeronautical University in Chicago in the mid-1930s,
- felt right at home when he joined TWA in 1937,
- gained varied experience on more than 150 ATC assignments around the globe during World War II,
- flew President Franklin D. Roosevelt to the Casablanca Conference in 1943, and/or
- saved the malfunctioning plane carrying General Patrick Hurley to the 1945 Yalta Conference in Crimea.

Instead, Al just shrugs as if he stumbled upon aviation at a career fair.

"Well," Sam says, "think about becoming a pilot. I can tell you have what it takes. I have an eye for that sort of thing."

"I don't know," the impromptu co-pilot says.

"Everyone should have a goal," Sam says.

A subtle, involuntary flash in Al's eyes indicates that he may already have one.

"What?" Sam asks.

Al hesitates. Sam insists.

"I want to own my own airline," Al says.

"Get in line behind the thousands of other WWII pilots who have the same idea," Sam says.

"Maybe I can bypass it," Al says.

~

It's a breezy early spring day at Port-du-Bouc in the south of France. Eddie Styrak, twenty-five years old—a tall, muscular Polish American WWII radio operator who looks like the linebacker he once was and sounds like the well-read human rights champion he's becoming—boards the SS *Ben Hecht*.

As he walks the gangplank, Eddie smiles at fragile refugees holding babies and lugging small bags that contain their lives' possessions. *What a blessing it is to be able to help*, he thinks.

At this point, all he knows about this sojourn are the basic facts:

- The ship is named after and funded by the playwright of *A Flag Is Born*, a 1946 pro-Jewish-state Broadway hit starring Marlon Brando.
- It's part of Aliyah Bet, an illegal effort by the Haganah (the Palestinian Jewish underground) to bring Holocaust survivors to Palestine.
- Its twenty American Jewish and non-Jewish crew members represent diverse backgrounds and WWII experiences.
- Uniting them is the drive to settle refugees who since their liberation from Nazi camps in 1945 have been stateless and homeless but, for the most part, not hopeless.

Raised in Detroit by antisemitic Polish immigrants, Eddie thought very little about the Jews until he liberated a Nazi concentration camp in southern Germany in April 1945. Standing among Dachau's straggling skeletons, he vowed to do whatever he could to help them. A *New York Times* ad pointed him toward his first stint: "Germany exterminates the Jews in Europe, and Britain bars the way to their rescue."

Great Britain, Eddie learned, has kept Holocaust survivors from relocating from Europe's DP camps to the only entity willing to take them: the Yishuv (Palestine's Jewish community). Mandated since 1923 by the League of Nations to control the Holy Land, the British have deployed their Royal Navy and Royal Air Force (RAF) to enforce an über-hawkish anti-immigration policy, the 1939 White Paper, praised by the Arabs and pilloried by the Jews.

At first, Eddie felt confused: Why would the United Kingdom, which put the possibility of a Jewish state on the table thirty years earlier by issuing the Balfour Declaration, reverse course as the need for such a haven reaches a critical level?

Eddie expected Britain to lift its blockade of Jewish immigration to Palestine after it announced the previous month that it plans to end its Mandate of Palestine and turn the matter of what to do with this narrow piece of land to the United Nations. But the British have shown no sign of letting up on the Holocaust survivors.

The more he reads about the subject, however, the more Eddie understands the UK position. He realizes that Britain's national interests lie squarely with the Arabs and dictate ensuring that Palestine's population (at that point, 1.8 million) remains no less than two-thirds Arab. Eddie can clearly see that the empire on which the sun is setting needs the Arab oil, money, and passageways to the East, including the Suez Canal.

Yet he refuses to accept nationalistic considerations as reasons to rob Holocaust survivors of the human rights they thought they had regained when the Allies deep-sixed the Third Reich (German for "Empire"). Besides, Eddie reasons, the British and the Arabs value their relations equally. Although letting in tens of thousands of Jews into Palestine would infuriate much of the Middle East, it's unlikely to burn the military and economic bridges built over decades of cooperation. To the Egyptians, Jordanians, and Iraqis, these cross-continental connections mean a great deal more than the Palestinian Arabs' political desires. In fact, it appears that some of the region's leaders have no intention of fulfilling the Palestinian Arab aspirations and are plotting war on the Jews as a land-grab ploy and a public-relations play.

Having grown up in an environment that unfairly characterized the Jews as greedy, Eddie suspects that bigotry may also be a factor in Britain's policies and actions. He cringes when he reads a newspaper article quoting British foreign minister Ernest Bevin saying, "If the Jews . . . want to get too much at the head of the queue, you have the danger of another antisemitic reaction."

Just as he harbors no illusions about the British opening the doors to Holocaust survivors, Eddie concedes that the Arabs have valid points: They should not be punished for a crime (the Holocaust) they did not commit, and they should not be subjected to a double standard. Western countries rejecting Jewish immigration to their lands while forcing it upon Palestine reeks of colonialism.

But none of this undermines Eddie's commitment to helping find a home for the Holocaust survivors. Boarding the SS *Ben Hecht* with the refugees instantly reinforces his dedication. He helps the passengers find space in the crammed ship. Built as a luxury yacht, it's designed to carry dozens, not hundreds.

The refugees are too anxious to respond or even notice Eddie's warm smile.

But he keeps smiling.

A green-eyed girl, her tattered dress draped on her thin frame like a ripped curtain, smiles back at him.

It is a smile so faint, so fragile, it saddens Eddie. But he maintains his reassuring eye contact.

He broadens his smile.

The girl's face lights up.

The ship blows its horn and sets sail.

~ .

US ATC officer Sheldon "Ike" Eichel, twenty-three, a WWII B-24 bomber pilot, puffs on a Chesterfield cigarette and sips seventeen-year-old Old Pulteney at a Royal Air Force officers' posh lounge. This is the posh lifestyle he pictured when he attended the Manhattan High School of Aviation.

One of Ike's hosts, a pipe-smoking flight instructor, asks what brings him to this part of the world. The American says he and his US ATC colleagues are transitioning control of the city's international airport to the Egyptians. When Ike notes that his job entails providing training, the British pilots indicate they have a similar task.

"The Egyptians have no idea," the RAF flight instructor says, "how to fly the forty Spitfires they bought from us."

"Why so many?"

The Egyptians, the British officers say, are preparing for the "threat" of a Jewish state.

The idea of a Jewish state has intrigued Ike since a Nuremberg trials legal assistant he dated showed him photographic evidence from Auschwitz. Having grown up in an assimilated Jewish home in Brooklyn, he's had little connection to Judaism. But the two hundred images taken by an SS officer, which helped convict twenty-four Nazi leaders of war crimes, ignited in Ike a lingering outrage—not just at the perpetrators but also at his "own people."

"If they ever grow hair on their testicles and fight," he told his girlfriend, "I will join them."

His girlfriend, an idealistic non-Jewish Swede, implored him to stop judging the victims and accept that systematic annihilation steadily paralyzes its targets. She told him a parable about a frog submerged in a slowly heating pot of water. The croaker is unaware that it's being boiled alive until it's too late. Ike pointed out that he expects Jews to be smarter and bolder than frogs.

"Whatever's happened to the Jewish warriors of the Bible?" Ike said.

"Look at you," she said.

Despite evidence to the contrary, Ike continues to deride what he perceives as a lack of a strong fighting spirit among the Jewish people. Keeping this sentiment to himself at the RAF lounge, he asks the British officers, "What does the founding of a Jewish state have to do with Egypt?"

"Egypt will be the first to attack," says an RAF fighter pilot as he cradles his whiskey.

"With your Spitfires?" Ike asks.

The RAF flight instructor nods, saying, "And some of our pilots."

"You mean," Ike says, his face reddening, "you'll fly combat missions against the Jews?"

The RAF officers answer the question with affirmative silence.

Unsure how to respond, Ike wishes his buddy, a fellow ATC officer, was here. A Brooklyn Jew like him, former WWII navigator Irwin "Steve" Schwartz, twenty-seven, seems to always know what needs to be said and how to say it.

Left to fend to himself, Ike does the only thing that comes to his mind—he pushes the issue, asking the RAF pilots point blank, "How could you do that?"

"Well, we'd take a leave of absence from the RAF and serve as 'technical advisors' to the Egyptians," the RAF fighter pilot says, downing his whiskey. "This would allow us to fly combat."

Ike strains to mask his disgust.

~

Inside the Lockheed Air Terminal in Burbank, California, Al leans against a pillar and Sam paces as they watch, through a glass window in their TWA boss's office, the bruised captain register his complaint.

Trying to ease his tension, Sam inhales deeply, bends his knees, sticks out his chest, throws up his arms, and exhales slowly.

"Maybe by 'your kind,'" Al says, "the captain meant hipsters?"

Ignoring him, Sam repeats the Lightning Bolt Pose, to little effect. Still restless, he checks his Rolex, saying, "My wife's expecting me home for dinner."

"She may get sick of you soon," Al says.

Sam gives Al a questioning look. Al spells it out: "I'm not married, and I've never gotten suspended, but seems to me most women aren't thrilled to have their husbands sit around the house."

To change the topic, Sam asks whether Al's heard of the SS *Shabtai Luzinski*. Receiving a headshake "no" for an answer, the TWA co-pilot describes it as one of the few Aliyah Bet ships to get by the British. Code-named "Susanna" and carrying more than eight hundred refugees, it reached the Palestine shore unscathed. British soldiers descended on the beach like seagulls at the sight of food. But the Haganah flooded the scene with Yishuv members who intermixed with the new arrivals and succeeded in sneaking several hundred illegal immigrants through the cordon.

The British, Sam says, arrested seven hundred Jews at the beach. They deported them to Cyprus but had to return nearly half after an ID check proved that they were legal residents of Palestine.

Sam beams at the Haganah "victory." Al's less impressed.

"So, bottom line," Al says, "hundreds of survivors of the Nazi camps are detained in a British camp in Cyprus."

Sam opens his mouth to say something, but, noticing that the captain's leaving their boss's office, he hurries in.

~

It's a windy, muggy day on the Mediterranean Sea. Running communications aboard the SS *Ben Hecht*, Eddie hears planes crisscrossing above. He believes they're RAF reconnaissance flyovers. He worries about a confrontation with the British. After the ship set sail, he learned that it's affiliated with the Haganah's extremist offshoot, the Irgun. Had he known this in advance, he would've reconsidered participating.

Much like the rest of the world, including most Jews, Eddie views the Irgun as a terrorist organization. He was horrified the previous year when the

Menachem Begin–led group killed ninety-one people, mostly British government officials and Arab staffers, at Jerusalem's King David Hotel. The radio operator has read that the head of the Yishuv, David Ben-Gurion, calls the Irgun an "enemy of the Jewish people."

Based on what he knows about the Irgun, Eddie expects the *Ben Hecht* to take a far more aggressive-defensive stand than the typical Aliyah Bet ship. So he's surprised to hear his captain—Bob Levitan, twenty-seven, a former US Merchant Marine—ordering him and the rest of the crew to not resist the British. Eddie finds it refreshingly ironic that a vessel affiliated with the Jewish Palestinian underground's most destructive group aims to be the least violent.

After a week at sea, the *Ben Hecht* runs up against the British blockade with nothing to protect itself except a false Honduran flag. Eddie hears a voice crackling through his radio. He ignores it.

The Royal Navy sailor repeats, "How do you read me?"

Despite catching every word, Eddie answers, "I read you badly."

"Permission to board your ship."

"Permission denied," Eddie says. "This is a US vessel, and these are international waters."

These facts fail to prevent the British from storming the German-built, 150-foot, 400-ton ship. Commandeering the *Ben Hecht*, they force Bob, Eddie, and the other crew members onto one of their three destroyers.

"Where are you taking us?" Eddie demands. It's the sailors' turn to ignore questions.

Several hours later, when he's led off the Royal Navy destroyer at the Port of Haifa, Eddie sees, in the distance, the *Ben Hecht* being towed in.

"What are you doing with the refugees?" he asks one of the guards.

"The Brits will probably take them to a detention camp in Cyprus," says Bob, the *Ben Hecht* captain.

British troops haul the crew members to the Acre Prison, an Ottoman citadel constructed over a Crusader fort. The next morning, they face a British judge. Their lone court-appointed attorney asks them just one question: "How do you wish to plead?" "Not guilty," they say.

Within an hour, they're found guilty of "aiding illegal immigration." The judge gives each of them a seventeen-year sentence. It's so out of bounds that it leaves Eddie numb.

In the dreary, dark prison, Bob urges the British guards to release Eddie and the other non-Jewish *Ben Hecht* crew members, saying, "They're Christian, for Christ's sake."

The guards remain stone-faced.

"Show them," Bob tells Eddie and the other non-Jewish crew members, pointing at their crotches.

They pull out their uncircumcised penises.

The guards keep their eyes straight.

～

It's a cold, early spring afternoon in Kearney, Nebraska. The sun hangs high in a sky that, thanks to the flat terrain, stretches as far as the eye can see. Standing on their front porch, FBI agent Bernarr McFadden "Pat" Ptacek, thirty-seven, and his only child, Edward, eleven, gaze at the heavens.

Pat's wife and Edward's mother, Valerie, thirty-two, summons them in.

Plopping down on his La-Z-Boy, Pat clicks on his wooden radio's plastic dial. Valerie and Edward sit on the carpet by him. They listen to a live broadcast of President Harry S. Truman, sixty-two, announcing a decree to examine federal workers' "loyalty." The president says failure to show "complete and unswerving loyalty" poses a "threat to our democratic processes."

Valerie tells Edward that his father provided much of the information President Truman needed to craft this executive order.

The FBI has shown Pat its appreciation by giving him a two-week vacation. He plans to spend all of it with his family—one week at home, and one week at the Grand Canyon National Park in Arizona. But he knows they need not go far to feel awestruck by nature. In the distance, he hears the rumbling of a grand flock of birds. He yanks his son by the shoulder and leads him to the porch. Valerie follows them.

They feel the porch's wooden planks vibrate beneath their feet. Then they see them: thousands of sandhill cranes crossing the sky.

The cranes block the sun and fill the air with thousands of throaty cries as they head to the Platte River cornfields to feast on spent grain in preparation for their Arctic journey. The annual spectacle never loses its impact.

～

As he watches Sam speak with their boss, Al thinks about "Susanna." He concludes that this exception to the rule—a Jewish refugee ship breaking the British blockade—illustrates Aliyah Bet's fundamental flaw. The long days the refugees and the crew members spend at sea make them easy prey for the Royal Navy.

"There's got to be a better way," he mutters to himself.

He thinks. He thinks hard.

Sam snaps him out of it.

"I can see why he's the boss," Sam says.

As Al starts toward the boss's office, he notices that it's dark.

"He went home to his second wife and three kids," Sam says.

Al stops and turns back toward Sam.

"What did he give you?" Al asks.

"A two-week suspension," Sam says. "And a promotion."

Al's reaction, which starts out with a "sounds about right" shrug, switches to a dropped jaw.

Sam shakes Al's hand. "Say hello to TWA's first Jewish captain."

2

April

In the weeks since visiting the RAF lounge, Ike has grown increasingly angry. The British pilots' pledge to participate in the attack against a new Jewish state has rewired the neurons in his brain. He's become determined to do something for the Holocaust survivors. What that might be, he's unsure. He wants to talk to his Jewish ATC buddy. But Steve's been MIA.

Every morning, Ike stops by the Cairo Airport's control tower, where Steve provides air traffic control training to the Egyptians. Every morning, he's told his friend's out that day.

Today, Ike runs into Steve as they enter the tower.

"Where have you been?" Ike asks.

"On assignments," Steve says with a Brooklyn accent that Ike has shed.

"Tell me," Ike says, "what do you make of all this talk about the creation of a Jewish state?"

Shrugging as if this is a foreign topic to him, Steve says, "Why are you asking?"

"Jews used to be warriors," Ike says. "They were farmers and shepherds, but they were also warriors. What happened?"

"What is this all about?" Steve asks.

Ike recounts how the RAF pilots told him they'd fly combat missions against the Palestinian Jews.

"That was just the alcohol talking," Steve says.

The RAF pilots, Ike says, were sober and serious.

"Even if they're crazy enough to want to do that," Steve says, "America would never allow it."

Steve excuses himself, saying, "My trainees are waiting."

This is not how Ike pictured the conversation going.

~

On a New York–bound flight, Al and Sam are joined by co-pilot Leo Gardner, twenty-eight, a prematurely balding US ATC veteran. He slaps the new captain on the shoulder, saying, "Now we can fly together again."

Leo and Sam became best friends during World War II when they transported bombers and supplies to Britain and other Allies. They have more in common than some married couples. They've served as flight instructors domestically and abroad, they each have two children, and although Leo's divorced, they paint the town as if they're both single.

But unlike Sam—an open book with a spotless flying and training record—Leo harbors a secret. During a training flight in Arizona, one of his trainees accidentally killed a man on the ground. As they landed, Leo never saw the victim due to the instructor seat's blind spot. Army Air Force investigators cleared him of wrongdoing and lifted his suspension after a few days. He returned to training cadets in the same plane. But he's never been able to shake the guilt.

"Who could've ever imagined?" Sam says. "Two Jews in the same TWA cockpit?"

Al clears his throat.

"What is it?" Sam says.

"You miscounted."

Sam and Leo exchange confused looks.

"You're Jewish?" Sam says.

Al nods. "I just don't go 'round roughing up guys 'cause of it."

"All these years flying together," Sam says, "and you never mentioned it?"

"It never came up."

"It came up several times."

"Yeah, about *you*."

"What are you?" Leo asks. "Reform? Conservative?"

Al's unsure of how to answer. Sam translates: "What kinda Jew are you?"

Al could say he's the kind of a Jew who, at his mother's request, visited several Nazi concentration camps and reviewed hundreds of documents after the war to investigate what happened to her side of the family. He could describe the sickening sorrow he experienced when he discovered that Hitler killed his Hungarian grandparents, uncles, aunts, and cousins. "Why didn't we try to help them?" he asked his mom as she cooked goulash in her modest Bridgeport, Connecticut, house.

But Al has something else on his mind.

"I'm the kinda Jew who wants to do something," he says.

"About what?" Sam and Leo ask.

"Remember how we talked about the British intercepting the refugee ships?"

Sam nods.

"I think we should fly them in."

Leo ponders it. He likes the idea. A lot.

"How you gonna get the planes?" Sam asks.

"The US military," Al says. "They're selling decommissioned transports for nothing."

"That might work," Sam says.

"I don't know where to start," Al says.

Sam's heard that the Haganah has set up a "front" office in New York. Al asks where. Leo says he thinks it's in the same building as a famous nightclub.

"Maybe the El Morocco?" Sam says. "On 54th, between Lexington and Third."

"Have you been there?"

Sam and Leo laugh. They have, but they had other things on their minds besides looking for the Haganah's secret US headquarters.

~

Pat walks through the Federal Triangle in Washington, DC, with a spring in his step. Although he enjoyed spending fourteen days with his family, he's eager to receive his new assignment. He expects to stick with scrutinizing American institutions for Soviet interference and infiltration.

Arriving at the seven-story Department of Justice building, he takes the elevator to the FBI offices, where his colleagues welcome him back with congratulatory handshakes and backslaps for his Loyalty Act work.

Skipping the pleasantries, his boss immediately gives Pat his new assignment: investigating the Palestinian Jews' acquisition of arms in the United States.

"What is the scope of their operation?" Pat asks.

"That's what you have to find out."

"That should take a week or two," Pat says. "What's my long-term assignment?"

"This is it," the boss says.

Pat is surprised.

Saying, "We expect Congress to pass it any minute now," his boss hands him a carbon copy of a hot-off-the-press White House "proposal for legislation."

Pat reads the one-pager. Signed by President Truman, it calls for the "supervision of the exportation of arms, ammunition, implements of war and related commodities."

"I never thought I'd ever see the Neutrality Act reactivated," Pat says.

The US government passed the Neutrality Act in 1935 to keep Americans from getting involved in the emerging global conflict that would become World War II. It issued stricter versions of the act in 1937 and 1939.

Two years later, the Neutrality Act became dormant when the United States joined the Allies in their fight against Japan, Germany, and Italy. Now President Truman has de-shelved it with a "stricter provision against arms exports," the boss says.

The revived act also calls for "more adequate information concerning the international traffic in arms."

"That's where you come in," Pat's boss says.

"Nowhere in this memo," Pat says, "does Truman mention Palestine or the Middle East."

"Read between the lines," the boss says. "Heck, read the actual lines. This is where they want us to focus."

"They?" Pat asks.

"The State Department," says the boss, who's beginning to lose patience. "They classified it a high-priority national-security issue."

"High-priority national security?" Pat says. "A tiny community on a tiny piece of land?"

"The Jews make up a tiny percentage of our population, too," the boss says, "and look how much trouble they cause."

Pat gives him a questioning look.

"Think about many of the Hollywood communists you're exposing," the boss says.

Pat opens his mouth to respond, but his boss raises his hand like a stop sign. To conclude the conversation, his boss reads aloud a key part of the

White House proposal: "'The international traffic in munitions . . . is a matter of major concern.' *Major* concern, Pat. Now get to it."

"I'm still . . ."

"Pat, this is about loyalty," the boss interrupts, his patience gone. "Loyal Americans cannot send weapons to foreign entities. It's that simple."

~

After landing with Sam and Leo at the New York Municipal Airport, soon to be renamed LaGuardia Field, Al takes a Yellow Cab to the El Morocco.

Examining the small building that houses the El Morocco, Al doubts he'll find a Haganah office here. Nonetheless, he goes in. As his eyes adjust to low lighting, he spots a club photographer sorting through his work at a half-moon-shaped, zebra-striped booth.

Initially unaware that he's speaking with celebrity photographer Jerome Zerbe, Al asks about the building's other tenants. "Are any of them Jewish organizations?"

Zerbe mentions a deli around the corner. Knowing that's not it—although he wouldn't mind a pastrami sandwich—Al asks whether there's a New York nightclub that shares a building with other offices.

"The Copacabana," Zerbe says, "is in the basement of the Hotel Fourteen, which I think also rents out office space."

Skipping the deli, Al, who's still wearing his TWA uniform, walks to 14 East 60th Street. Entering the Hotel Fourteen's marble-floored, baroque-columned lobby, he tips his fedora to showgirls taking a smoking break. On the building's office directory, he zeros in on "Jaffa Oranges."

Al senses this may be it. Eight years after his only visit to Palestine, he vividly recalls the citrus scent that infused the air and the whole fried fish he ate at a portside restaurant in Jaffa. He takes the elevator to the fourth floor and asks to speak with the Jaffa Oranges manager. The secretary says her boss is busy. She refuses to take a message.

The next morning, the secretary again stonewalls Al. This time, he insists that she take a message. She writes it down but tosses it as soon as the nudnik departs.

Returning in the late afternoon, Al lights a cigarette for a chatty showgirl who introduces him to that night's headliner: Francis Albert "Frank" Sinatra, thirty-three. Not one to be starstruck, Al shakes Sinatra's hand and exchanges pleasantries.

Little does Al know how useful this new connection will prove.

~

To sort out his unexpected assignment in his mind, Pat visits a duo of US foreign-policy experts he's befriended over the years. They explain that the State Department's implementation of the Truman Doctrine, an anti-communist guideline the president issued earlier that year, includes aiming to keep the Soviets out of the Middle East. Selling or even allowing the Palestinian Jews to get arms would spark an all-out war that could give the Russians an excuse to intervene and gain a foothold in the region.

With whom, Pat asks, would the Soviets side?

The Jews are their only option, the experts say. The Arabs are already taken—they're well entrenched with the Russians' Cold War adversaries, the British and the Americans.

This US-Arab alliance has gained a great deal of traction since World War II, the experts say. The Americans are leading an unprecedented global economic expansion and need all the oil they can get. Combined with several other factors, the lifting of war-era gas rationing has forced Washington to tap its oil reserves, Pat's pals tell him. The Truman administration is driven to stop draining the emergency supply. This has led to such developments as a ramped-up collaboration between American oil companies and the Saudis.

Even a short-lived slowdown in oil exploration could curtail global economic growth, they say. A crack in American–Middle Eastern relations could provide an opening for the Soviets and drag the US military into another global conflict only a couple of years after the end of World War II.

These are just some of the many reasons the State Department seeks to avoid upsetting the Arabs.

"That's why," the experts say, "we can't sell the Jews weapons."

Pat thanks his friends for giving him the insight he needs to do his job. He would still prefer to do something more important, like hunting down communist infiltrators, but he feels better about the Palestinian-Jewish assignment. He's helping to keep the Soviets out of the Middle East.

~

In Acre, Eddie keeps mostly to himself, reading any book he can get his hands on, including *The Jewish State* by modern Zionism founder Theodor Herzl. But when Eddie hears that the British plan to hang four prisoners, he reaches out to a couple of members of their organization—the Irgun.

After offering his sympathy, he starts engaging in long conversations with the two Irgun members, imprisoned for their roles in the King David Hotel bombing.

Although he admires the captain and crew of the SS *Ben Hecht*, an Irgun ship, Eddie remains critical of this organization. He asks the two Jewish terrorists about the bombing. They point out that they called in three warnings, urging the hotel staff to evacuate.

"Why didn't they?" Eddie asks.

"They wanted this to happen," says one Irgun member.

"They wanted the carnage, the destruction, the death of innocent lives," says the other. "They wanted to vilify us."

Eddie doesn't buy it. But regardless of why the British ignored the warnings—perhaps because they were tired of bogus bomb threats—he starts softening his attitude toward the Irgun. When his new friends ask him to help them with their planned prison escape, he says he'll think about it.

That night, the British hang the four Irgun prisoners.

The sound of necks snapping echo in Eddie's head the next morning as he approaches the two Irgun members.

A few hours later, he assembles a primitive transistor device from parts the Irgun has smuggled into the prison.

He completes the transistor just in time. That night, succumbing to increasing pressure from the US Congress, the British release the *Ben Hecht* crew members.

At first, Eddie's elated. But as he peers at the moon shining through the British lorry's flopping back-cover, he worries about the fate of the Jewish refugees and the Irgun prison escapees.

A fellow *Ben Hecht* crew member brings up another concern: Will they face criminal charges upon their return to the United States?

~

Pat goes to the Walnut Street Theatre in Philadelphia, the country's oldest such theater, to watch *A Flag Is Born*, which, after fourteen weeks on Broadway, now tours the country. The FBI agent is no fan of drama; he prefers fly fishing. He's here seeking insight into the Jews' arms acquisition attempts. He's looking into the activities of the Irgun, which playwright Ben Hecht supports with funds, deeds, and inflammatory words.

This extremist organization, Pat has learned, takes no measures to hide its presence in the United States. In fact, it's purposely conspicuous. The FBI has been investigating the Irgun—better known in the States as the Bergson Group, after the alias for its lead US operative, Peter Bergson, thirty-two (real name: Hillel Kook)—for most of the decade.

Born in Russia and brought up in an Orthodox home in a Galilee town where his father served as chief rabbi, Peter came to the United States in 1940 to raise funds and procure weapons for the Irgun. But a couple of years later, a story buried in the *New York Times* realigned his priorities. The page 10 article described the start of the Final Solution, the systematic effort to eradicate an ancient tribe. The Nazis had made substantial progress toward this unprecedented goal, the national newspaper of record implied, by already murdering two million Jews.

Pat learned from an FBI agent who had investigated the Bergson Group that Peter shifted his focus from raising funds and procuring arms to trying to save Europe's remaining Jews.

Peter scored his first victory when he recruited Ben to write and produce *We Will Never Die*, the Bergson Group's foray into what soon becomes its trademark—raising awareness about the plight of the Jews.

This musical, performed in arenas and concert halls in the Northeast in early 1943, opened the eyes of tens of thousands of Americans, including First Lady Eleanor Roosevelt. *We Will Never Die* bolstered the pressure the Jewish community put on the US government to take measures to try to stop the European genocide. In April of that year, American and British delegations met in Hamilton, Bermuda, to discuss solutions to this problem. But they came up without a single concrete step, maintaining their immigration prohibitions and quotas.

That's when the Bergson Group leaders took off the gloves, placing an advertisement in the *New York Times* declaring, "To 5,000,000 Jews in the Nazi Death-Trap, Bermuda Was a Cruel Mockery." Peter brought in 1,500 delegates from around the country to the Emergency Conference to Save the Jewish People of Europe in New York, which received a great deal of press coverage. He then highlighted American inaction in more than two hundred ads penned by Ben, who wrote *Scarface* and *It's a Wonderful World*, among many other movie scripts.

The Bergson ads included "Time Races Death: What Are We Waiting For?" and "How Well Are You Sleeping?"

Pat realizes Peter and Ben have continued pushing Americans' buttons in this vein after World War II. They now connect the Holocaust survivors' plight to the Jewish state's creation. In one of their postwar ads, they ask, "Is There Something You Could Have Done to Save Millions of Innocent People—Men, Women, and Children—from Torture and Death?" In another, featuring a photo of the SS *Ben Hecht*, they plead, "Give us the money . . . we'll get them there!"

To a certain degree, Peter and Ben have succeeded, offering road signs for Americans such as Eddie seeking to help Holocaust survivors. Liberating Dachau set him on this path; the Irgun's *New York Times* ad stating "Britain bars the way" led him to the SS *Ben Hecht*.

The ads, Pat has discovered, have generated a great deal of controversy in the Jewish community and beyond. *A Flag Is Born*, however, has sold out everywhere. As Sidney Lumet, who fills in for Brando on the play's national tour, accuses the Allies of letting Hitler turn the Jews into a "garbage pile," a mix of anger and sadness permeates the Philadelphia theater.

As he walks out, Pat wonders, *Why devote valuable resources to stopping the Palestinian Jews from defending themselves?*

He tries to shake off these doubts. He knows he must go all in. That's how he operates.

"All we have on the Bergson Group after years of surveillance, searches, and arrests," Pat tells his boss, "is that they do a lot of talking."

"That's why you're on this case," his boss says. "You're going to shut them up."

Pat gives his boss a questioning look.

"We know they're up to no good," his boss says. "We just have to finally prove it."

~

When they land in New York, Eddie and his *Ben Hecht* crewmates realize they have nothing to worry about it. The US attorney general has decided not to arrest them.

"Of course he did," says their captain, Bob. "Truman wouldn't want to risk losing the Jewish vote."

Bob is either unaware of or disregarding the fact Jews make up an insignificant percentage of the population—only about 1.5 percent. Regardless, the *Ben Hecht* crew members are met with a warm welcome in New York. Mayor William O'Dwyer, who two years later will work with the city's Jewish community to stage America's first Israel Day Parade, hosts a reception for the released prisoners at City Hall. From his vantage point of a couple of inches above the crowd, Eddie sees nothing but smiles. *This is a bubble*, he thinks, *removed from reality*.

Spending a couple of days removed from reality is exactly what Eddie and his fellow Aliyah Bet volunteers need. The next day, Ben Hecht throws them a party. In front of guests such as Milton Berle, Bob thanks their ship's namesake, noting that Ben, too, has paid a price for his efforts to settle Jewish refugees in Palestine.

"I hear the Brits have boycotted your work," Bob says.

"I wonder if that had anything to do with the fact that you compared them to the Nazis," Berle quips.

"The Brits are watching flicks I've written, and they don't even know it," Ben says, referring to using a pseudonym on several projects to avoid the boycott.

Eddie thinks, *If only getting around the British navy was this easy*.

3

May

PAT DRIFTS INTO HOTEL FOURTEEN. HE HAS FIGURED OUT WHY THE FBI investigations into the Irgun's activities in the United States have yielded no results: Most American Jewish organizations shun this extremist organization, refusing any association with it, much less providing it with assistance. For instance, Rabbi Stephen Wise, a Zionist and an advocate for Holocaust survivors, labeled Peter Bergson a terrorist.

The Irgun has achieved little more than making a great deal of noise in the United States, Pat concludes.

The same Jewish American organizations that the Irgun has failed to win over, Pat has learned, embrace a different, more mainstream Palestinian entity: the Haganah.

Although it criticizes the Irgun for being too violent, the Haganah also deploys paramilitary units to fight the British and the Arabs. But unlike the Bergson Group, it's in a position to actually purchase arms in the United States.

As he sits on a Hotel Fourteen lobby sofa pretending to read a newspaper, Pat watches who's coming, who's going, what they are carrying, what language they're speaking, and so on. He takes mental notes and jots down vital observations in his notebook.

There's no need for any of that so far today.

When Al enters the Hotel Fourteen lobby, he draws little attention from Pat or anyone else.

At Jaffa Oranges, Al receives the expected cold reception. This time, he camps out in the small waiting area. Ignoring the secretary's slanted stares, he reads the paper he's tucked under his arm. He reads one article over and over again: Yesterday in Flushing Meadows, Queens, the Soviet Union's surly UN representative, Andrei Gromyko, shocked the General Assembly by proposing partitioning Palestine "into two independent single states, one Jewish and one Arab."

Al gasps. Aware of the Soviet proposal's timing—on the eve of the General Assembly determining the mechanism for exploring a solution for Palestine—he senses the geopolitical tectonic plates shifting beneath his feet.

Aside from the British in 1917—when they issued the aforementioned Balfour Declaration, on which they have since reneged—no country has championed the Jewish cause. Until now. The Russians, longtime critics of Zionism, were never candidates to fill this role. Al wonders, *Why did they reverse course?*

What Al cannot imagine is that exactly one year after Gromyko's May 14 speech, Israel will declare independence. But, currently, he does grasp the magnitude of Russia's topsy-turvy turn.

"Did you see this?" Al waves the paper at the secretary.

She ignores him. He re-rereads the story. The Soviet proposal, approved and possibly even conceived by Joseph Stalin, aims to assist—in Gromyko's dramatic language—"not by word, but by deed" the hundreds of thousands of Holocaust survivors "wandering about in various countries of Europe."

How strange, Al thinks, *that the most vital development in the push to create a Jewish state should come from Stalin, one of the world's most antisemitic post-WWII leaders.* Al recalls hearing that, during the Yalta Conference, Stalin complained to Roosevelt about the "middlemen, profiteers, and parasites"—that is, the Jews. And here he is, acting like their best friend.

Drawing motivation from this unlikeliest of sources, Al leaps to his feet, ready to step up his own efforts.

~

The Central Cairo cabaret's cathedral-like ceiling dwarfs its dozens of foreign patrons, tuxedoed waiters, and eclectic entertainers. Three belly dancers thrust their hips this way and that as they shimmy past each other. One of them—her *bedlah* blue, her jewelry jangling—brushes up against Ike and Steve, who are engaged in a conservation over a legion of drinks.

They talk about the United Nations creating the Special Committee on Palestine and tasking its eleven member nations with issuing a recommendation by September.

"We've been dreaming about it for two thousand years," Steve says, "and they're going to decide our fate in three months."

"This is what I'm talking about," Ike says. "Why are we putting our fate in the hands of the UN?"

"Are you willing to do your part?" Steve asks.

Ike looks around. Everyone's immersed in his or her own conversation, and the musicians strum their *buzuqs* and hit their goblet drums with enough vigor to keep any talk private.

Turning back to Steve, Ike nods.

"Then I got something for you," Steve says.

Ike rubs his hands.

Steve leans in to whisper, "The Grand Mufti of Jerusalem."

Ike's never heard of the Islamic leader of Jerusalem. Steve says Mohammad Amin al-Husayni, who's attending an Arab Higher Committee meeting in Cairo the following week, is one of the Jews' biggest enemies.

"Help me kill him," Steve says.

Ike jumps back. But his curiosity keeps him from nipping this conversation in the bud and changing the topic to anything other than plotting a political assassination.

"If we start bumping off every Jew hater," Ike says, "we'd kill more people than the Nazis did."

Conceding that the Jews have a long list of enemies, Steve argues the mufti stands out for the unabashed support he showered on Hitler and the praise he's bestowed on Britain for curtailing Jewish immigration to Palestine.

About to ask Steve a question, Ike notices their ATC COO and his assistant searching the cabaret. As his eyes follow their movements, he wonders what or who they're after.

He soon finds out: himself.

They want him to fly to Saudi Arabia right away.

"I'm drunk," Ike says.

"We'll sober you up with black coffee," the COO says, signaling for a waiter to bring them some.

"It'd be illegal for me to fly right now," Ike says. "I already put in my hundred flight hours."

"Not according to my records," the COO says.

The waiter hands Ike and Steve cups of coffee. The COO motions for them to drink up.

Gulping the coffee, Steve burns his tongue.

"All you'll get," Ike tells his COO, "is wide-awake drunks."

"It's an emergency," the COO says, "and you're the only pilots we have."

Indicating that he'll give them the details on the way to the airport, the COO tags Steve for co-pilot/navigator and leads them out of the cabaret.

As their driver speeds through Cairo's crowded streets with authorized reckless abandon, the COO briefs them on their mission: yank an ATC communications chief from Saudi Arabia's oil capital, Dhahran.

"If we don't get him outta there," the COO says, "they'll cut off one of his hands."

The US ATC's Dhahran communications chief, Harold Livingston, punched a Saudi official for making an antisemitic comment. Now someone else, the COO says, will have to complete setting up the US radio operation in Dhahran.

"Did Harold knock out the Saudi?" Steve asks.

The COO nods.

"I would've done the same thing," Ike says.

"Then we'd be rescuing you."

Boarding a Douglas C-47 Skytrain, Ike and Steve are each handed a coffee-filled thermos. As they taxi to the runway, they see their colleagues stepping out to see them off. Or is that just an alcohol-fueled hallucination?

~

The Soviets' stunning proposal to allow the fulfillment of Zionist aspirations inspires Al to become more proactive. As soon as the Jaffa Oranges waiting room door opens to let out a visitor, he slips into the agency. The secretary chases after him, but he outruns her to the corner office.

"Mr. Rabinovitch?" Al says. "I have something important to discuss with you."

Shlomo Rabinovitch, thirty-two, a Russian Jew who served as a Haganah field commander before joining the British army's Jewish Infantry Brigade during World War II, gives Al a blank stare.

"I'm sorry," the out-of-breath secretary tells Shlomo. "I tried to stop him."

Shlomo—his thinning hair shaping the top of his head into an "M," and his narrow eyes appearing to squint permanently—pulls aside the secretary.

The investigator they sent to Bridgeport to do a background check on Al, she says, submitted his report a few days ago. She searches for it among the papers on Shlomo's desk. She digs it up, hands it to Shlomo, and leaves.

Although the report mentions Al's lack of a role in any Jewish affairs—local or elsewhere—it raises no red flags. Most important, it notes that the sister of the Haganah's chief fundraiser, Golda Meyerson, vouched for him.

Clara Stern has known Al and his family for years. Her husband saved Al's left leg—and therefore his aviation career—after he suffered a football injury as a kid. Fred Stern, head of the United Jewish Council of Greater Bridgeport, raised money to cover the costs of hospitalizing Al for months. His improved condition allowed the doctors to cut off "only" three-quarters of an inch of his leg instead of amputating it.

This explains Al's slight limp, thinks Shlomo, motioning for him to take a seat.

Remaining standing, Al introduces himself as a TWA flight engineer.

"Where do you fly?" Shlomo asks.

"All over," Al says.

"Good to know," Shlomo says.

Al presents his refugee-flying idea to Shlomo with clarity and conviction. Yet the Haganah representative pays him only partial attention, shuffling papers on his desk.

The Flying Tigers, the American airmen who helped protect the Chinese against the Japanese during World War II, could serve as a model for his proposed operation, Al says.

Now Al has Shlomo's attention. The Haganah representative knows that the Flying Tigers flew combat missions in China.

"You mean," Shlomo asks, "you'd take on the Arab air forces?"

"No combat missions, but it'd be similar to the Flying Tigers in that American volunteers would fly American planes to save another nation," Al says. "In this case, Jewish refugees."

"We're already bringing them in," Shlomo says.

"You're certainly trying," Al says. "But you're mostly failing."

"I spent eighteen months coordinating key parts of Aliyah Bet," Shlomo says. "I can tell you that it's extremely successful."

"How?"

"Well," Shlomo says, "for one thing, we sometimes break the blockade."

"Very rarely."

"What you don't understand," Shlomo says, "is that even when we fail, we succeed."

Al gives him a questioning look.

"When the British stop us, club us, maim us, deport us, or even kill us, they help raise awareness about the need for a Jewish state," Shlomo says. "Every ship they block helps turn world opinion in our favor."

"But it doesn't change the fact that the survivors of the Destruction need a home," Al says.

"Flying them," Al continues, "is the best option."

Shlomo says he'll think about it.

Al's disappointed. *What is there to think about?*

"Refugee relocation," Shlomo says, "does not fall under the jurisdiction of this office."

"Then put me in touch with the right office," Al says.

"We handle all US matters," Shlomo says.

"So it does fall under your jurisdiction," Al says.

Shlomo gets up to show Al the door.

"Look," Al says, "I just want to help."

"If you really want to help," Shlomo says, sitting back at his desk, writing a note, stuffing it into an envelope, scribbling an address on it, and handing it to Al, "hand deliver this for me."

"Where to?"

"The Haganah office in Rome."

"I'm not scheduled to fly to Rome."

"Then get yourself scheduled."

Al thinks. He has seniority at TWA. He can do that.

"I'll try to be there next week."

"Don't try," Shlomo says. "Just be there."

Al slides the note into his jacket pocket and heads out.

∼

By the time Ike and Steve refuel their plane in Baghdad, they're no longer drunk—they're hungover and, at the same time, wired from caffeine. They're also on the same wavelength on the mufti. Almost.

"You agree we need him dead?" Steve asks.

Ike nods.

"So you'll help?"

"No," Ike says. "We're not assassins."

In the distance, Dhahran pops out of the Arabian Desert like a pod of whales leaping out of the ocean. Starting to descend, Ike and Steve receive instructions from their ATC colleagues on the ground: keep your plane engine running, open your cargo door, watch for a Jeep, and take off as soon as Harold is onboard.

When they touch down, Ike runs back to open the cargo door. Soon Harold's bags fly in. He follows.

A small figure with a big presence, Harold sneers like a man who knows he's right but still regrets his actions.

Yelling "Go!" Ike jumps back in the captain's seat and takes off. No one utters a word until they clear Saudi air space.

Steve asks Harold about his background.

"Don't you want to hear what happened?" Harold asks.

"Knowing your background," Ike says, "will help us put your insane behavior in perspective."

Harold tells them he grew up in Haverhill, Massachusetts, a quaint town that borders New Hampshire. His father's a doctor. "I wanted to be a fighter pilot," he says. "But I'm as color-blind as an owl."

Ike and Steve inquire about his Jewish upbringing.

"Much to my father's chagrin," Harold says, "I got kicked out of Hebrew school."

"What do you have to do to get expelled from Hebrew school?" Steve asks. "Set the building on fire? Kiss the principal's daughter?"

"Question the existence of God," Harold says.

"Sounds like a perfectly Jewish thing to do," Ike says.

"They didn't see it that way," Harold says. "My father had to fight for me to have a bar mitzvah. They let me do it, but only on a Thursday."

Ike turns to Steve, "Is Thursday bad?"

Steve says, "You want Saturday."

"Now we know," Ike says, "why you still got something to prove."

4

July

A *CHAMSIN*, A SANDY, MIDDLE EASTERN HEATWAVE, HAS INFILTRATED CENtral Israel, drowning out the Mediterranean breeze. Yehuda Arazi, forty—a salt-and-pepper-haired Haganah operative who stays cool under almost any physical, psychological, or political pressure—arrives at Tel Aviv's Sde Dov Airport to survey the Yishuv's Shrut Avir (Air Service).

Neglecting on this day to uphold his reputation as the "King of Disguises," Arazi simply wears khakis, shirtsleeves, and a worried expression. The aircraft that make up Shrut Avir—small planes with long names such as de Havilland DH.89 Dragon Rapide and Fairchild Model 24 Argus/UC-61 Forwarder—inspire little confidence in him. This despite the fact that he brought in three of them during the years he headed the Haganah's arms procurement in Europe.

Arazi moved from Poland to Palestine as a child with his family before Hitler traded painting for genocidal mania. Yet Arazi is as obsessed with survival as any former concentration-camp inmate. He wonders, *How can the Yishuv defend itself with no military planes?*

Arazi watches a Piper J-3 Cub land. Lou Lenart, twenty-five—a WWII US Marine fighter pilot who grew up as Laszlo Lajos Lenorovits in Sátoraljaújhely, Hungary—jumps out. As a teenager, Lou immigrated with his family to the Pennsylvania coal-mining town of Wilkes-Barre, where his new classmates accused him of crucifying Christ. Besides black eyes and chipped teeth, they gave him a strong identity and a lifelong determination to fight back with whatever he's got.

About to introduce himself to Lou, Arazi pauses: Which of his factitious names should he use? He lacks the outfit for "Rabbi Lefkowitch," and he's too distracted to put on the proper accent for "José de Paz" or "Alon," the name of a *sabra*, a Jew born and raised in Palestine. He considers "Dr. Schwartz" and "Joseph Tannenbaum," but they feel a bit heavy. He settles on "Albert Miller," the nom de guerre he plans to use on his next assignment.

Shaking Lou's hand, Arazi—um, Albert Miller—asks in his subtle Polish accent about the young pilot's flying experience.

Lou, in his Hungarian accent, says that he spent World War II as a Marine fighter pilot in the Pacific. He felt frustrated missing the action against the Nazis. His aggravation turned into fury when he found out that most of his extended family perished in the Holocaust.

"Mine, too," Arazi says.

"I lost fourteen family members," Lou says. "Including my eighty-year-old grandma."

"Thank God you and your immediate family went to a safe place," Arazi says.

Lou never felt safe in Wilkes-Barre.

"I spent a lot of time behind the woodshed getting my face smashed," Lou says, wiping his lips as if they're still bloodied.

Arazi likes what he hears. This is the kind of deep-seated anger that can propel a young pilot to dogfighting greatness.

Lou asks about Arazi's background. Usually, the Haganah operative has a ready-made backstory for each of his identities. But he has yet to make up Albert's, and he feels a kinship with Lou, so he spits out a fact about his true self: "British intelligence."

Eager to shift the focus to Shrut Avir, Arazi asks Lou about his role.

"I mostly fly recon," Lou says. "You know, checking up on the British, on the Arabs. The one advantage we have is that they do not take us seriously. The disadvantage is that they're right."

"Can you help us recruit American pilots?" Arazi asks.

"I don't speak Hebrew, so I don't know exactly what *Shrut Avir* means," Lou says. "But unless it means 'Impotent Airforce,' it's misleading."

Arazi casts his eyes on the Pipers and Rapides. They appear less useful than when he brought them in.

"They're of no use in combat," Lou says. "I've been here a year flying these matchboxes, and I'm sick of it."

"What do we need to do?" Arazi asks.

"Buy military airplanes. You know, fighter planes, bombers, transports," Lou says. "I hear the US military is selling 'em for close to nothing."

Arazi likes this idea.

~

The conversation with the RAF pilots about a Jewish state haunts Ike. The former bomber pilot views their pronounced intention to fly combat missions against the Jews as a holstered declaration of war.

But Steve, the US ATC trainer, believes Ike had his whiskey goggles on and/or the British pilots had more drinks than even they could handle. Harold, who in his new role is upgrading the US ATC's communications station in Cairo, also doubts the crazy story but remains open-minded.

"I would think that, once they leave Palestine, the British would stay out of it," Harold says. "Then again, I thought the Saudis would treat Americans with respect and gratitude, and boy was I wrong."

"I know what you mean," Ike says. "I was certain that after Nazism, we were done with antisemitism, and boy was I wrong."

"I agree," Steve says. "You're both wrong."

Ike offers them a chance to hear firsthand what the British pilots plan to do if and when the Jews form a state in Palestine. Since Steve and Harold are enlisted men barred from officers' watering holes, he searches for proper attire to get them past the RAF lounge guards. He need not look farther than his own closet, loaning Steve, who's about his height and build, one of his pressed uniforms, and having another altered for Harold, who's half a foot shorter.

For this extreme-makeover alteration, Ike hires a Cairo tailor with a reputation for being discreet.

Putting on this uniform and observing his faux-officer self in the mirror, Harold says, "We could get court-martialed for this."

The tailor could only do so much with the dimensional discrepancy between Ike's uniform and Harold's body. But the radio-operator-turned-officer-for-a-day is all smiles. He likes the feel of the first-lieutenant bars on his shoulders.

He also enjoys being introduced by Ike at the RAF lounge as an ATC officer who "punches above his weight." His attention, however, drifts to a young, lanky British officer. She catches his glance from across the lounge. When he maintains surprisingly confident eye contact, she blushes. Although she's five inches taller than him, she flashes a friendly smile when he approaches her.

Shaking his head at Harold, Ike introduces Steve to the RAF officers. He mentions that, like them, this ATC "officer" also trains the Egyptians. This prompts the British pilots to complain about their trainees.

"They're a few sandwiches short of a picnic," the RAF flight instructor says, lighting his pipe.

Ike and Steve are confused.

"They show up bloody late, and they leave bloody early," says the instructor, his pipe dangling from his lips. "They act like we should take orders from them. It's hard to keep these blokes on task. What should take a day takes a week; what should take a week takes a month."

"In America," Ike says, "we'd wash them out on their first day."

"They're society boys," the RAF fighter pilots say. "They get in and through flight school purely on family connections."

"When the time comes," Steve asks, "how will they take on the Jews?"

The RAF pilots laugh. "The Jews have no air force."

Ike tries to steer the conversation toward the British flying combat missions against the Jews, but the RAF pilots never go there. He brings up the 1936 Anglo-Egyptian treaty, under which the United Kingdom must help this North African country in war. But the British officers won't bite. The American officer figures they've either realized that they should keep this vow to themselves or are simply tired of the subject. They're more interested in talking about Steve and Harold. They're surprised that they haven't seen them around before.

Steve and Harold, who rejoins the group with his new female friend, raise no suspicion about their ranks. This is despite answering the RAF pilots' questions about their roles in the US ATC truthfully. They may not be officers, but they do officer-level work.

As they leave, Harold and Steve point out to Ike that the RAF pilots never mentioned flying against the Jews.

"You must've imagined it," Steve says.

"Hard to focus in that place," Harold says.

But Ike knows what he heard.

~

Entering the Hotel Fourteen, Al thinks about how he persuaded his boss to let him mostly fly into and out of New York. When asked why, Al made up an excuse about having to care for his sick aunt. Feeling irrational guilt about cosmically putting her health in danger, Al reminds himself he couldn't give his boss the true reason—wanting to nag Shlomo about airlifting Holocaust survivors to Palestine.

So far, it's been a waste of time. Sure, Shlomo's now always "happy" to see Al and receive the written notes he brings in from Haganah operatives in places such as Rome, London, and Tel Aviv. He also always has envelopes ready to be delivered overseas. But he remains resistant to Al's fuller participation.

Today, as Al walks into the men's bathroom, he spots Shlomo—who, as usual, wears a white button-down and a dark tie—positioning himself at a urinal.

Al slides up to the urinal next to Shlomo's.

"Please stop by my office before you leave," Shlomo says. "I have a couple of things for you."

"I don't mind doing it," Al says, "but I'm not just a carrier pigeon."

Shlomo washes his hands.

"No matter what you use it for," Al says, "you need an air force."

As a licensed pilot, Shlomo knows Al's right.

"I can get it off the ground," Al says.

Shlomo exits. Quickly zipping up and washing his hands, Al chases after him. He says he'd buy decommissioned planes from the US military for the Haganah.

"How much are we talking about?" Shlomo asks.

"We can buy a transport for $10,000 [$113,000 in 2019]," Al says. "Maybe even as little as $7,500 [$85,000]."

Shlomo expresses skepticism. That's awfully inexpensive for a functioning military plane.

"The US military doesn't need these planes anymore," Al says. "They don't want to have to maintain them. There are way too many of them. So they're selling them for scrap."

"There's got to be a catch," Shlomo says.

"Well, we'd have to pick them up," Al says. "And we would have to fix them."

"How much would that cost?" Shlomo asks.

"About $20,000 [$216,000 in 2019]," Al says. "So, for $90,000 [$1 million], you could have three planes—your first fleet."

"That's beyond our means," Shlomo says.

"It's a fraction of what the US military originally paid for them," Al says.

"That's irrelevant. It's too much for *us*," Shlomo says. "Do you have a way to reduce the cost?"

"Me?" Al says. He notes that he'd get this operation going for the Haganah, but the Palestinian Jews would have to figure out the most cost-effective way to do the repairs.

"I thought you . . ." Shlomo starts.

"Don't you have people?" Al asks.

"No," Shlomo says. "We don't."

It suddenly dawns on Al what he's been proposing all this time. At first, it scares him. Would he have to quit his job at TWA? He's felt at home there for a decade. Move to Palestine? There was very little in that arid land that made him want to relocate.

Taking on this assignment would turn his world upside down at a time when he feels he stands on solid ground.

But as he leaves Shlomo's office—again empty handed except for the two packages he needs to deliver to Haganah operatives in Paris—Al remembers that nothing has changed. There is nothing to worry about, no big decisions to make. It's still all just talk.

~

A Pacific Ocean merchant marine since his release from the Acre Prison, Eddie finds himself alone in San Francisco one afternoon with nothing pressing to do. He goes to the Balboa Theatre to watch *The Homestretch*, a film about a topic that interests him—horseracing. But he's unable to focus on the cinematographic tour of the world's top racetracks, including Buenos Aires's Palermo and Louisville's Churchill Downs, or the protagonists' romantic ups and downs. Occupying his mind is the newsreel that played as he entered the theater. It told the story of the SS *Exodus*, the latest Aliyah Bet ship to run up against the British blockade.

The *Exodus* reminds him of his ship, the *Ben Hecht*. They each carried Holocaust survivors from Europe, waved false Honduran flags, faced Royal Navy destroyers, and succumbed to armed sailors. But it's the differences that grip Eddie:

- The *Exodus* carried more than four times as many Holocaust survivors as the *Ben Hecht*—4,515, including 1,600 children.

- The *Exodus*, a Haganah ship, fought back.
- One *Exodus* crew member—an American volunteer—and two Holocaust survivors died at the hands of the British.
- Unlike the refugees aboard the *Ben Hecht* and other intercepted Aliyah Bet ships, the *Exodus*'s passengers were not deported to Cyprus but to former Nazi camps in Germany.

It's the latter point, in particular, that causes Eddie to exit the Balboa before *The Homestretch* protagonists race their horses against each other in the climactic showdown. He pictures the Holocaust survivors who sought freedom when they boarded the *Exodus* locked up behind the same barbed wires that entrapped them during World War II.

What's kept Eddie from rejoining Aliyah Bet is the belief that whatever ship he'd board would probably end up like the *Ben Hecht* and that this time he'd have to complete the sentence he'd receive from the British. The US government is unlikely to intervene again on his behalf, and even if it did, the United Kingdom is unlikely to release a repeat offender.

Nonetheless, the *Exodus* story makes him want to take action. Eddie has no idea that, on the opposite coast, a Jew with a German name is working on that.

∽

Stepping into Shlomo's office with Haganah letters from overseas, Al gets right to the point: He believes he can pick up a couple of Curtiss C-46 Commandos for only $5,000 ($57,000 in 2019) each.

"Plus, what did you say, another $20,000 [$226,000 in 2019] each for repairs?" says Shlomo as he slices the envelopes with a sterling-silver letter opener.

"These planes are worth every penny," Al says.

Shlomo's unsure. To sway him, Al spews a slew of specs. He notes, for instance, that 2,000 hp Pratt & Whitney R-2800 *Double Wasp* engines power the C-46.

Sensing that he's losing the Haganah representative, who starts reading the letters, Al switches to describing the cargo plane's WWII heroics.

"Have you ever heard of the Hump?" Al asks.

Shlomo nods. Who hasn't heard of the Hump? Al points out that the planes that flew over the Himalaya Mountains to deliver supplies from Allied bases in India to their soldiers in China were C-46s. No other plane could have handled the massive mountains, the wild weather, and the awful airfields.

"I remember reading," Shlomo says, "that while flying over that Hump, many of those planes blew up for no clear, apparent reason."

Shlomo's right. ATC's India-to-China regulars dubbed the C-46 the "flying coffin" after several Commandos inexplicably exploded in midair and others caught fire.

"I don't recall hearing such horror tales about the C-47," Shlomo says.

The C-47, Al argues, wouldn't take them far. The C-46 can carry three times the weight. "Three times!" Plus, it has twice the cargo space, longer range, better engines, and larger cargo doors.

"We can't afford to buy and repair it," Shlomo says.

"We can't afford not to," Al says.

Reaching his wits' end, Al again asks whether there's someone else he could approach with his ideas.

Shlomo says no. But as Al exits, the Haganah representative says he may soon be taking on another assignment, in another country.

Al smiles. He's relieved to see Shlomo go and hopeful he can establish a better rapport with his replacement.

"Now," Al says, "I need you to deliver a note for me."

Al jots down a note, including the phone number and address of his parents' house in Bridgeport, where he often stays.

About to hand it to Shlomo, Al changes his mind, saying he'll leave it with the secretary.

On his way out, Al tells the secretary that Shlomo said she should give this note to her next boss.

"It's my quickest delivery yet," Al says.

The secretary nods with surprising gratitude. She knows Al has been the Haganah's most reliable carrier pigeon.

5

September

It's the start of Rosh Hashanah, the Jewish New Year. The Schwimmers sit down for a festive dinner devoid of any traditional elements. Instead of Manischewitz, they drink Cheerwine, Big Red Cream Soda, and other soft drinks that Al's father, John, bottles in his nearby factory. Instead of gefilte fish, matzah ball soup, challah bread, beef brisket, and pareve rugelach, they eat pork chops and cheesecake. And instead of going to synagogue, they plan to listen to *Strike It Rich* on the radio.

The conversation around the dinner table centers on the wedding plans of two of the Schwimmers' three daughters, one of whom is accompanied by her fiancé. When asked about their honeymoon plans, Celma jokes that they're considering Palestine. Everyone laughs except Al, who mentions that the UN Special Committee on Palestine has issued a report endorsing the United Kingdom's plan to vacate Palestine. The British, in turn, have announced that they will exit the Holy Land—removing its administrators, troops, staff, and equipment—within eight months: by midnight on May 14.

Perhaps even more important, Al says, the committee, echoing the Soviet proposal, recommends the partition of Palestine.

Al explains what that all means, including the possible formation of a Jewish state. His parents argue about the merit of such a development. John says that although he's never been a Zionist, he supports the formation of a haven for "those who escaped the Catastrophe." But Zippora argues that it will increase antisemitism around the world.

Celma wants to know what her big brother thinks. About to answer, Al hears the phone ring. He sprints to pick it up.

For the first time since he's visited Jaffa Oranges, Al's not disappointed. He hears the gruff voice of a Jewish Palestinian operative, Albert Miller (aka Yehuda Arazi), inviting him to meet in New York.

Tonight.

"But it's Rosh Soshanah," Al says.

"An apt occasion for a new beginning," Arazi says.

"I'll take the first available train," Al says.

"I'll wait in front of Grand Central Station," Arazi says.

Heading straight for the door, Al yells to his family that he has to run.

"But it's Rosh Soshanah," they protest.

A few hours later, Al steps out of Grand Central Station. He waits on the sidewalk, looking around for someone who fits the image he conjured up of "Albert Miller." Soon a tall, tanned man wearing a custom-tailored suit hobbles toward him.

Al smiles. They have at least one thing in common: they both limp slightly. But that's where their similarities may end. For instance, Al notices that "Albert Miller" wears a belt *and* suspenders.

"You don't take any chances, do you?" Al says as they take a walk.

Arazi motions that he's taking a chance on Al.

"One of the first things I was told was to waste no time on you," Arazi says. "I was told to give you packages to deliver around the world and nothing else."

"I knew Shlomo would one day prove useful," Al says.

"I have a different mission," Arazi says. "It happens to align with yours."

"Flying refugees into Palestine?"

"Flying in weapons."

"I don't know what Shlomo told—"

"Hear me out," Arazi says. He says the fight to control Palestine started the minute Britain announced its exit. It's about to get much worse. "First when the UN makes its final decision on what to do with this sliver of land, and then when the Brits finally get out. I can't wait for them to leave. But I'm worried."

Al asks Arazi to elaborate.

"We need munitions," Arazi says. "We need munitions just as we need air and water."

Arazi says he came to the United States for one purpose: to procure arms. He will need Al to airlift them to Palestine.

"This is about more than saving lives," Arazi says. "If we can demonstrate that we are viable, that we can defend ourselves, that we can build a self-reliant state, we just may get one."

"You mean," Al says, "the UN is more likely to vote for a Jewish state if it's already up and running?"

Arazi can already tell he's made the right decision in ignoring Shlomo's advice.

"We have plenty of able-bodied men with war experience," Arazi says. "They know how to handle weapons. We just have to give them rifles, machine guns, and bullets."

For more than a decade, Arazi has smuggled munitions from Europe into Palestine. Over the years, he's brought in thousands of guns, millions of rounds of ammunition, and dozens of machine parts to manufacture basic weaponry. His restless effort in every corner of the continent—under the guise of a Jaffa oranges exporter/importer—has allowed the Haganah's fighting arm, the Palmach, to engage in armed conflict with the British and the Arabs while offering a more "reasonable" alternative to the Irgun. But as the prospect of nationhood gains traction, the Yishuv's armament needs skyrocket, and Arazi's strung-together network of mostly fly-by-night suppliers cannot keep up. He seeks a better, bigger source, as well as a new way to deliver the weapons.

Arazi had relied on seafaring to smuggle arms and refugees. He spent a couple of years after World War II attempting to bring in tens of thousands of Holocaust survivors. But many of the ships he bought and packed with human cargo ran right into the Royal Navy in the Mediterranean. His biggest Aliyah Bet success—transporting more than one thousand refugees to Palestine—took leading a hunger strike and threatening to blow up the SS *Fede* and/or to orchestrate mass suicides unless the British let them depart from the Italian port in which they were held, La Spezia.

Arazi believes the future is by air, not sea. He tells Al that using cargo planes would allow the Jews to include landlocked countries in their search for weapons.

Al says he's in. Arazi tells him to come and see him at his Jaffa Oranges office in the Hotel Fourteen the next morning.

"Won't it be closed?" Al says. "You know, for—"

"Rosh Hashanah," Arazi completes his sentence. "Or, as you say, Rosh Soshanah. Most of the staff, including our financial officer, will be at synagogue. I won't have to jump through bureaucratic hoops. I'll be able to write you a check on the spot."

Al spends much of the rest of the night anticipating the size of that check and what he'll do with it.

~

The next morning, Al wakes up knowing what he needs to do: build, from scratch, an air transport command for the Haganah. Will Arazi support such an ambitious approach?

The punched train ticket on his hotel-room nightstand reminds Al that he left in the middle of his family's holiday dinner because, when he spoke with Arazi on the phone, he sensed a sea change. The Jaffa Oranges secretary confirms this when she whisks him into Shlomo's old office.

Arazi has his checkbook out on the desk. "What are you buying, and how much do you need?"

Al says that he can purchase a Curtiss C-46 Commando for $5,000.

"I know very little about planes," Arazi says, "but that sounds too good to be true."

"The repairs are the expensive part," Al states.

"How much?"

"Well, I've been thinking about it," Al starts. "We could save a lot of money and play it much safer if we do the repairs ourselves. I could set up shop, hire mechanics, and get it done faster, cheaper, better."

"It would also legitimize the operation," Arazi says. "Set it up as a commercial airline."

Al's eyes sparkle.

"A factitious one, of course," Arazi continues. "But pretend, outwardly and, in many ways, internally, too, that it's as real as the sunshine I left behind in Palestine."

Al says he needs to conduct more research to determine total, actual costs. For now, all he needs is a check to buy a C-46.

"Just one?" Arazi asks.

Al motions that he'd love to buy more.

"The Bible says two are better than one," Arazi says. "That means three are better yet. We'll be able to say we have a fleet."

He gets no arguments from Al.

"And as long as we're aiming for bigger and better," Arazi says, "is there a bigger and better plane we should buy?"

"The C-46 is good," Al says. "The Constellation is better. And bigger."

"How much?"

"About $15,000 [$170,000 in 2019]."

Arazi writes him a check for $45,000. Al stares at the payee name—Adolph W. Schwimmer.

About to leave, Al hears Arazi asking whether he realizes that he'll be breaking US law, including the recently reactivated Neutrality Act.

"Now I do," Al says.

~

The cool, early New York autumn morning reminds Pat of college football Saturdays in Lincoln, Nebraska. The FBI agent is back in the Big Apple after a few months in Los Angeles, where he worked to expose and undermine Hollywood's communist ties. His effort has helped lead the House Un-American Activities Committee to summon the Hollywood Ten to answer questions in Washington in a few weeks.

Now back on the Palestinian Jewish beat, Pat feels better about it. He has a renewed sense of focus and direction. He has been reassured by the emergence of a clear US State Department stance on the UN Special Committee's recommendation to split Palestine between the Arabs and the Jews. The State Department is urging the Truman administration to oppose partition. In a lengthy memo to Secretary of State George Marshall, Near East Agency Director Loy Henderson spelled out the reasons: keeping the Soviet Union out of the Middle East and protecting America's military and economic interests in this region.

Marshall, one of the most powerful men in the world, has gone public with these assertions, speaking against partition in major venues such as the UN General Assembly.

Pat restarts his assignment by stopping at the Hotel Fourteen. The FBI agent increasingly believes that Jaffa Oranges serves as a front for Haganah weapons acquisition in the United States. Now Pat's determined to "catch these people flat-footed." He notices Al coming in. He's seen him before. But there's nothing about this ordinary-looking man to keep his attention.

Al never notices Pat. He heads straight to Jaffa Oranges and Arazi's office to deliver good news: As he anticipated, the $45,000 check allowed him to buy three Connies from the US Office of Emergency Management's War Assets Administration in Washington, DC.

A pleased Arazi asks, "Where you setting up shop?"

"The Lockheed Air Terminal in Burbank, California," Al says.

"And you need money?" Arazi asks.

Al nods.

"You're on a lucky streak," Arazi says. "It's Yom Kippur, and our financial officer is at synagogue praying for our dwindling bank account."

"I hope to meet him one day," Al says. "If he exists."

Arazi writes Al a check for $20,000 ($226,000 in 2019). Again, Arazi makes it out to Adolph W. Schwimmer.

As he's prone to do, Arazi also tosses some caution into the mix. "Use code names," he instructs Al. "Call Palestine, oh, I don't know, Oklahoma. Tel Aviv, Tulsa. *Farshteyn* ['understand' in Yiddish]?"

Despite not speaking Yiddish, Al gets it.

"We need a code name for you, too," Arazi says. "How about Ervin L. Johnson?"

Al shrugs his assent.

"Speaking of names," Arazi says, "have you picked one out for the new 'airline'?"

Al shakes his head—not yet.

"How about Schwimmer Aviation?" Arazi proposes.

The excitement that Al has kept at bay for the past couple of weeks comes rushing in.

"*Mazel tov*," Arazi says. "You own an airline."

On his way out, Al stops by the Copacabana to get a raincheck for his date with a dancer whom he's taken out a couple of times. She jokingly says absolutely not, smiles, and gives him a warm hug.

Running into Sinatra on his way out, Al mentions he's off to Los Angeles to start an airline. The Sultan of Swoon suggests he look up Mickey Cohen.

"Mickey likes to help people," Sinatra says, sending his best regards to the notorious mobster.

Thanking Sinatra, Al rushes out. His transformation in less than two hours from an ordinary feller to a ball of energy and charisma draws Pat's attention.

The FBI agent follows the Schwimmer Aviation CEO.

When Al boards a train to LaGuardia Field, so does Pat. When the former enters the TWA office to speak with the supervisor, the latter hangs out in the waiting area.

Al asks to work the next available Burbank-bound flight. The supervisor tells him they could use a flight engineer for a red-eye that night.

Al thanks him and exits. When he boards a train to Bridgeport to quickly pack, grab his TWA uniform, and bid his parents farewell, Pat stays behind.

At this point, Pat figures it's a waste of time to continue following this guy. The dead giveaway, as far as the FBI agent is concerned, is that not once did Al look back to check whether he was being followed.

~

Landing at the Lockheed Air Terminal in Burbank, Al intends to quit his job immediately. But as he walks through the airport picturing where and how he'll set up Schwimmer Aviation, he rethinks his plan. Al figures his position with TWA, one of the world's largest airlines, may be helpful as he gets his own off the ground. He decides to delay his resignation by a day or two.

His first task is recruitment, and the first names on his list are Sam Lewis and Leo Gardner. He stops by the TWA offices to look for their names on the pilot-assignment board. He sees they're scheduled to fly in from Japan the following day. He plans to be there to greet them.

His next task is setting up shop. Stopping at airport administration, he requests space-rental information. The staff member, who's a bit surprised to receive such a question from a TWA crew member, nonetheless gives Al what he needs, including a pricing table, facility-layout options, and so on.

Returning to recruiting, Al starts looking for mechanics—right there at the airport. He spots a TWA employee whom he remembers from their WWII days: William "Willie" Sosnow, twenty-four, who grew up in a Russian Jewish home in New York.

Willie does not recognize Al. The Schwimmer Aviation CEO says they met in Yalta, Crimea, when the mechanic flew in to fix the malfunctioning plane that carried General Patrick Hurley to the post-WWII conference attended by President Roosevelt, Soviet leader Joseph Stalin, and British prime minister Winston Churchill.

Willie remembers Yalta, but not Al.

"I was the flight engineer on the plane you fixed," Al says.

"Wait," Willie says, "were you the one who kept it from crashing?"

Al nods humbly. He'll "brag" a little if it helps put together a team. Willie accepts his invitation for drinks after work.

Next, the Schwimmer Aviation CEO approaches another TWA employee with whom he worked during World War II: Ernie Stehlik, fifty, who was born in Czechoslovakia and grew up in a Roman Catholic home in Nebraska. This mechanic, who specializes in fixing and maintaining Connies, remembers Al.

That evening, they meet at a nightclub that reminds Al of the Copacabana: like the New York hotspot, the Rhythm Room makes its home in the basement of a hotel (in the LA club's case, the Hotel Hayward). Planning to keep his airline's true purpose a secret from the mechanics, Al describes it as a nimble outfit that can pounce on opportunities around the globe.

Willie says he's heard this kind of pitch before. Ernie hasn't, but he's not impressed, either.

Al pivots to talking about wanting to use his new airline to do some good in this world. Willie asks for specifics.

Avoiding giving a direct answer or lying, Al answers that he wishes to honor the memory of family members he lost during the Catastrophe.

Willie casts his eyes. Ernie says he feels as angry about the Holocaust as any of his Jewish friends.

Sensing he can open up a bit, Al brings up the possible creation of a Jewish state. Ernie says he's as supportive of it as any of his Jewish buddies. Willie says he stands for any logical entity that provides a safe haven to Holocaust survivors.

"We have Christian countries, Muslim countries, communist countries, every garden-variety country you can think of," Willie says, drinking a Hamm's beer. "Why not a Jewish country?"

Al offers Willie the position of Schwimmer Aviation's chief mechanic and Ernie the role of Connie supervisor. They ask about pay. Al says he may be unable to match their TWA compensation.

"I don't want to speak for Willie," Ernie says, "but you're going to have to do better than that to build an airline."

Willie agrees.

"Not just for us but for every mechanic you hire," Ernie says. "No one will take a pay cut just for the honor of risking their future with an unknown, mysterious new airline."

"What's the going rate?" Al asks.

"Between $1.70 and $1.95 [$19–$22 in 2019] an hour," Willie says.

"OK," Al says. "We'll pay mechanics $1.95 an hour. And each of you $2.15 an hour."

Willie and Ernie say they'll think about it. Then they order more beers and hang out with Al to talk about Palestine, the Jews, the Arabs, and the British, whom they despise for blocking the Holocaust survivors "from their home."

$\sim$

Greeting Sam and Leo as they disembark the TWA Connie in Burbank, Al presents the complete, true story of Schwimmer Aviation and asks them to join him in preparing to airlift arms to the Yishuv.

Although surprised and thirsty for details, they like what they hear. They slap Al on his back.

"It's senseless to fly in the refugees," Sam says, "if you can't protect them."

"Without weapons," Leo says, "even the most skilled soldiers in the world are dead meat."

When Al says he expects Schwimmer Aviation's first Connie to be released in a few days, Sam pumps his fist as if it's already his.

"Where is it?" Leo asks.

Al signals that he's waiting to hear.

"Wherever it is," Sam says, "I'll go fetch it."

By the time they reach the parking lot, they sign up—Sam as Schwimmer Aviation's lead pilot and Leo as his deputy.

"I can't believe you talked the Haganah into letting you start an airline," Sam tells Al.

"I can't believe I'm quitting TWA to become a gunrunner," Leo says.

Next on Al's list is Reynold "Ray" Selk, twenty-nine, a fantastic ATC mechanic whom he befriended during World War II.

Ray was born and raised in Montreal's Jewish quarter. When he was ten, his family moved to New Haven, Connecticut. The unexpected culture shock, which was coupled with homesickness, triggered a lifelong struggle with depression.

After a few weeks of holing himself up in the basement, he hitchhiked to his best friend's house in Montreal. Ray's parents brought him back that night. But over the following years, he ran away from home several more times. Eventually, he joined the US military as an airplane mechanic. He floundered after World War II, working at a liquor store in Los Angeles.

When Al shows up at the store, he gets right to the point, offering Ray the position of Schwimmer Aviation's shop supervisor.

Ray's surprised. Al tells him he brings a rare combination of strong technical and managerial skills. "And I trust you."

Ray quits the liquor store job on the spot. That day, he and Al rent space at the Lockheed Terminal and look for equipment. They go see Willie. They tell him the whole truth about Schwimmer Aviation.

Willie joins the operation.

Although he appreciates the candor, Willie says they should keep other mechanic prospects in the dark.

"I think they'll be able to concentrate better if they think they're fixing planes for a legitimate outfit," Willie says.

Nodding, Al asks whether he has any recruits in mind. Willie says he has several, including Bud King, who recently left TWA for a mechanic job elsewhere, and Robert Frieburg, who's still with the airline.

"I work with Robert. He's a good Jew and a good mechanic," Willie says. "Bud's versatile. I think he even has a flying license. He'd be extremely useful."

Al's eyes light up, not just because he's excited about the prospect of bringing Robert and Bud on board but also because his hunch that Willie's a team player has been confirmed.

Willie joins Al in speaking with Ernie, who has a similar reaction, signing up and promising to bring in other mechanics, starting with Bill Zadra—a "terrific technician right here in Burbank."

Before flying to New York to meet with Arazi, Al gathers his team. He charges them with generating a domino effect. Each must bring in at least one new pilot, radio operator, navigator, or mechanic and ask the new OZ member to do the same.

Since no one bats 1,000—not even Al's beloved Yankee, the Sultan of Swat, Babe Ruth, who hit 0.342—he asks that they contact at least three pilots, radio operators, navigators, or mechanics. He then lays out the rules of engagement: Tell the truth on a need-to-know basis, and even then, only when you fully trust the recruit.

Al asks for names.

Sam lists half a dozen aviators with whom he's flown over the years, including radio operator Eddie Styrak and mechanic Mike Ondra.

"I remember Mike. He'd be perfect," Al says. "Tell me more about Eddie."

"I've seen him fix the radio in mid-flight," Sam says. "I've seen him in all sorts of situations. I've never seen him lose his cool."

"Oh, yeah, Styrak," Leo says. "I think his parents are antisemites."

"Maybe he's a rebel," Al says.

The several people Leo plans to contact include two New Yorkers: resourceful flight engineer Shmuel "Sam" Pomerance, a manager at Ranger Aircraft Company, and Steve Schwartz, with whom he flew several missions during World War II.

"Steve's a reliable navigator," Leo says, "and an ardent Zionist."

"I hope by ardent Zionist you don't mean terrorist," Al says.

Leo gives Al a rebuking look, saying, "Don't believe everything you read in the newspapers."

"This isn't political, it's practical," Al says. "We have to carefully gauge these recruits' mind-sets."

"I'll reread the couple of letters he's sent me," Leo says.

Ray says the first person he'll call will be his cousin, Hank Greenspun, in Las Vegas.

"What does he do that could be helpful to us?" Al asks.

"He works for the mob," Ray says.

~

Sam urges Al to boost the budget to allow them to compete with established airlines and aircraft manufacturers for top mechanics.

"We will match any salary," Al says.

"We need to do better than that," Sam says. "Unless you want to settle for mediocrity."

Al agrees. Sam works closely with Willie and Ernie to assemble a strong mechanic team. As luck would have it, their top prospects work for the same company: Consolidated Vultee, San Diego's largest employer and one of the world's biggest aircraft manufacturers. Before it merged with Vultee, Consolidated Aircraft made two of the US military's most iconic planes: the amphibious PBY Catalina and the bomber that Ike flew during World War II, the B-24 Liberator.

Sam, Ernie, and Willie drive a few hours south to San Diego. They meet with Ernest Glen "Bud" King, thirty-one, a Christian WWII US Army Air Forces (USAAF) flight engineer now making his living as a mechanic. They ask why he switched.

"I just got married," Bud says, "and it keeps me close to home."

"Congratulations," Willie says.

"As a married man myself," Sam says, "I give you my condolences."

Willie and Ernie let out a nervous laugh. Playing with his wedding band, Bud says, "Knowing I go home to her every night keeps me grounded."

"Quite literally," Sam says. Willie kicks him under the table. He's worried that the chief pilot's lame jokes will cost them one of their best recruits. But Bud, basking in the glow of his first year of marriage, just continues praising the love of his life. "I don't know what I'd do without her."

Sam, Willie, and Ernie are happy to learn that Bud's beautiful wife grew up in Los Angeles and, as much as she likes San Diego, would love to return to the City of Angels.

They sell Bud not on the 5 cents extra an hour they offer but on the promise that he'll have opportunities to use his other skills and put his private flying license to use.

"I'd love to fly once in a while," Bud says. "As a flight engineer or a pilot. I miss it."

He signs up. They ask for recommendations. He mentions the "two best mechanics" he's ever met: Bob Dawn and Mike Ondra.

Sam says Mike's already on their list.

"That makes me feel like I'm dealing with people who know what they're doing," Bud says.

This doesn't stop him from giving them advice: approach Dawn and Mike with clear offers. "They don't like to mess around."

Taking Bud's advice—perhaps a bit too far—they come on strong to Bob Dawn, thirty-six, who grew up in a Southern Baptist home in Little Rock, Arkansas. He's suspicious of overgenerous proposals. Ten cents more an hour, plus an additional $200 a month deposited directly into his bank account? He says he needs to check out Schwimmer Aviation before he can decide. They encourage him to speak with Bud.

"Just don't give him the details of your offer," Sam says.

Their next meeting goes better. Ernie learns that Michael Ondra, thirty-four, a weathered grease monkey who dropped out of elementary school to become a Pennsylvania coal miner with his father, was also born in Czechoslovakia. They get into a rapid-fire, long discussion in their native tongue and, by the time they're done, Schwimmer Aviation has its third mechanic.

6

October

Behind Arazi's desk, Al finds a stranger. "Don't worry," the man says, "Mr. Miller's not been replaced, though maybe he should be." He introduces himself as Mr. Bernstein, Jaffa Oranges' treasurer.

To Al, Nahum Bernstein, forty, a partner in one of New York's top law firms and a Columbia University alum, looks nothing like an accountant. Decked out in a custom-made suit, a silk tie, and a matching pocket square, he projects the aura of a sophisticated assassin. A wiretapper for the CIA predecessor OSS during World War II, he's been using his spying skills to obtain information about Arab and British activities in the United States.

Nahum recently mentioned to Arazi that chatter among the Arabs about preventing the creation of a Jewish state has been increasing—a good sign.

"A *good* sign?" Arazi asked.

"The idea of us having our own country," Nahum said, "is transitioning from a pipe dream to a scary reality."

With Al, Nahum gets right to business. "Arazi gave you 8 percent of our total annual budget," he says. "*Eight percent.* Now you're coming back for more. You're going to have to convince me."

"Every dollar you give us goes toward building one of the most important parts of a future state—an air transport command," Al says.

Nahum is unmoved. Al triples down.

"You've given me a paltry $20,000 to start an air force," he says. "I need at least $60,000 more, right now."

"I don't see why I should give you a red cent," Nahum says. "I understand the need for an air transport command. I know you're trying to buy a few old planes. But to me, there's a big gap between the two objectives."

"We bought three transport planes," Al says. "We're going to fix them and get them ready to fly weapons, if and when the Haganah gets them."

"That's great," Nahum says. "Still not an air transport command."

"We're recruiting pilots, radio operators, and mechanics," Al says.

Al planned to tell Arazi that recruitment, despite being Schwimmer Aviation's primary current effort, has proven quite challenging. Most of the contacted pilots, radio operators, and mechanics refuse to meet. The majority of those who agree to catch up over drinks say no right there and then. Of the remaining few who accept the offers, only a handful make it through the arduous feat of telling their loved ones. Jewish mothers and wives, in particular, have put up a US version of the British blockade.

But Al knows better than to give Nahum another reason to doubt Schwimmer Aviation.

"With additional funding, we'll buy and fix more planes," Al says. "I also want to look for fighter planes and recruit fighter pilots."

"What about weapons procurement?" Nahum asks.

"That's not what an ATC—"

"But it should be," Nahum says. "An ATC is a military force. We need arms. Our ATC should help us find them."

"Munitions are not my expertise," Al says.

"Expertise?" Nahum says. "You're not putting on overalls and fixing the planes. You're not flying them. You bring in the experts and task them with fulfilling the needs of a true air transport command. Our biggest need, by far, is weapons. We need our ATC to participate in that effort."

Al thinks about it. Coming up with no valid counterargument, he reluctantly nods.

"Good. I want you to work with this guy," Nahum says, jotting down the name and phone number of one of Arazi's deputies, Reuven Dafni. "Also, hire an accountant to professionalize the airline and hold you accountable. Have him send me a biweekly report."

"Are we building an ATC," Al says, "or a bicoastal bureaucracy?"

"And buy insurance," Nahum says.

"For what?" Al asks.

"Our planes."

Al wonders which insurer would be crazy enough to do that.

"Try Lloyd's of London," Nahum says. "I hear they'll insure anything."

Again, Al nods reluctantly.

"Good, now we're on the same page," Nahum says. "How much do you need?"

"As I said, at least $60,000."

"I'll give you half," Nahum says.

Al shakes his head. Not enough.

"Come back in two weeks with an accounting report and some tangible results," Nahum says, "and I'll give you the rest."

"Make it out to Schwimmer Aviation," Al says.

Nahum writes and hands a check to Al, who pockets it and starts heading out.

"One more thing," Nahum says.

Al stops and turns around.

"What you are running is a front," Nahum says. "But a front for what? A military operation. No different from any other military operation. So let's give this operation a title."

Al motions, sure. "I'll see what I can come up with."

Exiting, Al pulls out the check, examines it, and rushes back into Nahum's office.

"It's only $20,000," Al says. "And it's made out to me."

Nahum gives him a blank stare.

Pointing at the top of the check, Al asks, "What is Foundry Associates?"

"Don't worry," Nahum says. "The check won't bounce."

~

Eddie receives a telegrammed invitation to Burbank from Sam Lewis. The radio operator figures that his skills are needed on a couple of TWA flights. He takes a few days off from his merchant marine job.

Flying to Burbank from San Francisco, Eddie reads the *Los Angeles Times*. A couple of articles capture his attention. The first is about the US Joint Chiefs of Staff, the executive branch's military advisory council. The generals who make up this new entity have taken a public position on the Holy Land's potential partition. In their paper, "The Problem of Palestine," they stress that supporting such a move would jeopardize US interests by threatening America's oil explorations and giving the Soviets a pretext to gain a foothold in the Middle East.

Eddie flips to an article about the Irgun: It made the British pay for deporting the *Exodus* passengers to Germany by blowing up their police head-quarters in Haifa, killing eight officers and an Arab couple.

Eddie wonders whether he'll ever again join the Palestinian Jews' struggle. On the one hand, a story like this makes him feel sick to his stomach. On the other, it also makes him want to help even more—to help put an end to all the violence.

When he arrives in Burbank, Eddie is surprised to see Sam and Leo, with whom he also flew during World War II, waiting for him. They take him to a house near the airport that Al has rented for the group and tell him what they're up to.

Eddie calls his shipping company to quit.

He hasn't felt this alive since he boarded the *Ben Hecht*.

~

At the Lloyd's of London office in New York, Al applies for an insurance policy for Schwimmer Aviation's three Connies. Then he meets Steve, the US ATC navigator and Cairo air-traffic-controller trainer, for breakfast at Katz Deli. They hit it off over mounds of peppered pastrami on mustard-soaked rye. When it's time to get down to business, they exit to avoid eavesdroppers.

Steve says he's been working for the Haganah for the past several years. Al tells him everything. Steve is impressed and excited. "This is exactly what we need," he says.

Al asks him what role he'd like to play. "We can certainly use an experienced navigator," the Schwimmer Aviation CEO says.

"Where I'd be most helpful at this stage," Steve says, "is in recruiting."

Al offers Steve the position of the operation's chief recruiter. Steve accepts. He says his first target is fellow Haganah member Irvin Schindler, a WWII transport pilot who flew into European battle zones with supplies and flew out with the wounded and dead.

Next, Al meets the Arazi deputy that Nahum asked him to contact: Reuven Dafni, thirty-four. The Croatian Jewish member of a small kibbutz nestled between the Sea of Galilee and the Golan Heights, who would have a babyface if he shaved off his thin mustache, introduces himself by his real name. He doesn't hide the fact that his job is to procure arms.

Ever since fighting the Nazis in North Africa, Greece, Yugoslavia, and his native Croatia as a British Army Jewish Brigade soldier, Reuven has felt the Yishuv and the Haganah should be more upfront about their activities. "When it comes to our missions and goals," he has argued, "we have nothing to hide."

This view clashes with Arazi's secretive, cautious approach. But Reuven respects the chain of command, keeps the arms procurement hush-hush, and heeds his boss's request to work with Al, saying, "Let's help each other in any way we can."

Meanwhile, Steve contacts Irvin "Swifty" Schindler, thirty-one, an almost obnoxiously cheery Floridian pilot whose unwavering can-do attitude annoys some people.

Swifty—who grew up in an upper-middle-class, Zionist home in Miami and learned to fly while studying business at the University of Florida in Gainesville—says he'll be right there. While he waits, Steve calls Ike, who's moved back to his parents' Brooklyn brownstone.

"Where are you?" Ike asks.

"A subway ride away," Steve says. "What are you doing?"

"Brushing up on my algebra," Ike says. "You know, for the college entrance exam."

"What for?"

"Engineering," Ike says.

"Sounds boring," Steve says. "How would you like to fly again?"

"Keep talking," Ike says.

They set up a meeting for later that day. Steve hangs up and calls Harold. No luck. He writes him a letter.

Steve is tapped on the shoulder by a man who's sneaked up on him. It's Swifty. They catch up. To the former's surprise, the latter says he's formed his own airline, Service Airways.

"We have no customers," Swifty says. "Which is not as bad as it sounds, because we couldn't fly them anywhere. The one plane we had, we sold."

Steve tells him about Schwimmer Aviation. "We have a built-in customer," he says. "And we're getting planes."

Swifty's in. He can help recruit. He can fly. He can assist with the business side.

Next, Steve meets with Ike, to whom he reveals his longtime Haganah connection.

"So all the days you were gone," Ike says, "all those 'assignments'..."

Steve nods.

"We believe that later this year, the United Nations will allow the creation of a Jewish state," Steve says. "We know that the Arabs will attack. The Egyptians, as you well know, but also the Transjordanians, the Syrians, the whole lot of them. We need pilots."

"I'm ready," Ike says.

That night, Steve and Swifty lead Ike into a nondescript, dark basement where they place him in front of a shadowy man who dons a Star-of-David flag as a cape and wields a pistol.

He interrogates the "pledge" about his background, WWII experience, flying skills, romantic status, and political opinions.

"You think Jews are cowards," the flag-draped man says.

"The Haganah is changing my mind," Ike says.

Steve, Swifty, and the man exchange visual cues to reach a unanimous decision. They place an Old Testament in front of Ike.

"What in the—" Ike says.

But, encouraged by Steve, he puts his hand on the Bible.

The man asks Ike to repeat after him: "Based on personal voluntarism and my own free recognizance, I am entering the Haganah. I swear to dedicate all my powers and even to sacrifice my life."

Ike's first assignment as a Haganah member is to fly to Burbank, where he's reunited with another US ATC buddy from Cairo. When Harold receives Steve's letter, he immediately calls. He wants in.

～

Lou, the fighter pilot, has mixed feelings about visiting his parents' farmhouse in Wilkes-Barre, a Pennsylvania coal-mining town. On the one hand, he's happy to see them and could use the rest and his mother's coddling and cooking. A week of doing nothing but sleeping, eating goulash and *csirke paprikás* (chicken dumplings), drinking homemade *palinka* (fruit-flavored alcohol), and playing checkers with his father is the break he needed after World War II but was too determined to help the Holocaust survivors to take.

On the other hand, Lou hates Wilkes-Barre. It's the memories of being bullied as a teenager. It's the feeling that nothing—not the Catastrophe, not

America's global expansion, not time—has altered, much less uprooted, the antisemitism and xenophobia. Disembarking a train from New York and walking home to surprise his parents, he feels suffocated. Returning a world traveler, he can sense the ignorance in the air.

Yet after a couple of days at his childhood home, he feels relaxed—even happy. He has no plans to leave any time soon. So when his father summons him to the household phone, saying it's from some guy named Steve, Lou drags himself to the living room.

"Hello?" Lou says.

"I got your name from Albert," Steve says.

"Never heard of him," Lou says.

"Albert Miller?" Steve says. "Regardless, I understand you're interested in flying."

"No."

"That's what you told Albert," Steve says.

"That depends on for whom and for what," Lou says.

Steve suggests they meet in person. He offers to come to Wilkes-Barre. Although amused by the idea of a Jewish agent recruiting fighter pilots in this antisemitic town, Lou says he'll take a train to New York.

As he leaves for the station, Lou tells his parents that he'll be back that night.

He won't return for two years.

~

On his way back to Burbank, Al stops in Las Vegas to meet with Ray's cousin, Herman Milton "Hank" Greenspun, thirty-nine, who worked closely with the late mafioso Bugsy Siegel and runs the public relations department at the Flamingo Hotel on the Strip.

Al, who is setting foot in Nevada for the first time, has heard that Vegas has failed to widen its appeal to hardcore gamblers. Many theorize that this is why the mob bumped off Siegel at his desert mansion. He had prevailed upon the likes of Lucky Luciano and Meyer Lansky to invest millions in the casinos, and they lost confidence that they'd ever see a profit.

Some say the opposite is true: The Flamingo flourished under Siegel, and he siphoned hundreds of thousands, perhaps millions, of dollars off the hotel's earnings. But Al cannot imagine that this savvy gangster was so dumb—after all, it was in his business interest to show and share profits and in his personal interest not to get shot.

The first thing that strikes Al as he enters the hotel, which has changed its name to the Fabulous Flamingo and displays fresh coats of green paint, is that it's packed with vacationing families. He joins Ray and Hank outside by a large rectangular pool surrounded by a grassy field dotted with palm trees.

Ray introduces Al as the operation's "mastermind and leader." The Schwimmer Aviation CEO would rather talk about Hank.

"I hear you helped Bugsy Siegel, may he rest in peace, reopen this casino," Al says.

Hank stays silent for a moment. He then orders everyone drinks and brings up the Yishuv's planned graduation into statehood. They agree that it could happen, that it could happen faster than expected, and that it could lead to an all-out war.

Al asks Hank whether he'd be willing to tap his mafia connections to procure engines, airplane parts, and perhaps even weapons. Hank says he needs to lie low for a while. He's still shaken up about his boss's killing. He's not quite ready for more trauma.

"We can have others do the dirty work," Al says. "We just need you to run our procurement."

"Why me?"

"You're the best and only option we have," Al says.

Hank looks to Ray, who motions that he agrees.

"Do you have any leads?" Hank asks.

Al nods. "A junkyard in Hawaii is owned and run by a friend of a war buddy," he says.

"I guess I could go there and see what he's got," Hank says. He agrees to do this one job—but to bring back only equipment. "No weapons."

They shake on it. Al writes down, "Universal Airplane Salvage Company, Nathan Liff."

Al still needs to recruit a weapons procurer.

～

On a bright morning in Burbank, Al meets a couple of new members of his team in the room he rented at the Lockheed Terminal. He remembers

Eddie fondly from World War II and is impressed with Ike's track record. He tasks them with finding pilots, crew members, mechanics—and an accountant.

"We need someone who's clever, cheap, and committed to the cause," Al says. "Someone who knows how to keep the books balanced and his mouth shut."

"In other words," Ray says, "someone my cousin's pals would hire."

Al realizes that he's starting to sound a bit like a gangster.

Ray calls his cousin in Vegas for an accountant recommendation, but Hank's wife says he flew on a "business trip" to Hawaii for a "couple of days."

"I wonder if he said a couple of weeks and she heard a couple of days," Ray says.

"How come he hasn't called us yet?" Al asks.

"He'll call when he has something," Ray says.

Meanwhile, Ike starts his search for an accountant by calling Steve, who puts him in touch with a member of the Los Angeles Jewish community, who in turn suggests Jay Leonard, forty-two, a "Zionist, gentleman, and one of LA's best accountants."

"None of his clients ever went to jail," the LA Jewish community member tells Ike.

That afternoon, Al drives Sam's black 1945 Plymouth P15S Deluxe to meet with Jay. He brings Ike, who asks whether they'll welcome their new accountant—whoever that will be—with a Haganah swearing-in ceremony.

Al's confused. Ike describes his recent rite of passage in New York.

Dismayed to hear about what he considers a counterproductive recruiting practice, Al pulls over by a pay phone. He calls Steve. No answer. He considers calling again, but, pressed for time, he returns to his car and drives off.

∼

Arriving at the Universal Airplane Salvage Company near Pearl Harbor on the Hawaiian island of Oahu, Hank stands back to take it all in: Hundreds of tossed US military airplanes—some intact, others taken apart, all piled on top of each other—litter a junkyard the size of a dozen football fields. At several spots, Asian laborers liquefy the wings, frames, and other aluminum parts and harden them into metal blocks to be shipped to mainland industries.

Hank sees Nathan Liff, fifty-seven—grey, bespectacled, a spec of a man in comparison to the size of his ingot empire—calling a lunch break for his dozens of workers.

As he introduces himself to Nathan, Hank notices that a navy surplus lot housing tens of thousands of discarded machine guns borders the Salvage Company. A Marine patrolling the US military grounds glances in his direction, or so it seems.

"Can I take you to lunch?" Hank asks.

Nathan nods.

~

Outside Jay's accounting office, Al speaks with Steve at a pay phone.

"You have to stop," Al says.

"Why?" Steve asks.

"I don't have enough change to fully explain it to you," Al says. "Let me just say we are not the Haganah. We are Schwimmer Aviation. *Farshteyn?*"

Al hangs up. A minute later, as he enters Jay's office, he's his old calm, composed, and persuasive self.

Jay agrees to join as the bookkeeper—pro bono. He's ready to start right away.

"I want to do more than just pray for my fellow Jews in Palestine," Jay says.

"Thank you for agreeing to be our accountant," Al says. "Please also keep praying."

Al and Ike return to the Lockheed Terminal with Jay, armed with a couple of spreadsheet notebooks, several sharpened pencils, and a pull-dial adding machine. Asking for the Schwimmer Aviation checkbook and signed agreements, he starts crunching numbers as soon as he gets situated at a desk in the corner of the room—all without a swearing-in ceremony.

At the same time, Ray introduces Al to a team member who just landed—Lou. Recognizing his accent, the Schwimmer Aviation CEO speaks Hungarian. The fighter pilot says he's *szívesen indul* [eager to get started].

Al hands him a $5,000 check and instructions on how to purchase a C-46, which they call "Dodge." A few hours later, Lou boards a plane to DC.

The next morning, Lou walks into the War Assets office in the nation's capital to buy a C-46. All he has to do is show his military discharge document and fill out and sign some paperwork.

When he calls Al afterward, Lou notes that "it seemed too easy."

"Don't worry," Al says, "now comes the hard part."

~

Nathan, the Salvage Company owner, takes Hank to a seafood restaurant, where they eat grilled moonfish and drink ice-cold Schlitz beer. They exchange war stories: Nathan reminisces about World War I, and Hank muses over World War II. But they know better than to romanticize death and destruction.

"Let's hope your children and my grandchildren never have to fight in another war," Nathan says.

This leads to a discussion of the possible creation of a Jewish state, for which they both express strong support. This cues Hank to put everything on the table. The description of the true nature of Schwimmer Aviation excites Nathan.

"I'd be honored to help," Nathan says.

"Great," Hank says. "How much for a couple dozen Pratt and Whitney engines and a similar number of assorted airplane parts?"

"I can't do that," Nathan says.

Hank's face falls.

"I can't take your money," Nathan says. "You're free to take whatever you want and as much of it as you can ship out."

Pumping his fist under the table, Hank thanks Nathan profusely. "May God bless you and your family," he says.

After lunch, Hank dashes into a pay phone to call Al with the good news.

Al says he's sending Willie to help take advantage of this unique opportunity.

~

Two weeks after his last visit to Jaffa Oranges, Al returns to New York with an accounting report, a Lloyd's of London insurance policy, and his chief pilot and his deputy. As Sam and Leo go on recruiting visits, the Schwimmer Aviation CEO walks into Arazi's office unsure what to expect. He feels relieved to see the Haganah operative and not Nahum at the desk. But soon the treasurer joins them.

Nahum reads the accounting report and examines the insurance policy, giving his highest compliment by saying nothing about them.

While Nahum reads the report, Arazi asks about the airplanes. Al says he will send his chief pilot and his deputy to fetch the first Connie as soon as he receives the green light from War Assets. He believes it will come in a few days.

Satisfied that things are moving in the right direction, Nahum asks Al whether he thought of a name for the operation.

"How about Operation Munitions for the Jews?"

Arazi laughs. Al does, too—in a delayed recognition of how bad it is.

"I was thinking Operation Yakum Purkan," Nahum says.

Al and Arazi exchange baffled looks.

"Biblical," Nahum says. "Means 'salvation will come from the sky.'"

"I don't know," Arazi quips, "I think I like Operation Jewish Munitions better."

Nahum and Arazi laugh.

"Operation Yakum Purkan it is," Al says, butchering the pronunciation.

Nahum hands a check to Al, who examines it right away. It's still made out to him, which brings a fleeting frown to his forehead, but it also spurs a smile on his lips: It's for $50,000.

"Good," Al says, pocketing the check. "This allows me to do what we need to do sooner rather than later."

"What?" Arazi asks.

"Set up shop in a second location," Al says. "Somewhere around here."

"Smart move," Arazi says.

"Yeah, hedge our bets," Nahum says. "I'm guessing you'll put half our planes here, half in Burbank?"

Nodding, Al shakes their hands and exits, saying he'll be back in two weeks.

That night, Arazi meets Al for drinks at the Copacabana, which they dub the "Copa*Haganah*." He brings the organization's Washington, DC, representative, Teddy Kollek, thirty-six, who was born in Hungary and grew up in Austria and Palestine.

Al bonds with Teddy over their background. They exchange a few sentences in Hungarian.

They return to English to discuss their goals. Al asks Teddy what he hopes to achieve in DC. "The same thing we're trying to get done everywhere else."

"Do you think we still have a shot with the US government?" Al asks.

"I wouldn't be here if I didn't think so," Teddy says.

Before they leave, Al takes Teddy and Arazi backstage to meet Sinatra. The singer mentions he's been reading about the burgeoning Jewish state. When asked whether he supports it, Sinatra answers with a resounding yes—as a haven for the Destruction survivors and as a homeland for a long-persecuted people. It's music to their ears.

~

Over the following days, Al, Sam, Leo, and Ike spread out across the Tri-state, scouting for their second location. They find it in southern New Jersey, just a few miles north of the Delaware Bay. The former Millville Army Air Field, where 1,500 pilots learned how to shoot the guns of the P-47 Thunderbolt fighter planes, is now eager to attract commercial clients.

The Millville Airport administrator offers Schwimmer Aviation a sweet deal, which Al takes.

The next day, Sam and Leo fly to a military airport in the South to pick up the first Connie, which they code-name "Cadillac." When they arrive at the air force base, they're horrified to see the plane's condition.

"It looks like a Constellation," Sam tells Al on the phone. "But it isn't. It's junk!"

"Is it flyable?" Al asks.

"We'll soon find out," Sam says.

Al keeps this information to himself when he meets with Steve and a few other team members at the Schwimmer Aviation office at the Millville Airport. He recognizes one of them: Harold, who greets him like an old war buddy. The couple of times they flew together during World War II take on extra significance.

Making the decision to join the operation was easy, Harold says. Telling his parents, however, proved nearly impossible.

"They were hysterical," Harold says. "My father said, 'You don't have to do this.' I said, 'You always wanted me to do something for the Jews. I'm doing it!' To which my father said, 'You don't have to get yourself killed!'"

Ike notes that he had an almost identical experience with his parents. Al asks what helped them get through it. They say the cause.

"That's not what drew me in," Harold says. "But that's what I used to try to calm my father."

"What drew you in?" Steve asks.

"I've missed the action," Harold says.

"What can we do to help future recruits deal with emotional parents and wives?" Al asks.

Ike and Harold stress that telling vetted recruits the simple, hard truth will help fortify them against grounding efforts by family members.

"We can do that," Al says, "whenever we gather enough credible info to trust the recruit."

Steve makes some other points about the recruiting process:

- Be selective about telling the truth—recruits who do not need to know the truth, such as many of the mechanics, are less likely to run into any interference from their loved ones because there's little danger in fixing commercial aircraft.
- Take into consideration that motivations for joining vary widely.
- Find the angle that appeals to each person—adventure to one, the humanitarian cause to a second, or the biblical dimension to a third.

At the same time, a new recruit—Ray Kurtz, twenty-nine, a Boeing B-17 Flying Fortress pilot turned Brooklyn policeman—spots a black Packard Clipper speeding through one of the 74th precinct's main thoroughfares. Flashing his lights, he chases it down.

Kurtz soon finds himself engaged in a personal conversation with the speedster, Norman Moonitz, twenty-six, a B-17 pilot turned Brooklyn fireman.

"As a kid," the policeman says, "I wanted to be a fireman."

"And now?" Moonitz asks.

Kurtz tells him he's about to join a new airline. Moonitz wants to hear more. Instead of a ticket, the policeman writes the name of a bar. The fireman says he'll meet Kurtz there that evening.

~

Willie arrives in Hawaii. He joins Hank at the junkyard, eager to help put together their equipment shipment.

"You'd be surprised how much we need," Willie says.

They work with a group of Asian laborers that Nathan has assigned them, selecting airplane parts to be packaged in a designated area. All the while, they keep glancing at the machine guns across the way. No fence separates the Salvage Company from the navy yard. The two could easily be mistaken for one giant field.

Hank and Willie exchange the kind of looks bank robbers throw each other before storming in guns blazing. But the Schwimmer Aviation members remain on the Salvage Company side—that is, until the sun starts to set. They explain to Nathan, as he and his men leave for the day, that a tight deadline forces them to keep working into the dark.

Once alone, Willie turns to Hank, asking, "I thought you didn't want to cross this line?"

"I didn't want to look for weapons," Hank says. "But they came looking for me."

As they observe the Marine guards, they pump hydraulic fluid from the planes into discarded metal cans. They plan to use it to preserve the machine guns. After a few hours of watching the navy yard, they detect a gap in the guard coverage of eight minutes every other hour.

This is their operational window: every 120 minutes, they have roughly seven minutes to raid the navy's machine guns.

The next night, they decide, they'll kick start the "Great Junkyard Robbery."

~

The improved OZ recruitment process has started generating results. It is particularly successful in bringing in transport pilots, crew members, and mechanics. Today, several new team members arrive in Millville. They include former TWA mechanic Robert Wayne Frieburg, twenty-six, who grew up in a Zionist home in Van Nuys, California.

Willie, who's worked with Robert since the United States entered World War II in 1941, dispatched him to oversee repairs on the East Coast.

Also arriving are Kurtz and Moonitz, the policeman and fireman, respectively.

Moonitz signed on while having drinks with Kurtz but then almost had to renege. The fireman told both his widowed mother and his pregnant wife while they were having dinner the previous night. The stereophonic crying and guilt charging nearly worked.

But this morning, he woke up predawn, kissed his wife, Lillian, goodbye, and scurried out. He had left her an apologetic explanatory note, asking her to share it with his mom, Ethel.

Kurtz slaps Moonitz on the shoulder. Robert heads to the hangar to prepare for the first Connie's arrival, which is expected the next morning at 7 a.m.

Kurtz and Moonitz are joined by three other transport pilots—a commercial-plane test pilot and two flight instructors, all from Philadelphia:

- Hal Auerbach, thirty-two, who grew up without a mother. During World War II, Hal served as a reconnaissance pilot in Pearl Harbor and Australia. He participated in the Battle of Midway.
- Coleman "Collie" Goldstein, twenty-four, who grew up in a poor Eastern European–immigrant home in South Philly during the Depression and flew B-17s in Europe during World War II.
- Collie's childhood friend, Phil Marmelstein, twenty-six, who grew up in a Russian Jewish home in South Philly. He graduated first in his class from US Navy pilot training and then became an instructor.

Hal, Collie, and Phil—like Kurtz and Moonitz—quit their jobs to join OZ.

"This reminds me of quitting my job at Douglas in 1940 to get into navy pilot training," Hal says.

"What did you do at Douglas?" Phil asks.

"Looked up and down the Santa Monica plant for airplane parts," Hal says. "It wasn't that I wanted to become a pilot. I wanted to join the war, and signing up for a pilot course seemed the best way to do it. I figured I could fly for the British or the Canadians if the Americans continued to stay out of the war."

"I always wanted to be a pilot," Phil says. "I lived near Mustin Field. I got my pilot license before the war."

Collie—who keeps his sunglasses on all day, and sometimes even at night—grew up in the same area at the same time but developed a different outlook.

"I never imagined myself flying in an airplane, much less as a pilot," Collie says. "I still pinch myself every time I get into a cockpit."

They ask him about his WWII experience. He says he crashed his Flying Fortress in Nazi-occupied France after taking anti-aircraft flak. A humble man, he never mentions that his expert landing saved the life of every one of his ten crew members. But Collie notes that they fought with the French resistors.

"We'd ambush the Germans in forests, farms, towns," Collie says. "We never stayed in any one place very long."

Kurtz and Moonitz ask Collie about his sunglasses.

"I used to have red, irritated eyes all the time," Collie recalls. "Then a buddy told me that my eyes are probably sensitive to sunlight and dust. The sunglasses changed my life."

"Are you sure you're not using them to *hide* your red eyes?" Moonitz says.

Collie raises his sunglasses to give Moonitz and Kurtz a glimpse into his perfectly clear eyes.

Moonitz and Kurtz ask their new teammates why they joined the operation. Phil says a story he heard from a European cousin, Lola Marmelstein, prompted him to do everything he can for the Holocaust survivors.

"Lola was in a Nazi concentration camp with her young daughter," Phil recalls, choking back tears. "They were bereft of water. She had to put urine on her daughter's lips to relieve her suffering."

The next morning, Sam and Leo land the Connie in Millville. To Collie, Hal, Harold, Ike, Kurtz, Moonitz, and Phil, the plane appears to need just a couple coats of paint. But Al and Robert know better.

Robert tries to dissuade them from taking the Connie for a spin above the bay.

"We shouldn't push our luck," Robert says.

Nonetheless, Sam leads the group into the Connie. Last to climb onboard is Robert.

Sam and Leo taxi the Connie back to the runway. It wobbles and coughs.

As it takes off, it sputters a bit, as if changing its mind. But Sam and Leo tilt it upward.

Sam glances at his boss. "Well, Al," he says, "it flies."

They reach altitude just below the clouds, to allow their passengers to take in the kaleidoscopic dance of sunrays on the water.

～

On their second day at the Salvage Company, Hank and Willie let the laborers do most of the heavy lifting. Like desert travelers rationing their water, they preserve their energy for the long, dangerous night ahead. Nathan notices that they seem on edge.

They admit it—the equipment procurement deadline's getting to them.

Noting that his wife makes schnitzel "so crispy it crackles in your mouth," Nathan invites them for dinner. Thanking him for his kindness, they say they cannot unwind until they get their procurement in shipshape. They ask for a raincheck.

"Having dinner with you and your wife gives us even more of an incentive to finish fast," Hank says.

As soon as Nathan and his men leave, Hank and Willie watch for their eight-minute window. According to their calculations, it's an hour away. But an hour seems to pass, and the guard lingers. They check their watches. Only fifteen minutes have gone by. To speed the time, they busy themselves with work, preparing the wooden crates for their expected new contents. They number the crates, which are marked "engines."

They weigh a crate containing an engine, scheming to maintain a similar weight once they replace it with machine guns. They line up the emptied crates like beer bottles at a firing range. They notice that the Marine guard has disappeared. They scramble onto the navy yard, gathering a dozen machine guns in four minutes.

In the mad rush, they neglect to hesitate before committing a federal felony that could land them behind bars for the rest of their lives.

The Marine returns a few minutes later. Hank and Willie regret not grabbing a few more machine guns.

Stowing the guns at a far corner of Nathan's junkyard, Hank and Willie dust them off, take them apart, and bathe them in the hydraulic fluid. The exhilaration that courses through their veins proves addictive. They do it again and again, each time cutting it closer and closer to the eight-minute mark.

They get more efficient—incorporating, for instance, a forklift—until they see the sun winking over the horizon. By then, they have packed five crates full of weapons, each with about forty machine guns, and each weighing the equivalent of an aircraft engine.

"These guns are indeed engines," Hank says. "Engines to statehood."

Willie rolls his eyes. He should cut Hank some slack. After a heart-pounding, sleepless night, they're both a bit delirious.

In the spreadsheet on which he indicates what each crate contains, Hank writes "engines" by the five they packed overnight. To make sure he'll know the difference later, he makes the "g" look more like a "q."

"Q?" Willie asks.

"For 'conquer,'" Hank says.

"That's hackneyed enough that I'll remember it," Willie says.

As they drive to their hotel rooms to get a couple of hours of sleep, Willie notices Hank shaking his head.

"We better watch out tonight," Hank says. "That was too easy."

"Yeah," Willie says, "our luck's bound to run out at some point."

Indeed, the next shift won't go so smoothly.

~

Since arriving in the United States, Arazi has pursued his Haganah mission on parallel tracks, aiming to reach an arms deal with the US government while also procuring weapons from less official sources. He is an operative who never, ever gives up; yet he also makes decisive strategic moves based on his reading of the landscape.

It's become clear to the Haganah representative that the first option no longer holds any promise. Even Pollyanna could see the dead end straight ahead. The US government has refused to sell the Jews one bullet. All indications show that this situation is extremely unlikely to change any time soon. The best Arazi can hope for is for the Americans to allow him to continue the second option.

On its face, this parallel track has gone exceptionally well:

- Al's buildout of an ATC is more than Arazi could have hoped for when he took on the US assignment. It allows the Jews to try to make arms deals anywhere in the world.
- Unlike their government, the American people have been trying to arm the Jews. Through various channels, they've sent in thousands of pistols and rifles, tens of thousands of rounds of ammunition, cannons, and even a tank.

Arazi recognizes that as helpful as these weapons are, they are not the ultimate solution. An army must fight using standardized, consistent rifles, bullets, and so on. It cannot function effectively with a hodgepodge of war instruments. Nonetheless, he stores these weapons in hole-and-corner warehouses at seaport cities such as New York and Miami while he determines how to ship them to Palestine.

He aches to get these arms out before the US authorities find and confiscate them—and before the need for them in Palestine triggers a widespread panic. The Haganah has a couple of ships that can take the weapons, and Arazi is working on getting more. In fact, he's finalizing the purchase of an aircraft carrier. Stripped of its flight deck, the 10,400-ton USS *Attu*, which the Haganah bought for $125,000, could deliver all the arms in one fell swoop.

But Arazi lacks the paperwork to allow the *Attu* or any other vessel to set sail. His applications have been and will continue to be denied. So he looks for other ways. He learns that the Port of New York Authority may be an entity of the state—two states, actually (New York and New Jersey)—but it is governed, for all intents and purposes, by Murder Inc. He knows that some of the mafia's major *machers* are Jews. He gets in touch with the most infamous: Meyer Lansky, forty-five.

Arazi has heard that Lansky, born Maier Suchowljansky in Russia, used to beat up American Nazis on the streets of New York before and during World War II. Meeting him in a kosher deli's smoky backroom, the Haganah representative looks the mobster straight in the eyes and makes his request as if ordering a pastrami sandwich.

Appreciating Arazi's straight-shooting style, Lansky agrees and quickly fulfills his promise, contacting the heads of the Port of New York chapter of the maritime union, the International Longshoremen's Association. The first Haganah ship packed with assorted weapons soon sets sail for Palestine.

Arazi and Teddy take precautions every step of the way. They officially send ships to destinations other than Palestine, such as Greece, and when they need to remit material or money to the Port of New York, they dispatch messengers who are not associated with the cause. For instance, one night, Teddy asks Sinatra to take a package to the docks. The singer readily agrees and hand delivers the cash-stuffed bag to an official, who releases a second Palestine-bound vessel.

Encouraged, Arazi and Teddy try a similar tack down South. They direct Dafni to meet with Lansky's Florida counterpart, Sam Kay. The Miami mobster agrees to help with the arms shipments out of the local port and then takes it a step further. Saying he's friends with Panama president Enrique Adolfo Jiménez Brin, Sam suggests he could cloak the Haganah ships with the Panamanian flag by registering them there.

Without checking with Arazi, Dafni accepts the offer on the spot.

"I would've done the same thing," Arazi tells him later.

Little do they know, all their port activity will soon backfire.

7

November

It is a quiet, chilly night at the Millville Airport. It's Ike and Harold's turn to guard Schwimmer Aviation's three C-46s. Despite having one less plane to protect after Sam flew the Connie earlier that day to Burbank, they scorn this task.

"My father told me I'd either get myself killed or waste my time or both," Harold says.

"It was my dad who got me into this," Ike says.

Harold gives him a questioning look.

"When I was growing up, the only entertainment he could afford was to take me to the Floyd Bennett Airfield," Ike says. "I was nine, maybe eight. I fell in love with aviation."

"I bet they didn't have a couple of bumbling Jews guarding those planes," Harold says.

As they speak, Harold grips the pistol Al gave him. The Schwimmer Aviation CEO also bought Ike a gun—but provided neither with any bullets.

"It's for your own good," he told them. "You're not trained marksmen. You'd probably miss the intruder and shoot each other."

Nonetheless, they demanded to have more than just toy guns. Al agreed to supply them with a few rounds of ammunition but never got around to it. So they bought bullets with their own money.

"I don't necessarily feel any safer with bullets in these pistols," Harold tells Ike. "But I do feel less like an idiot."

Their nights—and days, for that matter—at the Millville Airport have been uneventful. Every day or two, they take one of the C-46s for a test spin, checking such aspects as the takeoff, landing, and engine function at high altitude. When they land, the Schwimmer Aviation mechanics quiz them.

While Millville has been peaceful, the same cannot be said about Burbank. Pat, who's in LA continuing to investigate Hollywood's communist connections, heard about Al's operation and has been snooping around. This evening, he marches into Schwimmer Aviation to speak with Al. The FBI agent explains that Truman's reactivation of the Neutrality Act means no aid can be provided to a foreign entity.

"What aid?" Al says. "What foreign entity?"

"You know exactly what," Pat says.

"I don't."

"All right," Pat says, "I'll spell it out for you. We have reason to suspect you're helping the Palestinian Jews get weapons."

"Look, you're an FBI agent, you know about investigating and interrogating," Al says. "I'm a flight engineer. I know about planes. These used to be military, but we're turning them into commercial aircraft. If we happen to also fly in and out of Palestine, and if these flights happen to be beneficial to that community, then we're simply doing our job."

Pat shows Al the deposited $20,000 check he received from Nahum.

"What is Foundry Associates?" Pat asks.

"One of our investors," Al says.

"There's a problem," Pat says. "It doesn't exist."

"Then how was I able to cash this check?" Al says.

"That's what we're trying to figure out."

Al leads Pat onto a C-46 to see for himself. The FBI agent remains utterly unconvinced. He also has no proof to back up his assertions. But now he knows what he needs to do.

∼

On the second night of the Great Junkyard Robbery, as Hank and Willie haul machine guns across the invisible navy yard/Salvage Company line, they are stopped in their tracks by a blinding light.

A man driving a Jeep onto the property slams his brakes.

Hank and Willie inch their way toward him, aiming their flashlights and pistols. The driver throws up his hands. They recognize him. He's one of

Nathan's laborers. At first, they feel relieved; then it hits them that they may still be in trouble.

They ask the laborer whether he wants to live. He nods vigorously. They give him two choices—scram and forget what you've seen or join them for $7 an hour.

The laborer, who makes $1 an hour, chooses the latter.

A few days later, Hank and Willie possess fifty-eight crates of engines, aircraft parts, and machine guns. They're almost ready for Mrs. Liff's schnitzel. They have to figure out how to get the priceless packages to America's Port in San Pedro.

A friend of Nathan offers to ship them with no questions asked and with symbolic inspection. The price: $7,000 ($80,000 in 2019). Hank calls Al, who says he'll speak with Jay and get back to him.

But by then, the problem has been solved. Arriving at the Liffs' for dinner, Hank and Willie are surprised to see the house, which overlooks the ocean, packed with members of the local Jewish community. Nathan has turned this into a fund-raiser.

Hank and Willie leave full, buzzed, and with more than enough donated funds to pay for the shipment.

~

Flying one of Schwimmer Aviation's just-released C-46s from a US air base in Panama to Burbank, Sam and Leo get into a rare argument: whether the United States will vote for or against the UN committee's partition recommendation in a few days. Eddie stays out of it.

Leo predicts the United States will vote no. He notes that the State Department and the Joint Chiefs of Staff have been increasingly critical of the idea of a Jewish state. He also notes that the British effort to paint the Palestinian Jews as "Reds" has started to color the way some Americans feel about the issue. Secretary of State Marshall just wrote a memo to Congress repeating what he heard from the United Kingdom's anti-Jewish state foreign secretary, Ernest Bevin: Many of the Jews trying to immigrate to Palestine illegally are "communists."

"It doesn't matter," Sam says. "Truman loves the Jews. He'll vote yes."

Leo shakes his head; Sam nods.

"I'm sure Truman's getting a ton of pressure from the Jewish community," Sam says.

Sam is right. American Jews have sent Truman 35,000 letters urging him to support the creation of a Jewish state. By his own admittance, he's read none of them. He told Senator Claude Pepper (D-Florida), "I put it all in a pile and struck a match to it—I never looked at a single one."

But Truman's decision making is far more complicated than his missive bonfire makes it seem. The president is caught between his best friend and his most valued cabinet member.

Since finding out about the Catastrophe in 1945, his best friend, Edward "Eddie" Jacobson, fifty-six, has been imploring President Truman to help the Jews. They've been close since they met forty-two years earlier in Kansas City. They did their military basic training together and became business partners after World War I. Now a traveling salesman, Jacobson sometimes stops by the White House to catch up with his buddy, the president. The son of poor Lithuanian Jewish immigrants rarely neglects to bring up the Yishuv.

One of the main reasons Truman has taken little action on this issue rests with his deep respect for his secretary of state. Although not as passionate about it as Jacobson, Marshall has been just as determined to influence the president. The architect of the administration's post-WWII, early Cold War strategy has made it clear that the State Department believes the formation of a Jewish state would harm America's interests in the Middle East.

Thus, Truman's torn. This situation has led to contradictory statements and mixed messages. The president goes back and forth on a weekly basis. Beyond being pulled in opposite directions, he's conflicted inside. His heart—the heart of a God-fearing, Bible-loving Baptist—beseeches him to side with Jacobson and do more, perhaps a great deal more, for the Jews. His mind—the mind of a practical country judge and WWI artillery commander—favors Marshall.

Even Sam, who remains optimistic about the United States voting for the UN Partition Plan, admits that Truman has a tough choice to make.

"We should drop leaflets on the White House," Sam says. "Vote Yes!"

This is something Sam, Leo, and Eddie can all agree on: They better not.

~

Pat's conviction about investigating the Palestinian Jews' arms procurement grows when he hears that the biggest supporter of the UN Partition Plan is the Soviet Union. He recalls what his friends, the experts, told him when he started on this assignment: The Russians view a Jewish state as a chance to gain a foothold in the Middle East.

Three days before the decision, the Soviets' UN representative, Gromyko, strongly advocates this creation. A vote against the Partition Plan, he says, would represent a "historical injustice."

This statement draws clear lines for Pat. He knows which side he's on.

But the lines blur again when Pat finds out that, at Truman's direct insistence, the US delegation has been working behind the scenes to convince countries that are on the fence to support partition. It remains uncertain whether this effort—coupled with the Jews' and the Soviet Union's—will win over enough votes to yield a two-thirds majority of the UN's fifty-seven members. But the FBI agent finds it strange that three years after World War II, the Americans are indirectly rejoining the Russians on a pivotal international issue.

Maybe his work, he thinks, could persuade Truman to finally take his State Department's advice and oppose the creation of a Jewish state. Meeting with his boss, Pat asks for help stopping the weapons shipment to the Yishuv from US seaports, particularly New York and Miami. The FBI gives him all the resources he needs, including a couple dozen agents. Within days, they shut down the Haganah's arms smuggling. Even the mafia cannot override this interference.

It's all up to Al and his men now.

∼

When he wakes up in the Burbank house he rented for his core team on Saturday, November 29, 1947, Al feels like a child about to listen to his favorite team—in his case, the New York Yankees—play in the World Series' decisive game. Later that day, the UN General Assembly is set to vote on whether to adopt its Special Committee's recommendation to split Palestine between the Arabs and the Jews.

Al's plan calls for barbecuing, hosting his team and their guests (mostly attractive women), and listening to the UN vote live on the radio.

"Feels like a national-championship game day," says Sam, a college football fan.

"Except your team's playing for the first time in 2,000 years," Eddie says.

"And if we lose," says Hank, who's back from Hawaii with Willie, "we may never get to play another game ever again."

Tossing burgers and hot dogs on the grill in the backyard, Willie greets guests with a wave of his spatula.

When the vote starts, everyone goes inside to gather around the radio. They holler when the reporter notes that the UN General Assembly's six Arab nations walked out in protest. They gasp when the first country—Afghanistan—votes no. They grunt when the second—Argentina—abstains. They cheer as Australia shifts the momentum in the Jews' favor by casting the first yes vote. The next five countries—Belgium, Bolivia, Brazil, Byelorussian SSR, and Canada—all support partition.

Other notable yes votes come from Czechoslovakia, France, Panama, and the Soviet Union.

When the United States' turn comes up, Leo and a few others hold their breath.

The US votes yes.

Sam whispers to Al that he hopes the US vote indicates that the government will lessen its scrutiny. The latter wants to believe that, but even cautious optimism feels like a luxury he cannot afford.

By a final count of thirty-three to thirteen votes, with ten abstentions, the United Nations passes Resolution 181, paving the way for the creation of a Jewish state. The Schwimmer Aviation house erupts. The aviators pump their fists, hug, sing, and dance. Their guests—some bewildered, others amused—join in, with more restrained hoopla.

Sam puts his arm around Leo and leads him back to the yard as if they just beat the Big Ten representative at the Rose Bowl.

"I've never been happier to be wrong," Leo says.

Only Al remains subdued. Watching the celebration, he wonders: How long before this joy turns into grief? How long before the new reality of the manifestation of the Jewish dream deteriorates into a nightmare? The UN may allow the Yishuv to become a full-fledged state, but it's not providing the means for the Jews to defend themselves. As of now, no entity on the planet is willing to do that.

These apprehensions also keep Al's future friend from joining the thousands of Jews flooding the streets of Tel Aviv and other parts of Palestine with singing, dancing, and flag waving. Yishuv leader David Ben-Gurion, sixty-one, concedes that although the UN vote marks a dramatic new chapter, it could also spell the beginning of the end.

~

In the days following their celebration, the OZ members sober up to the realization that the Partition Plan may not pave the way to the establishment of a Jewish state after all. The Yishuv might declare independence, but it may be unable to establish it where it counts the most—on the ground.

The British have announced that they'll leave May 14. The Arabs have announced they'll invade May 15.

"What can we do?" Leo asks Al and Sam.

"Recruit more pilots," Sam says. "And train them."

"Redouble our efforts to find weapons and spare parts," Al says.

That evening, Al and Leo visit Abraham J. Levin, forty-one, a dealer who may be able to get them the engines and spare parts they desperately seek. An overnight Zionist who grew up in a traditional Jewish home in San Francisco and discovered a new kind of happiness when the United Nations passed the Partition Plan the previous day, Abe asks for a list of Schwimmer Aviation's needs.

Kicking themselves for not having it on them, Al and Leo say they'll be right back. They go get Willie, who writes a long list in the car while Al drives.

They leave Abe's feeling optimistic. They remain so even after finding out that, citing an investigation that has revealed the "questionable nature of this enterprise," Lloyd's of London has canceled their Connie insurance.

Walking into the OZ shop in Burbank, Al notices a familiar face that nonetheless looks out of place. Examining the oil-smudged mug of this mechanic, the Schwimmer Aviation CEO realizes it's Arazi, who's paying him an unannounced visit.

"Let me know when you're done fixing our planes," Al says. "We have a lot to catch up on."

Arazi remains at the repair shop. There's a great deal he wants to explore before reassuming his Haganah representative role.

When he meets with Al, Arazi has a simple message: The war in Palestine has begun. As soon as the Jews finished celebrating partition, they encountered an angry, violent backlash from many Palestinian Arabs. This has ignited a civil war with streets and roads as battlegrounds and civilians as main targets. Jews have been killed riding buses, driving cars, walking down the street, and sitting at home minding their own business. Arabs have been blown up while lining up for work and shopping in marketplaces. It's ugly, and it's getting uglier.

"Whatever you're doing," Arazi tells Al, "do more. A lot more."

~

Al clashes with Nahum about the way Schwimmer Aviation spends money. The Haganah treasurer complains that the airline's monthly payments and allowances vary too widely, at times even wildly, and appear to be randomly allocated. The OZ boss says the pay grade depends on recruitment needs. For instance, Zionist aviators receive the least and mercenaries the most.

"Doesn't sound fair," Nahum says.

"It's not," Al says. "But we have a limited budget and almost limitless needs."

"How do you keep everyone's salary straight?" Nahum asks.

"I let Jay worry about it," Al says.

Tired of flying over a dozen states to beg for a check every other week, Al tries to bring in dollars on his own. Why depend exclusively on Nahum's whims? But his first stab at fund-raising proves more daunting than he imagined.

It starts out promising enough. Hank sets up a meeting with a "friend of Bugsy's" who's interested in helping. Through Reuven's connections, the family that owns and runs Carter Brothers Hardware—which sells high-end plumbing metalware, glass tiles, and other fixtures to LA's top contractors and wealthiest homeowners—hosts a reception in their Beverly Hills mansion.

Hank advises Al to bring operation members who can answer this mystery man's questions.

"He likes to ask whatever he wants of whomever he chooses," Hank says. "He doesn't like to follow protocol, unless it's his."

Al arrives early at the Carters' with Hank, Reuven, Eddie, Willie, and Ray. The well-dressed hosts invite them to sit on one of their Chesterfield couches in one of their living rooms, drink Napa Valley wine, and eat crackers with cheese. They make big talk about the UN's historic decision.

Reuven raises his wine glass. "Each one of us must do everything we can," he says. "Something like this only happens once. It has never happened before, and it will never, ever happen again."

Across the way, Ray notices a dark-haired, blue-eyed, porcelain-skinned teenager doing her homework at the kitchen table. He moseys over, pretending to look for a tray of drinks or food.

"Hello," he says. "I'm Ray."

"Hi," she says, blushing. "I'm Fanya."

They hear the doorbell ring. As soon as the Carters' butler opens the door, five gangsters canvas the house, sending a couple of the women, including Fanya, into a tizzy. Ray shields her with his body. Her arm rubs against his.

The gangsters check every nook and cranny. For what exactly, the non-mobsters can only guess.

Hank whispers to Al, "He's just survived an assassination attempt."

Once they're satisfied, the goons reconvene in the lobby like ducklings summoned by their mother.

～

While the Schwimmer Aviation leaders are away, Pat snoops around their Burbank shop. He overhears some of their mechanics talking about the CAA (Civil Aviation Authority) demanding that they outfit their Connie and C-46s with modern fuel-injection systems.

Senior mechanic Bill Zadra, thirty-one, knows what it takes to upgrade a large airplane. He worked on two presidential planes—the Dixie Clipper and the Sacred Cow. The former flew Roosevelt to the Casablanca conferences in 1943; the latter to Yalta in 1945.

"I don't know that we have the means to outfit our old planes with these new fuel injections," says Zadra, who has earned his co-workers' respect with his hard work and attention to detail.

Mechanic Mike Ondra, twenty-nine, says the CAA representative who stopped by earlier that day gave them no choice.

Pat speaks with Mike, Bill, and a few other mechanics. They appear to be in the dark about their airline's true purpose.

The FBI agent's questions surprise Bill.

"This is a legitimate airline," Bill says, pulling Pat aside, "isn't it?"

Pat senses an opening. "Why don't you find out?" he says. He instructs Bill to take notes on everything and to get his hands on some of Schwimmer Aviation's documentations. "Then we can evaluate it together."

"What exactly do you suspect?" Bill asks.

Pat outlines it for him: Schwimmer Aviation may be an illegal front for an arms-smuggling operation.

~

The gangsters who inspected the Carter mansion open the front door and let in their boss, Mickey (born Meyer Harris) Cohen, thirty-four, who's shorter than his shortest goon, smaller than Fanya, and only slightly taller than the Carters' eighty-year-old matriarch, who's succumbing to osteoporosis.

A former boxer, Mickey enters the mansion with the bravado he unleashed on the rings in Cleveland and Chicago a decade earlier when he won seven fights and lost eleven. He's done much better in his current profession. He's brokered a mafia deal with the Teamsters Union and has taken over Bugsy's loan-shark and gambling ventures in Los Angeles. A mafioso at the top of his criminal activities, he poses a growing threat to more established names. Although his rise to the near top has swelled his ego, it has also weighed on him. After what happened to his boss, Bugsy, Mickey is willing to trade some success for security.

As his goons stand at attention like British Queen Guards, everyone lines up to greet Mickey. Hank plants a kiss of respect on both of his pudgy, scruffy cheeks.

"Can't handle the Vegas heat?" Mickey asks.

"All the action's here, Mickey," Hank says.

Al passes along Sinatra's long-distance greeting. Mickey pauses with genuine appreciation.

"How do you know the Voice?" Mickey asks.

"They sing together in a church choir," Hank says.

A beat. A nervous beat.

Mickey lets out a laugh. Everyone follows. The mobster plops down on an empty sofa, placing his briefcase on the carpet. He summons Hank to sit by him. Making eye contact with each person in the room, the little feller says, "Hit me. Don't leave out no juicy parts. In fact, skip everything else."

But when Al gives Mickey a summary, he never mentions the juiciest part—the weapon procurement.

"You make it sound almost legal," Mickey says.

Al notes that the airline they have set up is legit. What it may do in the future is a different story. But right now, it is kosher.

"I grew up in a kosher home," Mickey says. "I still eat kosher, whenever I'm at a Jewish deli that doesn't serve pork."

The goons chuckle. The rest follow.

"Do you work with the Irgun?" Mickey asks.

A murmur spreads through the room. Mickey demands to know what the problem is. Several chime in, calling the Irgun a terrorist organization.

"What some people call terrorism," Mickey says, "I call self-defense."

"I indirectly volunteered for the Irgun," Eddie says.

Mickey signals he wants to hear more. Eddie shares his *Ben Hecht* story. He notes that although the Irgun members with whom he came in contact treated him well, he finds their violent techniques appalling and counterproductive.

Mickey directs his next question to Ray: What are they raising funds for?

"We need spare parts like Pratt & Whitney R-2800 Double Wasp engines to fix our Dodges and Cadillacs and prepare them to fly anywhere in the world," Ray says. He's trying to impress Fanya—and he succeeds.

"Let me see if I got this," Mickey says, turning to Hank. "You're organizing a sort of a waste management racket for aeroplanes. Is that it?"

Hank and Al nod.

"I like it," Mickey says, placing his briefcase on a coffee table.

He pops it open. It's full of cash.

"Here's $25,000," Mickey says. "I want all of it, every penny, to go to the Irgun."

Before Al and Hank could protest, Mickey and his henchmen are gone.

That night, Al and Eddie fly to New York—the former to ask Nahum for more money, the latter to hand Mickey's briefcase to the Irgun.

~

When Ray returns from Beverly Hills, he gathers the mechanics for an impromptu meeting. He starts by letting them know that War Assets continues to delay the release of the rest of the Connies and C-46s they purchased.

"It's all right," Ray says, "the Connie and two C-46s we have here will keep you plenty busy for a while."

Next, he asks what it would take to satisfy the CAA.

"A fuel-injection upgrade," Willie says, "which would cost a fortune and take forever."

Bill jots notes in a small notebook. Ray notices it. He wants to say something right then and there, but he waits, pulling aside the mechanic after the meeting.

He's simply trying to keep up with the work, Bill says. "There's a lot going on."

"Why didn't you take notes on your first day?" Ray asks.

"Things seemed simpler then," Bill says.

Ray remains suspicious.

"I'm committed to this job," Bill says. "I want to do more. I see you staying here at night to do paperwork. I did paperwork at TWA and the ATC. I'd be happy to give you a hand."

This only intensifies Ray's suspicion. He declines Bill's offer. About to mention this to Al, he decides to watch Bill a little longer first.

After everyone leaves, Ray locks the Schwimmer Aviation office door. It's unusually cold. At a corner of the large room, he finds a gas heater. He turns it on and moves his desk closer to it. Going through a few drafts of several repair plans and schedules, he crumples papers and tosses them into a metal garbage can.

His long to-do list includes coming up with an estimate for meeting the CAA's fuel-injection requirement. His calculation yields a way-out-of-reach figure: $80,000 a plane.

At around midnight, a couple of hours before he planned to stop, Ray falls asleep.

He's awakened by a panicked Bill, who tells him that he's saved him from certain death.

The heater leaked gas and knocked Ray unconscious.

His head pounding, Ray thanks Bill. As he rises to go home, he notices that the garbage can is half emptied and that a couple of written plans are missing. Did Bill take them? Or is the gas poisoning messing with his head?

8

December

THE NEXT MORNING, RAY CALLS AL FROM A PAY PHONE. HE STARTS WITH the $80,000 fuel-injection estimate.

Al listens and asks a few questions but offers no indication about the next steps. Nahum would have a coronary if he brought it up. So Al needs to think it through.

He has more to say about Bill, whom Ray describes as a "possible spy." Al agrees that the mechanic is acting suspiciously but says they should leave him alone for three reasons: one, he may be innocent; two, they need his skills; and three, if they fire him, he'll definitely talk. Instead, Al advises Ray to keep Bill away from any sensitive information.

Before getting off the phone, Ray asks Al whether he's having more success raising funds in New York than he did in Beverly Hills. "Yes," Al answers. Nahum just gave him $40,000.

Ray asks what has made the difference with Nahum.

"The Partition Plan," Al says. "It's changed everything."

Now Nahum focuses less on budgeting money and more on boosting the operation's efficiency. He wants to see the Schwimmer Aviation planes filled with American weapons.

Al pointed out to Nahum that the American government has repeatedly turned down the Yishuv's requests to purchase arms.

"I would argue that when the United States voted for partition, it assumed the responsibility of making sure this plan can be implemented," Nahum said. "That means providing the weaker side with the means to defend itself."

Before the United Nations passed the Partition Plan, the US government would have broken international law by selling arms to a stateless entity, Nahum argued. But the authorization of the Jewish state has freed America to arm a would-be ally.

"Why would America support our statehood at the UN," Nahum said, "but not on the ground, where it counts the most?"

Al shrugged. All he knows is that Schwimmer Aviation had better speed up the repair and preparation of its planes.

"That's always the bottom line for us," Al tells Ray.

When Ray returns to the Schwimmer Aviation hangar, he treats Bill differently. He tells the mechanic to take detailed notes.

Bill becomes an even more crucial member of the team by serving as its point of reference.

When Bill gives Pat the notebook, the FBI agent nearly hugs him. But his heart sinks once he starts reading it. He can't make heads or tails out of the technical gobbledygook. Bill helps him zero in on a few revealing—perhaps even incriminating—paragraphs.

Bill also gives the documents he lifted from Ray's desk and garbage can to the FBI agent.

These documents alone, Pat thinks, should give him plenty of ammo.

~

Sam and Leo greet Al in Burbank with bad news: The United States has placed an arms embargo on the Palestinian Jews.

"Just on the Jews?" Al asks.

"Well, technically," Leo says, "on the whole Middle East."

"But this won't affect the Arabs," Sam says. "They'll still get their weapons from the British."

The Truman administration imposed this embargo despite pleas from Representative Jacob Javits (R-New York) and Senator C. W. Tobey (R-New Hampshire), the Democratic president's strongest Republican allies in Congress. The State Department has argued that selling arms to the Jews would kill any chance of finding a nonmilitary solution to the problem of Palestine.

New York mayor William O'Dwyer, who hosted Eddie and his fellow *Ben Hecht* crew members at a welcome reception upon their return from the Acre Prison, has questioned this "logic" in public, noting that war has already started in Palestine. It's not a matter of preventing violence: It's a matter of not letting one side annihilate the other.

Nonetheless, the State Department has stuck to its guns.

Hearing about the embargo, Al chokes back tears. His response throws Sam and Leo a curveball. They've never seen him upset, much less on the verge of sobbing.

"Maybe it's for the best," Sam says.

Al gives him a questioning look.

"If we armed the Jews," Leo says, "maybe we'd also have to arm the Arabs."

Seeking more practical answers, Al enters a phone booth to call Arazi, who tells him to wait for him to call back from a street pay phone. A few minutes later, the Haganah member tasked with procurement in the United States says he anticipated "something along these lines" and is "working to find another source."

"We'll do the same," Al says. "I hear Mexico's nice this time of year."

After hanging up, Al rushes to meet with his chief mechanic.

"Forget the fuel-injection upgrade," Al says.

Willie gives Al a questioning look.

"We won't be picking up anything in the States," Al says. "We don't have to worry about the CAA anymore."

Willie wonders who they need to worry about now.

"The State Department," Al says.

～

Pat goes to the FBI office in Washington, DC, to file his latest reports, receive new directives, and ask questions. Recent political developments have again left him a bit confused.

"Help me sort this out," Pat tells his boss. "We appear to be going in opposite directions at the same time. On the one hand, we reactivate the Neutrality Act and impose an arms embargo; on the other, we vote for the UN Partition Plan."

"That's just one thing."

"No," Pat says, "that's everything."

"I agree," his boss says. "And so does the State Department. Supporting partition is a mistake."

A State Department report the boss hands Pat concludes that the Partition Plan is "impossible to implement" and proposes that America's UN delegation reverse it.

"So, the UN can say yes to a Jewish state one day," Pat asks, "and no the next?"

"I doubt it's that simple," his boss says. "But the State Department thinks it can take the UN in a new direction, away from mayhem and toward stability."

"Speaking of a new direction," Pat says, handing his boss a folder marked "classified" and "S.A." (Schwimmer Aviation), "let's shut her down."

Pat's boss smiles. For the first time, he feels his top investigator is fully onboard with this assignment.

～

The fifty-eight equipment and machine-gun crates arrive from Hawaii. His arms outstretched, Hank runs toward them like a child greeting a father returning from war.

In what may be a show of superstitious gratitude, Willie knocks on a crate.

With the help of practically all their Schwimmer Aviation teammates, Hank and Willie haul the forty-two equipment crates on a couple of trucks to their Lockheed Air Terminal hangar—quite a task, considering that each crate weighs nearly a ton. To narrow the window during which the FBI may take notice of this shipment, the crew works around the clock.

Their muscles—even Sam's and Lou's—hurt for weeks. No number of pushups could have prepared them for this.

With Steve's assistance, Al arranges storage for the sixteen machine-gun-containing crates—in Mexico City.

Hank tells Al he'll deliver the guns to Mexico. "I've come this far," he says, "I'm going all the way."

Before setting out to Acapulco, Hank drives to Vegas to save his marriage. His wife, Barbara, whom he met and married during World War II in her native Ireland, has been taking care of their one- and two-year-old babies on her own for weeks.

While Hank patches things up with Barbara, who jumps into his arms when he surprises her at their modest Vegas home on Fifth Street, Al tasks Ray with hiding the machine guns and Leo with finding a boat to take them to Mexico.

Ray removes the guns from the wooden crates. He burns the latter and transfers the former into heavy sacks. He spreads the sacks across two warehouses and two basements in the homes of LA Zionists.

Ray tells his crew to relocate the sacks every few days, "just to be safe."

Meanwhile, Leo speaks with a few boat captains. The one who asks the fewest questions and offers the most flexibility is Lee Lewis, thirty-two, a member in good standing of the LA Jewish community. They make a deal to take sixteen "airplane engines" on his sixty-foot sailboat, the *Idalia*, to Acapulco.

Leo returns to the Lockheed Air Terminal eager to deliver the good news about the *Idalia* to Al. But he arrives just as a bevy of US Customs agents raid Schwimmer Aviation to seize the Salvage Company equipment.

Most of the engines and other airplane parts are still in the crates.

The Customs agents demand that the Schwimmer Aviation employees put back all the equipment in the crates. They reluctantly and painfully do as they're told.

"Good thing Hank isn't here to see this," Sam says.

"No matter when or where he finds out," Willie says, "it will break his heart."

The next day, when they finish confiscating everything in sight, the Customs agents demand, "Where are the other sixteen crates?"

Al says the discrepancy stems from different packing styles. The Customs agents do not buy it.

"Most of the other crates contained engines," the lead Customs agent says. "One per crate. There's really only one way to pack them."

Al shrugs. "This is all we have," he says. "Take it or leave it."

No one's happy. The Customs agents leave feeling duped, and Al and his men have to scramble for engines and parts at a time when the authorities' scrutiny heightens by the day.

Al, Leo, and Willie revisit Abe, who has yet to fulfill his promise to deliver engines and parts. He notes conveniently that the lack of action on his part so far has proven to be a blessing in disguise.

"They would have taken the equipment I'd had given you, too," he says.

He's ready to give them whatever they need.

Al proposes that they pick up engines and parts from Abe on a per-need basis.

"So, when we need an engine, we come get an engine," Al says. "When we need a spare stick, we come get the spare stick."

"Sounds like a lot of extra work," Abe says.

"It's the only way I can think of to make sure we get to keep the parts," Al says. "When can we start?"

"What can you take with you right now?" Abe asks.

~

With a hop in his step and an official order in his hand, Pat storms into the Schwimmer Aviation hangar like a Wild West sheriff bursting into a saloon. Feeling a tap on his shoulder, he turns to see Willie.

"I'm looking for Adolph Schwimmer," Pat says.

Willie says Al is out. Pat asks when he'll be back. The chief mechanic has no idea. Pat says he'll wait.

After a couple of hours, Pat leaves.

Willie calls to inform Al—and ask what they should do.

"We should stay a step ahead of them at all times," Al says.

The chief mechanic asks for more specifics.

"They know what we're up to," Al says. "They're trying to catch us. So we have to be unavailable. When they're here, we should be there; when they're there, we should be here."

Pat returns the next day, and the next, and the next . . .

Finally the FBI agent tapes the note to the airline's front door.

It's a closure notice. Schwimmer Aviation is history.

Hearing the news while in New York, Al rushes to the Hotel Fourteen to consult with Nahum. The defunct aviation company CEO mentions that one of his pilots owns a dormant airline: Service Airways. They summon Swifty to Manhattan and fill out and file the necessary paperwork to transfer Schwimmer Aviation's airplanes to this revived entity.

They keep Swifty as president and CEO, but only on paper. Al remains the boss.

Nonetheless, Swifty takes pride in the fact that the airline he formed, which until now never had more than one plane, has nine.

To test the water, Al sends the Service Airways president/CEO to the War Assets office in DC the next morning to buy a "Dodge" (C-46).

As Swifty exits, Al and Nahum exchange concerned looks. They sense that Service Airways' days, too, may be numbered.

∾

When Hank returns to Burbank, he has no time to mourn the loss of the engines and parts. With Customs and FBI agents closing in on the machine guns, he has to move fast. He tells Lee to get his sailboat ready and gathers the team to help him load.

They transfer the machine guns into new crates. They load them onto the *Idalia* at America's Port in San Pedro. This task proves just as hard as it sounds. Every crate fights them, tests them, and mocks them. When they take a break at the halfway mark, Lee tries to turn it into the stopping point.

"This is all my boat can handle," Lee says.

"We're taking every one of these crates to Acapulco," Hank says.

"One, maybe two more," Lee says. "That's it."

"We're not leaving even one create behind," Hank repeats.

"This boat will sink, and none of the crates will make it," Lee says. "Probably none of us, either."

"That's a chance we have to take," Hank says.

As the tensions rise, it occurs to Lee that he should find out the nature of this transport. "What's in them that's so important?" he asks, pointing at the crates.

"None of your business," Hank says.

Lee cracks open a crate. Staring at the machine guns, he calls off the "whole thing."

Hank presses his pistol against Lee's temple with one hand. With the other, he motions for his OZ teammates to continue loading the *Idalia*.

Several hours later, as they again collapse to the floor, they have completed placing every crate on the boat. Sure enough, Lee was right: The *Idalia's* waterline covers its portholes. It struggles to stay afloat. It could sink at any point during the 1,800-mile voyage.

Again, Lee protests. But again, Hank makes it clear that they're taking every crate, pulling out his pistol anew.

The *Idalia* captain gives up. For now.

The *Idalia's* main halyard snaps onto the middle mast a hundred feet above the deck, the sail catches the wind, and the gunrunner sets off.

∾

Chanukah—a minor holiday elevated in America for its proximity and superficial similarity to Christmas—has come and gone without Al noticing, much less lighting a menorah candle or biting into a latke (traditional potato pancake). But this morning, a few days before Noël, he soaks in the festive atmosphere as he walks to the Hotel Fourteen.

When he enters the hotel, he's surprised to find Arazi in the lobby, pacing.

"Waiting for someone?" Al asks.

"Yeah," Arazi says, taking Al back outside for a walk, "you."

Passing by spellbound shoppers schlepping shiny store bags, the Haganah representative tells Al, "I got a Christmas gift for you."

It appears that the Jews, Arazi says, have found a country willing to sell them weapons.

"That's the best gift I've ever gotten," Al says.

"Glad you like it," Arazi says. "It's going to cost us $11 million."

That's $10 million more than Al would have guessed.

"I guess they didn't accept any coupons," Al says.

"The Czechs know they're our only option," Arazi says.

"The Czechs?"

Arazi nods, saying, "The value of the air transport command you're building just skyrocketed."

This, they both know, stems from the fact that Czechoslovakia is landlocked. The only way to get the weapons out is to airlift them, and the only one who can do that is Al.

"I just hope we won't have to sell our airplanes to help pay for these weapons," Al quips.

Arazi assures him they have the funds to pay the Czechs.

"Forget fund-raising," Arazi says. "Focus on your job."

"What kind of weapons are we buying?" Al asks. "And how many?"

Arazi says they bought 34,500 rifles, 7,000 machine guns, more than a hundred million rounds of ammunition, 10,000 bayonets, 500 pistols—and ten fighter planes.

"What kind of planes?"

"Bf 109s," Arazi says.

"Messerschmitts?"

Arazi nods. Al's floored. The Bf 109 served as the workhorse for the Luftwaffe during WWII's first half. In the second, the German air force switched to a jet, the Me 262.

"The Czechs built hundreds of Bf 109s," Arazi says, "and have quite a surplus." The Czechs named their version the Avia S-199.

"How much are we paying for them?"

"Including bombs, guns, ammunition, repairs, and training, $180,000 each," Arazi says.

Al nearly gags. "We can buy forty P-51s for the price of one lousy Messerschmitt."

Arazi would love to have North American Aviation Mustangs. They far outgun the Messerschmitts, which have only two machine guns and one cannon and can carry bombs totaling no more than three hundred pounds. Powered by Rolls-Royce Merlin engines, the P-51s feature three times as many guns and more than triple the bombload.

"Good luck finding someone willing to sell us Mustangs," Arazi says.

Al gives him a questioning look.

"I mean it," Arazi says. "I hope you can get some P-51s. For any price."

To avoid sounding too optimistic, Al changes the subject.

"The bang-bangs and bullets," Al asks, "are they also—?"

Arazi nods, noting that all the weapons the Jews are buying from the Czechs are basically Nazi surplus. The Czechoslovak Arms Factory in Brno made them for the Germans and now has enough to arm not just the Jews but also the Arabs.

"Which Arabs?" Al asks.

"The Syrians," Arazi says.

"I thought they were getting their weapons from the French," Al says.

"They used to," Arazi says. "The French now arm the Lebanese."

"And the British arm?"

"And train the Egyptians, Transjordanians, and Iraqis," Arazi says. "Looks like the Saudis will also buy weapons from the Brits, now that the US has turned down their request for fifty fighter planes."

"I'm stuck on the Czechs selling weapons to the Jews *and* the Arabs," Al says.

"It doesn't matter where the Arabs get their weapons, because they'll always find some source," Arazi says. "For us, this is a lifeline. The Czechs are also letting us use an air base. For repairs, training, loading. A minor miracle. It's in a town called Žatec. We're calling it Zebra."

Al smiles. His operation now has airfields in Burbank, Millville, and Žatec—umm, Zebra.

But the smile disappears as he thinks about how to get his planes from the United States to Eastern Europe. The obstacles include the FBI, the State Department, and the Treasury Department. What flight routes will they be able to obtain? Where will they refuel? How will they evade the constant interferences from the likes of the CIA and its British equivalent, MI5?

This, too, may take a miracle. A major one.

II

JANUARY–APRIL 1948

9

January

THE *IDALIA* ARRIVES IN ACAPULCO. IT DROPS ITS ANCHOR IN THE HARBOR, which is dotted with boats, some in sync with the still water, others with the whales that come up for air as they pass by on their annual migration.

Hank pays Lee half his fee, $2,000, in cash, promising the *Idalia* captain the rest as soon as the machine guns reach the shore.

Instructing his men to keep Lee onboard, Hank hops on a speedboat to go into town to call Al and pick up supplies. While he's away, the OZ gun-smuggling effort gets exposed by none other than the Wizard of Oz.

The actor who played the Wizard of Oz (and four other roles) in the 1939 classic film—Francis Phillip Wuppermann, fifty-seven, known as Frank Morgan—happens to be on his yacht in the Acapulco harbor. He recognizes his friend Lee's boat.

The boat's low waterline alarms Frank. He rows his dinghy to the *Idalia*. Seeing how stressed Lee appears and how strange he acts intensifies the actor's suspicion. He invites his LA friend to his 117-foot yacht.

Lee looks to Hank's men. To avoid telling Frank, a household name, that his friend is under boat arrest, they motion for the *Idalia* captain to go ahead.

On the *Chita*, Lee tells Frank and his wife of thirty-five years, Alma, everything.

They're shocked. Frank takes Lee to town to alert the authorities.

At the same time, from a pay phone overlooking the harbor, Hank calls Al, who gives him the address of a Mexico City warehouse. They'll meet there once all the crates are stored.

"Bring lots of *bakshish* [a tip; essentially bribe money]," Hank says.

Al is thinking bigger. Since they have to deal with the Mexican government about an arms shipment, they may as well try to get more. They may as well try to purchase weapons from the southern neighbors.

Hank likes the idea, but he's too exhausted mentally and physically to start tackling it.

"Take your time," Al says. "You can get going on this tomorrow morning."

Hank laughs.

Meanwhile, Lee gives the US consulate workers something to report home: The machine guns that the FBI has been chasing have surfaced.

~

In Millville, Harold goes to see Steve with a request. The radio operator starts by reminiscing about their days in Cairo. "Remember when Ike took us to the RAF officers' lounge?"

"Don't bring it up with him," Steve says. "He's still sore about it."

Harold nods. He's seen it.

"Hey," Steve says, "what happened with that pretty British officer?"

Harold motions that it did not work out.

"The height difference?" Steve asks.

Harold shakes his head. "She didn't like my politics," he says. "Especially on Palestine."

"You told her?"

"I can't sleep with a woman unless I reveal all my innermost fears and aspirations."

Harold asks for the Service Airways plane tally. Steve notes that several employees bought C-46s for $5,000 each, bringing the aircraft total to thirteen—three Connies and four C-46s in Burbank, and six Commandos in Millville.

Harold expresses concerns that this is an unlucky number. But Steve assures him that in numerology, the number thirteen carries a positive charge.

Harold asks how many pilots they have. Steve says nine.

"That's a third of what we need," Harold says.

"I'm working on it," Steve says.

"Maybe I can become a pilot," Harold says.

Steve gives him a questioning look.

"I have a flying license," Harold says. "I got it right after the war."

Steve asks to see it. Harold reluctantly shows him.

"Light planes don't count," Steve says.

"I could learn to fly the Dodge," Harold says.

"What is this about?" Steve interrupts.

"I've always wanted to become a pilot," Harold says. "I was always reading aviation magazines and making model airplanes. I studied the Battle of Britain."

Steve's unsure what the 1940 Battle of Britain, when the RAF beat back a would-be Nazi invasion of the British Isles, has to do with this.

"What we need you to do is train our radio operators," Steve says. "We have only eight, and most of them are merchant marines brought in by Eddie. They need airplane training."

This new assignment softens the blow of the rejection for Harold. Although he'd rather become a pilot, he's excited to whip the radio operators into shape. He takes this assignment seriously—some say too seriously. Acting like a drill sergeant, he breaks down his trainees so that he can "rebuild them."

Eddie tries to talk to him about it, but Harold solicits no feedback.

Eddie drops out of the training. He remains worried about the radio operators he convinced to join. They tell him they're fine; they can handle a rough trainer. They've been through basic training, and they've been through a long war. Nonetheless, Eddie tries to figure out how to fix the situation.

He also continues to read everything he can find about Palestine. He learns that the American leaders who oppose their country's arms embargo believe they can lift it. For instance, former first lady Eleanor Roosevelt, a member of the Truman administration's UN delegation, has urged the State Department to scrap it.

America's official support for the Partition Plan, Eleanor Roosevelt wrote, puts a "responsibility on us to see the UN through in actually implementing its policies." She has urged equipping the Palestinian Jews "with modern armaments, which is the only thing which will hold the Arabs in check."

Her words, however, do little more than embolden Jewish-state supporters like Eddie, who rushes to tell his OZ team members about it like a kid who just received confirmation that Santa Claus is real. The first person he runs into is Harold. He skips telling him.

The next day, Eddie reads that the Arab League has made it official: It plans to invade Palestine as soon as the British leave. Although far from a surprise, the appearance of this announcement in the newspaper makes it all too real. An all-out war is coming, and the Jews are ill prepared.

~

Arazi updates Al about the Czech arms deal. It's official. The agreement has been signed by both sides.

"How did it get done so fast?" Al asks.

"Ethiopia," Arazi says.

Al gives him a curious look. Arazi explains the weapons are supposedly going to this northeastern African country, which had won its independence from Italy the previous year. The Haganah had purchased, from a Russian prince, embossed Ethiopian stationery signed by one of its government officials.

"Do the Ethiopians know that?" Al asks.

Arazi shakes his head. He has more good news: "The American Jewish community gave us $50 million to buy weapons."

Golda Meyerson (later Meir), fifty, who grew up in Milwaukee and moved to Palestine in her early twenties, came to the United States with the goal of raising $5 million from American Jews. Thanks to her candid, charismatic speeches, she received ten times as much.

The Czech arms, Arazi says, are thus paid for and ready to be delivered to Palestine, where they're needed more than ever. The Arab invasion has "informally" begun—five months before the British are scheduled to leave and the Jewish state is expected to be formed. With fighters from throughout the Middle East—as well as a small number of volunteers from Germany, Poland, and Yugoslavia—Syria has launched the Arab Liberation Army (ALA).

Two ALA battalions totaling more than one thousand troops attacked Jewish positions and set up camps in Palestine, Arazi says. Knowing that the OZ planes need at least a couple more months to get to Czechoslovakia, he's bought a ship—the SS *Nora*, an Italian-built vessel that can carry 600 tons—to deliver the first Czech arms shipment to Palestine.

"Don't worry," Arazi says, "there'll be plenty for you to take, too."

"How will the ship get through the British blockade?" Al asks.

"With the 200 tons of potatoes and onions that will cover the 400 tons of weapons," Arazi says. "And with the original Greek owners still on the books."

Al smiles. Arazi knows what he's doing.

"We still have a lot to figure out, including the originating port," Arazi says. "And we still have to fool the Royal Navy. Regardless, even if this succeeds, we'll only use ships when we have to. It's too complex, risky, and slow."

Arazi doesn't tell Al that the Haganah is negotiating to buy a second cargo ship, the SS *Shayo*.

Speaking to his men later, Al says the number of trips the *Nora* will have to take will depend on how fast they can prepare the Connies and C-46s.

"It's on us," Al tells the OZ members.

10

February

Steve asks Harold to welcome aboard new team member William "Bill" Guy Gershon, thirty-four, a married father of two who served as a US ATC pilot in Europe during World War II. A devout Zionist, Gershon was the first to seek out the operation.

"How'd you hear about us?" Harold asks as he gives Gershon a tour of the facility.

"Word's getting around," Gershon says.

Gershon and Harold hit it off. The pilot becomes the radio operator's mentor, guiding him on personal and professional matters. He soon plays a similar role with several other OZ members, including Eddie.

One day, Eddie tells Gershon about Harold's overly aggressive training.

Gershon talks with Harold, who, far from denying it, takes pride in it. "It's how you *teach*."

"It's how you teach if you want resentful radio operators," Gershon says.

He urges Harold to change his pedagogy. The radio operator listens. Gershon repeats his point until it sinks in.

"You cannot treat human beings this way," Gershon says. "We need them. We need you. You've got to back off."

"You mean," Harold says, "become a nice guy?"

"A *mensch*, even," Gershon says.

"Now you're pushing it," Harold says.

Harold doesn't like it, but he dislikes the idea of losing Gershon's mentorship even more. So he tries this new approach. Harold's trainees have no idea where the change comes from, but they're too relieved to care.

When Gershon hears about this, he thanks Harold and makes him an offer: "Do you still want to fly a Dodge?"

Harold nods.

"I'll train you," Gershon says.

Harold gives him a bear hug.

~

During his biweekly meeting with Arazi at the Hotel Fourteen, Al asks about the *Nora*. The ship, the Haganah representative says, has faced numerous obstacles and has yet to come close to picking up the Czech armaments.

Arazi tells Al about the *Shayo*, which the Haganah bought from the Francesco Parisi company in Trieste, Italy. Although it has moved faster than the *Nora*, it has made even less progress. As it left Venice loaded with enough weapons to give the Palestinian Jews a fighting chance, the MI5 figured out its true purpose.

Knowing that the Royal Navy was pulling out all the stops to keep the *Shayo* from delivering its cargo to Palestine, the Haganah unloaded the weapons, hid them in Yugoslavia, and sent the ship in a new direction.

"The bottom line is that the weapons we bought are still not in our hands," Arazi says.

Al apologizes, saying his men are moving as fast as they can.

"Our mechanics work around the clock," Al says. "I've seen several of them sleep by the planes."

Arazi asks Al to help find a small European airline to start airlifting the weapons.

"With all due respect to you and your hardworking crews," Arazi says, "we can't wait."

Indicating that he understands, Al says he has a couple of options in mind—tiny airlines created and run by former TWA colleagues. Arazi asks him to conduct due diligence, evaluate their interest and trustworthiness, and connect their decision makers with one of the Haganah's arms procurers in Europe, Freddy Fredkens.

"These are stopgap measures," Arazi says, referring to the charter airlines and ships. "None of them should take away any of your operational urgency."

Speaking of urgency, Al says, the OZ team needs assistance recruiting fighter pilots. Having only one—even a top gun like Lou—is worse than embarrassing. It's troubling.

"It's difficult to recruit fighters," Arazi says. "They're settling down after the war, and we're asking them to upend their lives for what most believe is a losing cause."

"But that's also true for the transport pilots, flight engineers, navigators, and radio operators," Al says, "and we're still bringing them in."

Indeed, Al has just recruited several strong aviators, including two who flew B-17s for the USAAF during World War II: pilot Bill Katz, twenty-eight, a Loyola University journalism freshman, and flight engineer Max Kahn, thirty-two, who bombed enemy military factories in Germany and France. The Clevelander kept his crew's oxygen masks from freezing with one of his numerous inventions.

Responding to Al's concern about the fighter pilots, Arazi assigns his most reliable assistant, Hyman Shechtman, twenty-eight, to work full time on OZ.

Shechtman, who grew up in a secular Jewish home in Philadelphia and moved to Palestine after serving as a logistics officer in the US military during World War II, had no intention of coming back to the United States for more than a family visit. He took this assignment because he knows this is where he can best use his skills and connections to advance the cause.

Excited to work on what he considers the most important part of the Haganah's enterprise in the United States—supporting the operation to build a Jewish ATC and air force—Shechtman jumps right in. The experienced Haganah operative, who goes by the code name "Norman," thinks, *Where could I find fighter pilots?* At universities, getting their degrees on the GI Bill. Since he's based in New York, Shechtman starts with the city's top institutions of higher learning, Columbia and NYU.

At Columbia, he connects with Jewish students. Several show interest in volunteering for the Jewish state's war efforts, but none is an aviator, much less a fighter pilot. Shechtman has better luck at NYU, where he meets Milton Rubenfeld, twenty-eight, a stunt pilot who trained RAF and USAAF air combatants in aerobatics during World War II. The son of Russian Jewish immigrants, Milt's on track to graduate next year with a business degree but misses the thrill of flying. He's also deeply concerned about the future Jewish state's chances of survival.

"I tend to be an optimist," Shechtman says, "but I share your concern."

Milt, who makes up for short stature with braggadocio, asks what's being done about that. Shechtman counters with a question about the stunt pilot's flying experience. At first, Shechtman's disappointed to hear that it included mostly helping others prepare to fight. But when the NYU student explains what that entailed—for instance, teaching pilots dogfighting maneuvers—and that he's perfectly capable of flying combat, the Haganah operative asks whether Milt would be interested in fighting for the Jews.

Without asking another question, Milt says yes. The spark in his eyes indicates this is a resounding yes, the kind that could withstand interference by loved ones.

Shechtman sends Milt to the Millville Airport, where he's greeted by Al.

"We've been waiting for you," Al says.

"I got here as fast as I could," Milt answers, taking Al literally. "I just met with that feller of yours yesterday."

Al inquires about his background. The fresh NYU dropout says he grew up by the Hudson River in Westchester County, New York. The OZ leader asks whether Milt would be willing to fly transport while they figure out how to get him and Lou to Czechoslovakia for their Messerschmitt training. Again, with no hesitation, Milt says yes.

Meanwhile, back at NYU, Shechtman recruits one of Milt's business school classmates: Gideon "Giddy" Lichtman, twenty-five, an acid-tongued WWII fighter pilot with a chip on his shoulder.

As a troubled teen, Giddy often got into bloody schoolyard tussles over girls, baseball, and antisemitic comments. As a WWII aviation cadet, he broke records and rules at an equally dizzying pace, routinely getting into trouble. He dreamed about skirmishing against Nazi planes. So when the US Army Air Forces sent him to the Pacific instead of Europe, he became bitter. Nonetheless, he developed into an exceptional fighter pilot.

Shechtman cannot mask his excitement. Here's a bona fide fighter pilot ready to fight for the Jews, whether he knows it or not. Shechtman asks Giddy whether he's interested.

Recognizing this as his chance to release his WWII frustrations, Giddy becomes elated. So much so that the usually private pilot opens up to Shechtman, fully answering his questions about his background and motivation.

"I grew up in a lower-middle-class home in Newark," Giddy says. "My father was a Russian immigrant and a Zionist, and there were always meetings about Palestine in the house. His friends were socialists. My father would give me one of those Jewish National Fund boxes, and I'd stand on street corners when I was seven or eight collecting coins for Palestine."

"Besides the *pushka* [Yiddish for little tin can] charity collection," Shechtman asks, "what else did your family do?"

"My father bought fifteen acres in Palestine," Giddy says. "He and my mother sent a good chunk of their modest income to plant and maintain an orange grove there."

Giddy pauses.

"I looked forward to moving there," he says. "I looked forward to running around in our orange grove. That was my fantasy."

Shechtman signs him up and sends him to Millville, where he's greeted by Lou, who has flown in to meet Giddy and Milt.

Giddy and Lou initially bond over their WWII frustrations.

"Just imagine how many Nazis you and I could have blasted out of the sky," Lou says.

"I don't want to think about it," Giddy says. "It makes me want to cry."

But what starts out as a potentially strong friendship quickly deteriorates. Milt thinks the problem is that they're too alike. Eddie notes that jealousy and clashing dispositions—Giddy keeps the details of his life locked up, and Lou shares stories of war and romantic conquests like cigarettes—have turned the fleeting connection into OZ's biggest—and silliest—rivalry.

Lou's "brashness" irks Giddy.

This confuses Lou. Giddy shows just as much swagger. It's an occupational hazard for fighter pilots not to.

~

Al had hoped that recruiting in Canada, away from the US State Department and FBI, would prove easier. But Ottawa has adopted Washington's antagonistic stance, including enforcing the arms embargo and threatening to revoke the citizenship of any Canuck who gets involved in the Middle Eastern conflict. Thus, months of targeting prospects, making cold calls, visiting college campuses, and spreading the word at synagogues and Jewish organizations throughout the Great White North have yielded not a single new OZ member.

However, Al presses on. His faith in Canada stems from its long engagement in World War II, a strong Jewish community, and a proximity to the United States. He travels to Montreal, Quebec, to meet with hometown hero Sydney Simon Shulemson, thirty-two, the most famous of the Lumberjack Country's 17,000 Jews who served during World War II.

Co-creator of a rocket-launching system, Sydney flew Bristol Beaufighters against German battleships and Messerschmitts in Northern Europe.

Needing just a couple semesters to graduate from McGill University with an engineering degree, he declines to fly for Al. But he agrees to help recruit aviators.

Sydney recruits two of his McGill classmates, starting with business major Jack Goldstein, twenty-four, who served as a Royal Canadian Air Force (RCAF) communications specialist and air gunner during World War II. Unlike Giddy and Lou, "Smiling Jack," as he's known for displaying the same happy-go-lucky disposition as the comic book character, had plenty of chances to take out some of his anger at the Nazis by participating in more than forty WWII bombings of Germany. He quits college midsemester to join the team in Millville.

Premed student William Novick, twenty-four, who served as an RCAF bomber pilot during the Big One, appears to be a tougher sell, mainly because he's just earned admission into medical school. But growing up in a motherless home, he found comfort at Young Judaea, a Zionist youth group, and developed an emotional tie to the notion of a Jewish state.

Taking some time to think it through, Novick quits McGill before the end of the spring semester, indefinitely delaying his graduation and putting his med school future in flux.

"After what I've learned about the Catastrophe," he tells Sam upon arriving in Burbank, "this is the least I can do."

Sam takes Novick under his wing, teaching him to fly the C-46 and Connie.

"I have to warn you, I'm rusty," Novick says. "Last time I did any flying was 1945."

Jack, meanwhile, trains with Harold, who's happy to have an aviation communication specialist among the maritime radio operators.

The addition of Jack, Novick, and other recruits frees up other original OZ members to focus on new areas. For instance, Eddie has become the operation's geopolitical analyst. While most of his teammates tend to shun newspapers to avoid the constant stream of bad news, he dives deeper into them, reading several a day and many periodicals a week.

Eddie tries to pass along as much good news as possible. Today, he tells OZ members that thirty US House of Representatives Republicans sent Secretary of State Marshall probing questions about the arms embargo.

"So what?" Sam asks.

"This is a big deal," Eddie says. "This is the first time national public officials publicly questioned why the Brits are continuing to arm the Arabs."

"Are they taking any steps to stop them?" Sam asks.

"Not that I know of," Eddie says.

Sam shrugs to say, "Then it's just talk."

"The congressmen also asked what the UN plans to do about implementing the Partition Plan," Eddie says.

"Did the UN answer them?" Willie asks.

"Not yet," Eddie says. "I don't think."

"Everyone already knows the UN's answer," Leo says.

"Yeah," Sam says, "a big, fat 'no.'"

This prompts Sam to pull Willie aside. The OZ chief pilot tells the chief mechanic that he's worried about what he considers the "lack of progress on repairs of the Cadillacs" and wants to know what can be done and what he can do to help.

Willie assures him that the mechanics are moving as fast as possible. Somehow, this news only increases Sam's stress.

"If this is the best your boys can do," Sam says, "we're in trouble."

This is a slap in the face to Willie, whose team has been working 24/7. Remaining calm, the OZ chief mechanic asks where Sam gets his intensity.

"All the men in my family were rabbis and furriers," Sam says. "I don't believe in God, so after high school, I went into the fur business with my dad."

Willie fails to see the connection to Sam's ferocity.

"I hated being a furrier," Sam says. "I became a pilot to get out of that business. And I never want to go back."

Now Willie gets it.

"I love our airplanes like my children," Sam says.

"Just remember," Willie says, "we have joint custody."

"For now," the OZ chief pilot says. "One day soon, I will take them and never bring them back."

~

Al and Sam differ sharply in their leadership styles. The OZ boss projects a quiet, confident authority, asks many questions, gives few answers, maintains a proper distance from his subordinates, rarely cares about anything other than the mission's objectives, delegates as much as he can, and commands respect. The chief pilot displays overconfidence, tends to speak in declarative sentences, forges warm relationships with everyone around him, shows empathy for others, and seeks collegial approval. But they share one trait: They lead by example.

They practice what they preach. Al pounces on tasks while Sam takes good care of himself, making sure he's always sharp in the cockpit. And they both always fulfill their promises.

In the midst of the Czech arms airlift, for instance, Sam attempts an insane gambit to keep his vow to do everything to protect his beloved Connie. It begins while he's on the ground watching another OZ pilot bring in the transport plane back from Israel.

One of the Connie's wheels refuses to go down. Sam flies up in a borrowed Czech Vultee BT-13 Valiant to try to dislodge it with the tip of his wing.

The Connie's pilot—Marty Ribakoff, thirty-one, a Brooklyn native and WWII USAAF veteran as experienced and skilled as Sam—watches the twisted Valiant effort with befuddled horror.

Like everyone on the ground, Marty, who flew C-46s over the Hump in China during World War II, breathes a sigh of relief when Sam gives up.

Marty lands on one wheel. The Connie requires days of extensive repairs, and Sam solidifies his reputation as a risk taker who keeps his word at any cost.

In less ostentatious fashion, Al puts his life on the line when he tests a new kind of explosive. One of Hank's friends connects them with a chemist who claims to have created a bomb "ten times more powerful than TNT."

They test it in a New Jersey ravine. When the two homemade bombs fail to detonate, the inventor insists that Hank go down to check the wiring. Knowing the explosives could still go off at any moment, Al insists on doing it himself.

Hank counters that it's his responsibility. Hearing Al's reason—that he's single while Hank's married with two children—the inventor sides with the OZ boss.

They both agree to go. They fix the wires, return safely, and watch the chemist detonate the bombs to Kingdom Come. In the end, this type of explosive proves too unstable to use in battle. But the OZ boss solidifies his reputation as a leader who never asks anyone to do anything he wouldn't.

At this point, Al aims to fulfill his promise to Arazi to search for a European charter to start airlifting the Czech arms. He believes he's found the right one: Paris-based Ocean Trade Airways, created and run by former US ATC and TWA navigator Gerald Rowland, twenty-nine.

Remembering Al, Gerald agrees to speak in person with Harry "Freddy" Fredkens, thirty-two, who was born and raised in the Belgian Congo, flew transport planes for the RAF during World War II and joined the Yishuv after the war.

Gerald meets Freddy—who uses "Julius Lewis" as a nom de guerre and pretends to be a pastry chef—at one of the City of Love's best Moroccan restaurants, Jour et Nuit. The Ocean Trade Airways CEO calmly answers the Haganah representative's detailed questions: The charter carries a Panamanian registration, has one plane (a Douglas C-54 Skymaster), flies out of Paris–Le Bourget Airport, and transports luxury goods such as custom-made clothes and limited-edition whiskey.

"We're used to being very discreet," Gerald says.

Freddy gives him a questioning look.

"In postwar Europe," Gerald says, "$1,000 dresses and $500 bottles of perfume are considered so untasteful, we treat them as contraband."

Freddy proposes that Gerald go all the way and start smuggling arms. The Ocean Trade Airways CEO does not flinch.

"Usually, we charge a minimum of $2.50 a mile," Gerald says. "This is going to be at least $3.50."

"Palestine is about 2,000 miles away," Freddy says. "That would make it $7,000."

Gerald's eyes light up.

"How about we give you $10,000 a flight?" Freddy says.

Gerald extends his right hand.

~

The Haganah's move to find other ways besides OZ to bring the Czech weapons to Palestine has made some of the operation members more determined. Sam, in particular, has taken this as a personal challenge. He has stepped up the C-46 and Connie training, making it more structured and rigorous. He wants to prepare the pilots, none of whom have flown these planes, as fast as possible but not compromise quality.

Much as he does in every endeavor he pursues, Sam aims for perfection as a trainer. Besides being fanatical about preparing OZ pilots for every possible scenario, he also knows that the best way to earn their respect is to excel in all aspects of flying. He's heard them making fun of his quirks, including his yogurt making and amateur boxing. But he believes they're just showing him affection. For the most part, he's right.

If he could hear them now, he'd beam and cringe at the same time. Meeting with new pilots, Ike and Lou prep them for their trainer.

"He's got the most flying experience of any of us," Ike says.

"He's vain," Lou says, "but with good reason."

"He's a pilot's pilot," Ike says. "He can carry out any flying mission, no matter how tough."

They also warn the new recruits about a different side of Sam—the overly competitive, sometimes sore loser.

"He works out with weights," Ike says. "When he found out that I work out, too, he wanted to arm wrestle. I was starting to beat him, and he looked like he was panicking, so I let him win."

Lou cautions the new recruits to think twice before accepting Sam's invitation to compete.

"Whenever he sees me, no matter where we are, he challenges me to pushups," Lou says. "I do a hundred pushups every day. The first time, I beat him. But he looked so sad that, since then, I've let him win."

Sam shows up. To get going, he leads the group in doing pushups. Ordering them to do fifty, he keeps up with the slowest members, helping them complete the set.

He pumps out a couple more—bringing his total above fifty—and starts the flight training.

11

March

Packing a loaded pistol, Al flies into Mexico City's Aeropuerto Internacional Benito Juárez carrying a briefcase stuffed with $250,000 in cash. It's more than *bakshish*—it's money to secure an arms deal, the prospect of which has been made possible by Hank's chutzpah.

After unloading the crates from the *Idalia* and storing the machine guns at the Mexico City warehouse, Hank evaded the US authorities long enough to gain protection from the upper echelons of the Mexican defense complex, whom he's charmed and befriended. His new contacts shield him and show a willingness to sell him weapons. They've even discussed specifics.

It's not blind trust that has won them over. They know Hank's lying when he proclaims that the weapons will go to China. What's drawing the Mexicans to the Vegas operative is his dazzling style (he wines and dines them), mobster reputation (he sure looks and plays the part), and free-flowing cash (he tosses around $100 bills like pesos).

Landing in Mexico City, Al tries to think about anything other than his cash-filled briefcase. He considers how this purchase complements the Czech acquisition by giving the Jews a different set of weapons: thirty-six artillery pieces, seventeen thousand artillery shells, and two thousand aerial bombs.

The Mexican deal also includes seven million rounds of machine gun ammunition.

Recalling the Zebra $11 million price tag, Al considers the Mexican deal a bargain. Getting into a taxi, he tells himself that if he and Hank had negotiated with Czechoslovakia, they would've saved the Jews millions. He knows what he would do with that extra cash: buy P-51s.

Al has heard that the Mexicans have Mustangs for sale. He hopes to convince them to sell him some of them. But first he has to reach the defense officials' office at a Federal District building in the Zócalo, Mexico City's main square.

A policeman stops the taxi for an unspecified—and, as far as Al can tell, trumped-up—violation.

The policeman opens a back door and plops down next to Al, who slips the briefcase to the floor.

Realizing that Al is an American, the policeman asks why he's here.

Al says he's a UCLA researcher coming to an academic conference to present his findings of how northern wind currents affect post-WWII commercial flight patterns. He whispers that he'll "make it worthwhile" for the policeman to "let him go."

The policeman says he has no idea what Al's talking about and demands a bribe.

When Al reaches for his wallet, he inadvertently reveals the pistol. The policeman points at it.

Al reluctantly gives it up. The policeman examines it. He grips it. It feels good in his hand. He pockets it. But he lingers. Al hands him $20.

The policeman jumps out of the taxi, shuts the door, and motions for the driver to drive on.

Al turns to watch the policeman playfully aiming the pistol.

At first, Al is miffed. What if he needs the pistol during this trip? But when he looks at his briefcase, he grasps the magnitude of his good fortune.

He cradles the briefcase like a baby.

~

Sam and Lou enter a USAAF base in Tulsa (not the code name for Tel Aviv but the real Tulsa, in the real Oklahoma) to pick up a C-46. They present their War Assets certificate of purchase to the commanding logistical officer, who leads them right to it.

"What's taken you so long?" the officer asks.

"We came as soon as we got the notice," Sam says.

The officer shrugs. He's just happy to get rid of this giant piece of scrap.

As they enter the C-46, Lou reminds Sam that he still needs training.

"You've never flown a Dodge?" Sam says.

"Sam," Lou says, "I've never even seen one."

"That's all right," Sam says. "Get in the right seat, and I'll teach you on the way."

Sam gives him the kind of detailed, patient, hands-on training that sticks. When they go into this era's equivalent of autopilot, the OZ chief pilot tells Lou that they've recruited one of the world's best fighter pilots.

"The Falcon of Malta. Canada's most famous WWII hero." Flying Officer George Frederick "Buzz" Beurling, twenty-nine.

Lou's impressed. He's heard of Buzz.

During World War II, Buzz shot down thirty-two German and Italian warplanes, including seventeen in a whirlwind two-week span over the British-controlled, Axis-besieged Mediterranean island of Malta. His kills included enemy aces such as Italy's Furio Doglo Nicolt—who stalked the RAF, downing six Spitfires—and several Bf 109s.

"Does he know he'll be flying a Messerschmitt for us?" Lou asks.

Sam shrugs.

When he approached the Haganah representative in Montreal to offer his services, Buzz (who never answers to that nickname) had no idea he'd be slated to fly a Bf 109. Ben Dunkelman never revealed the type of fighters the Jews were buying. But the Canadian ace would have most likely agreed to fly any plane. He was desperate. After earning a reputation as an extremely difficult feller, the Distinguished Flying Medal honoree has failed to secure gainful post-WWII employment. Even the USAAF and commercial airlines have all turned him down.

Separated from his wife due to his wandering eye, which started bothering her during their honeymoon, Buzz needs a new mission.

"Is Al aware of his reputation?" Lou asks.

Sam nods. They know he clashed with his British and Canadian commanders, that he's single-minded and odd, and that he's a lone wolf in a pride of lions. But they don't care. They are as desperate as him.

Sam and Buzz share a few traits, including a commitment to a strict exercise routine and diet. But for the Canadian ace, it's not about his overall health. It's about keeping what he believes to be his number-one edge: his 20/10 eyesight. He'll do anything to preserve his hawkish visual acuity.

"This is his third air force," Sam says. "But it's the first to appreciate him."

"We have an air force?" Lou asks.

They certainly have an ATC. And by the time they land in Burbank, they have another pilot who can fly their C-46s: Lou.

~

Al arrives at the Mexican defense office to find Hank waiting impatiently. He sticks a few $20s in the Vegas operative's jacket pocket.

"What this for?" Hank asks.

"In case you need to shake off any Mexican cops."

"When will our planes pick up the machine-gun crates?" Hank asks.

Al says the weapons he hopes to buy from Mexico and the guns Hank stole from the US Navy will have to go to Palestine by sea.

"That smacks up against everything you stand for," Hank says.

Al notes that he does what's needed, even at the expense of looking hypocritical. He explains that the machine guns are ready to go, but the planes are not. Hence the need for a ship.

Arazi bought it—Al's argument and, soon after, the SS *Kefalos*, a tramp steamer. They registered the ship, code-named *Dromit* (Hebrew for "South"), in Panama and staffed it with Spaniards who escaped their country's dictator, Francisco Franco. Now in San Francisco, it's preparing to sail to Brooklyn's Todd Shipyards for repairs.

"But—" a disappointed Hank protests.

"I prefer to fly the weapons, too," Al says. "Our planes are stuck in the US for now. We need export licenses to get them out."

Al and Hank meet with the Mexican defense officials.

The Mexicans are charmed by Al's easygoing, authoritative manner, as well as the crisp cash. They shake hands, accept the payment, and, despite refusing to sign any documents, guarantee the delivery of the arms.

Sensing an opening, Al brings up the P-51s. The Mexicans surprise him by saying they have fifty Mustangs for sale and would be happy to begin negotiating. Oh, and they also have a few Republic P-47 Thunderbolts they'd be willing to unload for the right price.

This American-made fighter plane packs even more firepower than the P-51. Propelled by Al's favorite kind of airplane engine—a Pratt & Whitney— the P-47 has two more machine guns and carries more than twice the bombload.

The Mexicans offer to sell twenty-five P-47s for $1 million. Al says he will get back to them.

As they leave the defense ministry, Al asks Hank to wait for the *Kefalos*. The look he receives in response indicates that Hank never considered any other option.

Al flies to New York to update Arazi and Nahum about the Mexican arms deal and put together an offer for the P-51s and P-47s. This time, it's the accountant/attorney who's more enthusiastic.

Al examines Arazi, who says it's simply too late.

"We already made the deal with the Czechs," Arazi says. "And we're already exploring buying more."

"More Messerschmitts?" Al asks.

Arazi nods.

"Why? They're, at best, mediocre," Al says. "Who knows how well the Czechs built them? The P-51 and P-47 are two of the best fighter planes in the world. Why wouldn't we do everything we can to get them?"

"Because the P-51s and P-47s are just talk," Arazi says. "The Messerschmitts are real."

"The P-51s and P-47s can become just as real if we make a quick offer," Al says.

"Let's see how the Mexican arms delivery goes first," Arazi says, "before making any more deals."

"I didn't realize we had the luxury of waiting," Al says.

Although he remains unconvinced, Arazi says he'll bring it up with the Palestinian Jewish leadership. "I may have a chance to speak about it with HaZaken," he says.

HaZaken (Hebrew for "The Elder") is Ben-Gurion, the Yishuv leader.

"Please present it in a factual way," Al says.

"Believe me," Arazi says, "I'd love to be proven wrong and send American fighter planes to Palestine. I could retire after that and go live in a kibbutz in the Galilee, knowing that Mustangs and Thunderbolts are keeping my country safe."

~

Like Swifty, Ike's ingrained enthusiasm infuses everything he does. He even looks back fondly at the days he spent breaking his back helping load Hank's machine guns onto the *Idalia*. But today he feels particularly excited. His operational task calls for meeting—and hopefully signing up—recruiting prospects at UCLA.

He's heard that Jackie Robinson, who integrated Major League Baseball by joining Ike's beloved Brooklyn Dodgers the previous year, got his start at UCLA. In the OZ member's playful mind, venturing to the campus abutting the Santa Monica Mountains is a little like stepping onto Ebbets Field in Flatbush, and recruiting pilots is a little like bringing up star minor leaguers to the majors.

What Ike doesn't know is that, while at UCLA, Robinson excelled in football, track and field, and basketball but not baseball, hitting .097.

Lou, who joins Ike on the UCLA recruiting visit, is confused: "It's not like Jackie's there now."

Arriving at UCLA expecting to find a pristine, peaceful campus, Ike, Lou, and Milt are surprised to see bulldozers tearing up sidewalks and trucks dumping construction material on communal areas. Had they checked with Eddie, he would've told them that he read that the school is undergoing a $38 million expansion.

"At least we won't have to worry about anyone overhearing our discussions," Lou says.

They have three targets:

- Art major and LA native Bob Vickman, twenty-six, a six-foot-two-inch son of Russian Jewish immigrants. During World War II, he served as a pilot in the USAAF's photography unit in the Pacific.
- Art major Stan Andrews, twenty-five, son of Russian Jewish immigrants to the Bronx. During World War II, he flew B-25 bombers for the USAAF in the Pacific.
- Business major Lee Silverman, twenty-one, son of Polish Jewish immigrants to Cleveland. As a high school senior in 1945, he signed up for a US Navy pilot course, which was canceled as World War II wound down. He was in basic training during the war's final couple of weeks and never saw action.

Lee recoils in speech class as a classmate argues against the creation of a Jewish state. When she concludes her talk, she receives faint applause and an instant, impassioned rebuttal from Michael Chlavin, an intense young man with dark features, bushy eyebrows, high cheekbones, and a booming voice.

When Michael finishes, he receives a standing ovation, led by Lee.

Meanwhile, Ike, Lou, and Milt look for Vickman and Stan, who are best friends and roommates, in the art school. The first student they ask knows them. As former combat pilots who are proud of their service, Vickman and Stan stand out among the beatniks who dominate their major.

Ike, Lou, and Milt hit it off with Vickman and Stan, who are interested in joining the operation but need to think about it. They invite the OZ members to Stan's twenty-fifth birthday celebration that evening.

Ike, Lou, and Milt never locate their third prospect, who, as a walk-on point guard on the UCLA basketball team, should be easy to find. Maybe they're just too excited about Vickman and Stan. Regardless, Lee, inspired by Michael's speech, finds his way to the future Jewish state's military. Although he never joins OZ, he volunteers through the Cleveland office of Land and Labor for Palestine, a nationwide effort set up by Teddy Kollek to recruit all kinds of volunteers, not just aviators.

Lee leaves UCLA for Palestine, where he serves as an Israeli Air Force (IAF) intelligence specialist.

Back at UCLA that evening for the birthday party, Ike, Lou, and Milt answer Vickman and Stan's questions, including whether they can use their artistic skills as part of the Jewish state's war effort.

"What do you have in mind?" Ike asks.

They say they'd like to do some designs for the Jewish military, take some photos, that sort of thing.

"We'd bring our cameras, drawing pads, sketching pencils," Vickman says.

"I don't see why not," Lou says.

They sign up.

~

As he drives to Burbank, Pat hears a radio news report about the American UN delegation, in essence, rescinding its vote for the Partition Plan. On the world stage, America now seeks to shelve the creation of a Jewish state for ten years and, in its place, set up an international trusteeship in Palestine.

Shocking everyone outside the US State Department, including President Truman, America's UN ambassador, Warren Austin, explains that a trusteeship "would establish the conditions of order which are essential to a peaceful solution."

According to the State Department, which crafted this proposal, the trusteeship would allow the United Nations to take control of Palestine after Britain's mandate ends in mid-May.

The need for the trusteeship, Austin and the State Department official imply, is clear: the Partition Plan cannot be implemented without a major armed conflict. It has already ignited a civil war, and it's projected to touch off an unprecedented Middle Eastern conflict that could force countries outside the region to intervene. So, to a large degree, this proposal is a preventive measure.

Pat likes it. By eliminating the prospect of war and the creation of a Jewish state in one fell swoop, the trusteeship would take away Service Airways' raison d'être. This would allow the FBI agent to focus on crushing America's growing communist community.

Walking into the Lockheed terminal, Pat sees Swifty. Without saying a word, he hands the Service Airways CEO a note threatening to shut down his company. It includes probing questions, which the airline's figurehead boss later passes on to its real leader, Al.

"Every answer must be backed up with documentation," Swifty says, passing along Pat's directive.

Al skims the note and questions, crumples the paper, and tosses it in the garbage. He tells Swifty they must come up with a new solution. Launching another shell airline, he says, will lead them down the same dead-end avenue, only this time it will be faster. The FBI would most likely shut down whatever entity they form in a matter of days. Even if it lasts a few weeks, a domestic regular airline will no longer serve their growing needs. They need a way to get out of the United States without export licenses, which they're extremely unlikely to get. They need a cover for making stops for refueling and repair around the world. They need an international airline.

Al looks to Swifty for an idea. Swifty has come through before, and maybe he can come through again.

They gather the team to figure this out. They ask, "Does anyone have any idea? Know anyone? How can we create an international airline?"

Al urges his men to brainstorm. What have they heard about international aviation?

Eddie says he's read a story in the *LA Times* about Panama building an $8 million international airport despite lacking its own national airline.

"Maybe we can be their national airline," Al says.

Swifty says the wife of one of his WWII buddies, Martin Bellefond, roomed at Radcliffe College in Cambridge, Massachusetts, with the girlfriend of the nephew of the president of Panama.

Although this seems a bit of a stretch, it encourages Al. Recalling how relatively easy it was for Arazi to register the SS *Kefalos* in Panama, he tells Swifty, "That sounds like just enough of a connection to get us going."

"How close are you to Bellefond?" Harold asks.

Swifty met him at RAF station Deenethorpe in Northamptonshire, England, where Bellefond front-gunned USAAF bombers.

Al asks Swifty to contact Bellefond right away. He also gives Panama a code name. If America is Detroit, then the Isthmus is Latin Detroit.

It takes Swifty a couple of days to track down Bellefond, who's eager to hear what his old friend has in mind.

Swifty and Al fly to New York to meet with him. They tell him they want to provide Panama with a ready-made national airline. Bellefond, who's been floundering since World War II, likes the idea. He remembers the president's nephew well. Gilberto Arias, he says, returned to Panama City after graduating from Harvard Law School to open his own practice.

They ask a Haganah connection in Panama City to look up the president's nephew. She reports that Gilberto Arias's law office specializes in government contracts. This well-positioned attorney has built a reputation as an honest broker.

Bellefond calls Gilberto, who remembers him. The attorney says he's willing to meet.

Al and Bellefond fly down with a proposal for a new airline that includes a mockup of a brochure and a drawing of a Connie featuring the Panamanian flag on its tail with the words *Lineas Aereas de Panama* across its body. They impress the usually reserved Gilberto. He agrees, for a large fee, to pitch the idea to the right people in the government.

~

The OZ members have been tuning out Eddie's news briefings. Unless he comes in flashing a happy smile—a rarer occurrence in Burbank than rain—they ignore his depressing updates. But today he acts differently enough to make them stop what they're doing—figuring out flight routes, recruiting pilots and crew members, reviewing training manuals, learning basic Czech, and so on—and listen. Running in, the radio operator breathlessly announces that they've just received their deadline: April 15.

Sam, Leo, Lou, Gershon, Harold, and others gather around Eddie, who says Truman has given the State Department far-reaching authority to ground their planes after Tax Day indefinitely.

"How?" they ask. They usually do not have to milk Eddie for information. But because this piece of news is so relevant and crucial, he's reverted to using the journalistic communication method known as the inverted pyramid, starting with the bottom line. He says they have less than three weeks to finish repairing their planes, load them, set up refueling and repair stopovers around the world, and arrive in Czechoslovakia.

Now that he has their undivided attention, Eddie delves into the details. Truman, he says, has issued a proclamation (2776) listing all the categories that will require export licenses starting April 15. They include "all commercial type aircraft and all aircraft components, parts, and accessories."

Knowing that military planes have long necessitated export licenses, the OZ members have been arguing—through documents, deeds, and disagreements with Pat—that they're preparing *commercial* aircraft. Now, that no longer matters.

Truman has made it clear that any plane exceeding 35,000 pounds, including all of Service Airways', must receive State Department permission to leave the country.

"They'll shoot us before they'll give us permission," Leo says.

"What are the other restrictions?" Sam asks Eddie.

Eddie starts reading them: "rifles, carbines, revolvers, pistols, machine guns, mounts, breech mechanisms, howitzers, cannons, mortars, rocket launchers, flame throwers, pyrotechnic projectors."

The list goes on and on and on. Eddie loses most of the OZ members' attention. However, Sam stays to the end. He's fascinated by this leave-no-war-instrument-behind list, which ends with "tanks, armored vehicles, artillery trucks, half-tracks, tank-recovery vehicles, turrets, tank engines, tank tread shoes, and tank bogie wheels."

Little do they know, at the same time, a non-Jewish arms dealer is trying to get them tanks. Fifty of them. American made. It was Lou who contacted US Marine colonel Larry Ives, whom he met during World War II and heard has started dealing arms. Working with Al and Hank, they have set it up as a purchase for the Mexican military.

Now they're waiting on State Department approval of Ives's export license application.

12

April

AL RECEIVES THREE PIECES OF NEWS—THE FIRST, MOSTLY GOOD; THE SEC-ond, bad but not unexpected; the third, good and eagerly anticipated.

The *Nora* and the C-54 have made it to Palestine with their arms ship-ments intact. The former tricked British destroyers into assuming it was an innocent merchant ship. The latter flew nonstop from Prague International Airport to Byat Daras, Palestine, where Haganah troops made its landing possible by capturing a former RAF airfield from the Arabs. This will be the only time they use this airstrip.

Together, the *Nora* and C-54 deliveries increase the Jews' munitions inventory by a third and boost their ammunition stockpile tenfold. The ship and the plane bring in 4,500 rifles, 240 machine guns, and 5,190,000 rounds of ammo.

It's a shot in the arm that fortifies the Yishuv in all ways physical and psychological.

But the *Nora* and the C-54 have been exposed. The Haganah's repeated failed attempts to arrange an originating seaport gave rise to suspicion across Eastern Europe.

The sea shipment appeared at last ready to go when Yugoslavia agreed to let the *Nora* dock, load, and depart from Šibenik and Romania agreed to allow the Czech arms to reach this Adriatic Coast port by boat on its part of the Danube River. But the Romanians reneged, and the Haganah had to scurry to nail down another, less ideal option. It reached understandings with Hungary and Yugoslavia, but that meant delays and such complications as having to transfer the weapons to a train during the final leg.

Using the *Nora* again would mean having to remap its route and renegotiate its points of transfer. It would likely again take months. By the time it's ready, the OZ planes are expected to have completed delivering the Czech munitions and Messerschmitts.

The C-54, meanwhile, arrived in Palestine relatively quickly and with few snags. However, a Prague International Airport official notified the US embassy's military attaché, who pushed the Czech government to never allow Ocean Trade Airways in and out of the country without a thorough inspection.

Freddy contends that they can overcome this obstacle. But Gerald refuses to take such a risk, even for $10,000 a flight.

The sum and substance for Al: His ATC has become the only viable option for bringing in the Czech arms.

The second piece of news Al has received shows that the Czech weapons may be the only ones on which the Jews can count. The delivery of the Mexican arms is, at best, delayed for several weeks, or, at worst, held up indefinitely. Several factors are contributing to this situation, including bureaucracy and pressure from the US State Department and Mexico City's well-established Arab community on the Mexican government to abort this deal.

Despite accepting the quarter-of-a-million-dollar payment and guaranteeing the weapons' release, the Mexicans are singing a different tune these days. To Hank, it sounds like a grating melody composed by the US State Department. His contacts refuse to be seen in public with him and, lately, to even see him privately.

This, Al understands, most likely kills the chance of the Haganah signing off on a P-51/P-47 deal. Arazi has reiterated that the Mexicans must deliver the purchased weapons before he pushes Ben-Gurion to buy fighter planes from them.

Hank asks Al to return to Mexico to help break the arms impasse. But the OZ leader must devote his energy to setting up the Panamanian airline and beating the US State Department's April 15 deadline. And the other piece of news he's just received means moving full speed ahead. Gilberto called saying he hasn't seen Panamanian leaders this excited since they proposed, at the conclusion of World War II, that the United States give up its control of the Panama Canal. Now they have cleared Lineas Aereas de Panama for takeoff.

When adding the Spanish designation for a limited liability company, Sociedad Anonima, the new airline even has a catchy acronym: LAPSA (pronounced lap-sah).

"LAPSA, LAPSA," Al says to himself. It sounds weird, yet just right. Service Airways has turned into the national airline of Panama.

The vision of his planes breaking through clouds bearing the Panamanian flag allows Al to exhale. He realizes that this could solve many problems—seen and unseen. Of course, it could also cause troubles. For instance, how should he manage the Panamanians' anticipations? They're expecting a real airline. They're getting a farce.

But Al has no time for deep reflection. He must move fast to transfer Service Airways' thirteen planes into Panamanian registry, secure Panamanian numbers for each of them, obtain a LAPSA franchise, and mobilize his teams in Burbank and Millville to load the planes with equipment and spare parts.

~

The Czechs propose several Messerschmitt training sessions, each lasting six weeks and composed of seven participants. To accelerate the time frame while maintaining quality, Al and Arazi ask them to reduce the number of weeks to four and the group number to five. The Czechs agree but stress that a month is the bare minimum needed to prepare a fighter pilot—even an experienced one—to be battle ready in a Messerschmitt.

Flying out of New York, Lou, Milt, and Giddy—especially Giddy, who has yet to fly anything for the operation—are anxious to get to Czechoslovakia and train on the Messerschmitts. But first, they're told, they must stop in Rome to receive new identities and passports.

Giddy mocks Lou's Hungarian accent. Lou's attempt to imitate Giddy's New Jersey accent backfires, exposing the lingering grip of his native inflection. Sick of both of them, Milt buries his head in George Orwell's *Animal Farm*.

Arazi greets them at Rome's Ciampino Airport, which has transitioned in recent years from a USAAF base to Italy's main commercial hub. Dressed as a Catholic priest, the Haganah operative takes them to Rome's highest vantage point, the swanky Hotel Mediterraneo. Nestled on Esquilino, the city's tallest hill, the ten-story Art Deco building overlooks landmarks such as the Colosseum and the Forum.

Arazi checks them in and asks them to meet him at the rooftop restaurant in a few minutes.

They drop off their bags and head right up to meet the other pilots, who, besides Buzz, include four experienced air combatants from Palestine:

- Mordechai "Modi" Alon, twenty-seven, grew up in Safed, the Holy Land's highest city, and Tel Aviv, and helped found a kibbutz, Hanita, near Lebanon. During World War II, he flew RAF Spitfires in Italy. After the war, he majored in architecture at the Technion in Haifa and helped create the Shrut Avir.
- Edward "Eddy" Shlomo Cohen, twenty-five, grew up in a wealthy Johannesburg household. During World War II, he flew for the South African air force. Since the Great War, he's harvested vegetables at Kibbutz Ma'ayan Baruch near the Lebanese and Syrian borders.
- Ezer Weizman, twenty-three, grew up in Acre in an academic household. His father, Yechiel, is an agronomist, and his uncle, Chaim, is a biochemist who will become Israel's first president. During World War II, Ezer flew Spitfires for the RAF in Egypt, India, and Rhodesia. After the war, he studied economics at London University and joined the Irgun.
- Leonard Cohen, twenty-eight, was born in Liverpool and grew up in Haifa. During World War II, he flew Spitfires for the RAF, earning the nickname the "King of Lampedusa" for single-handedly conquering this Mediterranean island. Like Buzz, he did most of his dogfighting over Malta.

Several other Palestinian Jewish pilots—including Jacob Ben-Chaim, Pinchas Ben-Porat, Itzchak Hennenson, Misha Kenner, and Nachman Me'iri—are due to arrive in Rome in coming days.

Taking in the sights of the Sistine Chapel, St. Peter's Basilica, and the Vatican Museums from the Hotel Mediterraneo's rooftop, Lou and Milt strike up a conversation with the four aviators from Palestine, while Giddy hits it off with Buzz.

"What's your optimal firing distance?" Giddy asks.

"Two hundred and fifty yards," Buzz says.

"You always shoot when you're in that range?"

"No," Buzz says. "I only shoot if I know I have a kill."

"How do you know?"

"I feel it."

Arazi interrupts them to ask Buzz to test-fly a Noorduyn C-64 Norseman, a Canadian single-engine airplane that Freddy is trying to purchase from the USAAF in Germany, purportedly for his place of birth, the Belgian Congo.

Buzz peppers Arazi with technical, strategic, and logistical questions. The Haganah representative has most of the answers. The Jews set up a fictitious firm, Somaco, to buy as many of the fifty available Norsemen as they can. They plan to use the hardnosed planes, which can carry more than 3,000 pounds and take off from and land on any kind of runway, for transporting supplies and weapons throughout Palestine, especially the Negev Desert. They hope to complete the first purchase any minute now.

Almost satisfied, Buzz asks why him.

Arazi says Buzz is the best they got, and this is a challenging assignment. Although reliable once tamed, the Norseman is notoriously difficult to handle.

Buzz asks Giddy to be his test-flight co-pilot. Giddy says he's honored.

Buzz invites Giddy to his hotel room to show him how he stays in mental shape. The Canadian ace shines a light on a hung sheet to produce silhouettes of various fighter planes. He angles them this way and that to figure out the best ways to shoot them down.

"Did you do this when you were in the RAF, too?" Giddy asks.

"Every night," Buzz says.

"And people say you're odd," Giddy quips.

~

Pat has set up 24/7 monitoring of the operation in Burbank. He and his FBI colleagues—usually two at a time—run eight-hour shifts sitting in an unmarked black Buick Roadmaster Cruiser watching the OZ members.

The FBI agents pass the time smoking, yawning, dozing off, talking about their wives and kids, and writing boring reports that no one ever reads. Yet the original-and-still-lead agent on this case, which has grown in importance and urgency in recent weeks as war in the Middle East has become not just probable but actual, is not discouraged. Something is about to happen. Pat senses it. He's doing everything he can to make sure he's here when it does.

The other reason for the new close surveillance: Pat lost his inside OZ man when Ray finally talked Al into firing Bill, their suspicious star mechanic. The FBI agent has failed to replace Bill, as Operation Zebra has become more tight knit, sealed lipped, and impenetrable.

This evening, as the sunrays transition from dancing on the airplanes to caressing them, Pat notices Sam marching to his favorite Connie, a once giant piece of scrap metal that the OZ mechanics have restored into a beautiful beast. Nothing unusual about that, or about the fact that he's accompanied by several teammates. No, what prompts the FBI agent to grab the binoculars from his partner are the objects Sam and his teammates are carrying: ladders, paint buckets, and brushes.

On the side of the Connie, they draw "RX-121."

Sam stands back, his chest filling with renewed optimism. He's ready to do 121 pushups.

Pat's binoculars race from the jazzed-up Sam to the new registration marking to another ladder, off which Leo paints "LAPSA" on the underbelly of one of the Connie's wings.

Jotting down this information, Pat jets off to investigate, instructing his partner to alert him immediately about any more suspicious activity. He races to the FBI's LA office.

Suspicious activity has been taking place under the FBI agents' noses for days—Sam and his teammates have been loading the Connie with spare parts and equipment. They've made the process seem like ordinary repair by going back and forth with equipment. They've also sneaked on hundreds of LAPSA brochures.

As Pat frantically searches for the origins of LAPSA and RX registration numbers, Sam, Leo, and several OZ ATC crew members prepare to take off.

Pat's partner leaps out of the Roadmaster waving his arms. He jumps the fence to chase the plane down the runway. The Connie clears the ground before he gets on the tarmac. He reaches for his holster but lets his arm drop to his side.

~

It's an unseasonably suffocating spring in New Jersey. For days, the Millville OZ planes and members have been monitored around the clock by US

Treasury Department agents in dark overcoats that would overheat less cool customers. Watching from a black Ford Mercury just outside the airport fence, the T-Men never try to conceal their presence or intentions.

Swifty waves to them. They wave back.

"We should bake them cookies," Swifty tells Ike and Robert.

"Yeah," Robert says, "and fill them with rusty nails."

"I don't think they eat," Ike says. "I think they just get plugged into an electric socket and recharge."

To calm his increasingly shaky nerves, Swifty reminds himself that the airline formerly known as Service Airways has written authorization from the Panamanian government to fly its Connies and C-46s to Tocumen. He realizes that this Machiavellian tiptoe is unlikely to sidestep the US authorities after the April 15 deadline, but that's a couple of weeks away. Still, why wait? He summons Robert to his office.

"I want to start loading the Dodges tonight," Swifty says. "Can you be done with the repairs by the end of the day?"

Robert bolts to the shop.

Al drives in from New York. The instructions he gives his team are as alarming as they are clear.

"Leave *nothing* behind," Al says again, "even if you have to overload the planes."

Swifty gives him a disapproving look.

"We need every spare part and every piece of equipment we can take," Al says. "We have to keep these planes in the air, we have to set up at least one shop along the way, and then, of course, another, more permanent one in Zebra."

"We won't be able to do any of this if our planes are so overloaded that they crash," Swifty says.

"Get their center of gravity right," Al says, "and they'll be fine."

Continuing to the executive office, where his Millville team has gathered, Al turns back to Swifty and adds, "Don't exceed 10 percent."

Swifty shakes his head. If they overload the C-46 by more than 10 percent, they might as well stay on the ground.

In the office, Al announces the C-46 assignments to the Millville team. Expecting to captain one of the C-46s, Ike is surprised to hear he's co-piloting. His Commando captain is Moonitz. Their radio operator is Eddie, and their navigator is newcomer Moses "Moe" Rosenbaum, twenty-eight, who was born in Poland, grew up in a Zionist home in Brooklyn, and, as a USAAF navigator during World War II, spent thirteen months in a German prison. To join OZ, which he wanted to do as soon as he heard about it a few days ago, he put his mechanical engineering education at Cornell University on indefinite hold.

Moe's such a gentleman that, when he overhears Ike speaking with Eddie about Moonitz, he steps out of earshot.

Ike tells Eddie, with whom he has forged a close friendship, that he's concerned about Moonitz. "He's a great guy, but I've seen him panic in the cockpit."

Eddie finds this hard to believe.

"I know, he's so suave and sure of himself," Ike says. "But I'm telling you, under tense conditions, he loses his cool."

"What does he do, exactly?" Eddie asks.

"He yells," Ike says.

"What is this about?" Eddie asks. "Are you angry Al didn't make you captain?"

Ike shakes his head. He admits he's a little disappointed, but he insists that's not coloring his judgment.

"I'd be perfectly happy co-piloting for a captain I respect," Ike says.

"Well," Eddie says, "you better show Moonitz respect, or he'll really lose his marbles. And he'll be right to do so."

This is why Ike considers Eddie a good friend. He smacks him upside the head with the truth and shakes him out of his cloudy, often self-defeating musings.

So when Al pulls him aside, Ike never questions his decision. Instead, he carefully considers the boss's request: that they transport some of the weapons that the Haganah has received from US citizens but no longer attempts to ship by sea because the FBI has shut down all port access.

"Are any other pilots taking weapons?" Ike asks.

Al shakes his head. Ike motions, "Why me?"

"You're a member in good standing of the Haganah," Al says.

Ike lets out a nervous laugh. Although he was sworn into the Jewish underground, he's never considered himself a Haganah representative.

His membership has just been reactivated.

"Have you asked my captain, Moonitz?"

"Moonitz will go along with whatever you decide," Al says. "He respects you."

~

When Al announces assignments and lineups in Burbank the next day, he disappoints another original OZ member: Harold.

Having been making good, steady progress on his C-46 training, Harold was hoping to be Gershon's co-pilot. To add insult to injury, the ATC aviator who gets this assignment is a mechanic—Bud.

Harold has nothing against him. In fact, like the rest of the OZ team, he has a great affinity for Bud. But Harold was hoping that he had made enough progress in his flight training to earn that front-right seat.

Noting that Bud has a flying license and a great deal of experience as a WWII USAAF flight engineer, Gershon tells Harold that he's not quite ready. "But you will be soon."

Harold calms down until he hears that another mechanic—Bob Dawn—will co-pilot a C-46.

"Maybe instead of learning how to fly them," he says, "I should learn how to fix them."

"Be careful what you volunteer for," Gershon says.

Gershon reminds Harold that his radio operating experience and expertise are vital to this flight, which is fraught with risks and requires everyone's top skills.

Overhearing them, Marty asks Harold to join his C-46 crew as a radio operator.

Seeing mechanic Templeton "T" Taylor climbing onboard Marty's C-46, Harold snaps, "Why don't you just have him do it?"

A disapproving glance from Gershon prompts an apology.

"I'd love to be your radio operator," Harold tells Marty, "but Al wants me to go with Phil and Ted."

Harold huddles with his group, RX-133: captain Phil Schild, twenty-eight, who grew up in a Zionist home in Los Angeles and flew US ATC cargo missions during World War II; co-pilot Ted Applebaum, twenty-nine, a New Yorker who flew Boeing B-29 Superfortress bombers for the

USAAF; navigator Jules Cuburnek, thirty, a Chicagoan who served a USAAF bombardier; and flight engineer Sam Pomerance, thirty-eight, whom he's gotten to know in Burbank and Millville.

~

On the way to Panama, Sam and his crew stop in Mexico City's Aeropuerto Internacional Benito Juárez to refuel. They meet with Hank, hand him $15,000 in cash, and tell him that the US government has rejected Ives's export license application for fifty tanks.

He invites Sam and Leo out for the night, but they're eager to leave before drawing the attention of the US authorities.

Hank laughs, saying, "Everyone already knows you're here."

Pat has alerted US authorities in several Latin American airports to be on the lookout for LAPSA RX-121. Hank has used his connections and cash to allow the Connie to refuel and its crew to be safe from arrest in Mexico City.

"This may be the most expensive one-plane refueling in history," Hank says, smiling.

"Money's just paper," Leo says.

"Lately," Hank says, "it feels like water."

Nonetheless, Sam and his crew take off as soon as the Connie's four fuel tanks are full. Besides aiming to avoid pushing their luck, they're increasingly eager to return to Burbank to help get the C-46s out before it's too late.

At the same time in Burbank, having been given the same push-it-to-the-limit-and-beyond orders from Al, Ray oversees the loading of the C-46s. With Pat now fully aware of their Panamanian scheme, they no longer try to hide anything.

Nonetheless, Pat—who kicks himself for missing the Connie's escape—is determined to stop any more OZ planes from leaving the country.

~

In Millville, the four C-46s are ready to take off. But the T-Men are not quite ready to deal with this crisis. In a knee-jerk reaction, they drive onto the tarmac to block the first Commando in line.

The C-46's radio operator, Jack, alerts Swifty.

True to his nickname, Smiling Jack speaks calmly and clearly. It's enough to set off Swifty like a match to a barrel of firecrackers.

Rushing to confront the T-Men, Swifty yells, "You can't prevent Panamanian planes from going to Panama."

He has to repeat himself a couple of times—and point at the Central American country's flag on the tail of the C-46—to cut through the airplane-engine noise.

The T-Men direct Swifty's eyes to the US numbers still emblazoned on the Commandos.

Swifty leaves in a huff. He returns a few moments later with Robert and the other mechanics hauling ladders and paint buckets and brushes. They draw Panamanian registration numbers on each of the C-46s, from RX-135 to RX-138.

Returning to the T-Men on the tarmac, Swifty points at the visual representations of the Panamanian authorizations. The government agents chuckle. Swifty turns to see the paint dripping down the sides of the planes.

No amount of fresh paint will move the T-Men.

"You can camp out here as long as you like," Swifty says. "We're taking off."

Swifty instructs his pilots to back up to allow the first C-46, RX-135, to go around the Mercury. Awkward and bumpy at first, they ultimately succeed. But by the time they complete this maneuver, the T-Men have simply driven further down the runway.

The C-46s remain blocked.

Swifty gets into the RX-135 to speak with its captain, Arnold Ilowite, twenty-seven, who grew up in a Romanian Jewish household in Queens, New York, and served in the US ATC during World War II.

"Can you take off over them?" Swifty asks.

Arnie stares straight ahead, calculating his odds.

∼

Sam, Leo, and their crew members arrive in Panama to what they would later describe as "great fanfare." High-ranking government officials greet them on the tarmac, put them up in exquisite lodging, wine and dine them, and grill them: When will the rest of the planes arrive?

"To help make that happen," Sam says, "we must get back to the States right away."

But the Panamanians want it both ways: They demand the other planes' timely arrival while expecting Sam and his crew to stay and start operating their new national airline.

Sam, who had planned to return on a commercial flight with Leo and leave the crew members to guard and maintain the Connie, reluctantly proposes a compromise: asking his co-pilot to stay behind.

Hearing this for the first time during dinner with the Panamanians, Leo nearly chokes on his *carne guisada* (beef and potatoes drenched in *sofrito* sauce). But he gets it. So Leo composes himself, smiles, and announces that he'll set up the LAPSA office in coming days.

The Panamanians, in turn, say that they'd like to welcome the other planes with a presidential ceremony. Leo says that won't be necessary, but they insist.

As Sam flies back to Burbank, Leo starts building the LAPSA office, a fully "functional" front that will soon feature a ticket counter, a C-46 model, and a rack of postcards.

～

At the Millville airport, Swifty gives the T-Men a final warning. When they call his bluff, he returns to the C-46s on the tarmac, makes eye contact with the first captain in line (Arnie), drops to his left knee, and points forward with his right index finger.

Arnie taxis the Commando, startling the T-Men. He speeds down the runway. The Mercury driver slams on the accelerator, zipping out of the way at the last second. It's an unnecessary move—Arnie takes off just in front of where the T-Men vowed to stand their ground.

The other C-46s soon follow.

Swifty jumps into the left seat in the last C-46. As much as he'd love to, he's not hanging around to see the T-Men's reactions.

The next morning in Burbank, having heard what went down in Millville, Al gathers his transport pilots and crew members at dawn to go over procedures.

Walking to his C-46, Harold is surprised to see Sam heading to a different one.

"I thought you were in Panama with the Cadillac," Harold says.

Sam is fulfilling his promise to fly out a C-46. He walks to the first plane in line—RX-130—to join co-pilot Elliot Polansky, twenty-seven, a New Yorker who flew US ATC cargo missions during World War II.

As the C-46s line up, Pat drives onto the runway, daring them to cross him. Al approaches. The FBI agent jumps out of the car to confront him. Their conversation echoes Swifty and the T-Men's, revolving around the US authorities' lack of jurisdiction over Panama's national airline, with similar results.

The only difference is that, after Al returns to the C-46s, Pat summons another FBI vehicle, doubling the size of the makeshift wall.

Sam smiles as he prepares to break the FBI blockade. The vehicles scurry out of the way as he races down the runway. Good thing, too, or he would've smashed them to smithereens.

Pat jumps out of the car to watch six C-46s take off in quick succession and become silver dots in the sky.

It occurs to him that he could justify arresting Al, who, he believes, has stayed in Burbank. He searches throughout the airport and puts out an alert to his FBI colleagues around Southern California. But they find no trace of the de facto president of "Panama's national airline."

Pat expands the call for Al's arrest throughout the country and, soon enough, throughout the globe. He turns the OZ leader from a minor target to one of the FBI's Most Wanted.

Retreating to the shadows, Al takes great measures to navigate these new stormy waters. For instance, he sleeps in a different place every night and avoids interactions with US authorities.

One night in Manhattan, while staying at a friend's twenty-second-floor apartment, Al hears that two FBI agents are taking the elevator to arrest him. Slipping away in his pajamas, he shoots down the stairs, which spit him out to a back alley. He races to another friend's home in New Jersey.

~

Moonitz, Ike, Eddie, and Moe, who carry a lighter load (weapons) than the other pilots (equipment and spare parts such as engines, etc.), outpace the group. This is despite the captain and co-pilot clashing the whole way.

The problem starts soon after they level off over the Atlantic. Moe points out that they're off course.

"Already?" Ike says, glaring at Moonitz.

"What's the big deal?" Moonitz says calmly. "We'll do what we always do. We'll correct."

On the 1,500-mile flight to the Millville group's refueling stop—Kingston, Jamaica—the uneasy interaction repeats several times.

Ike and Moonitz lecture each other.

"There are no downdrafts and headwinds to knock us off course," Ike says. "If we can't have a smooth flight now, what's going to happen later?"

"Being off course is par for the course," Moonitz says. "And so is correcting. They go hand in hand."

Although they mostly agree on the facts, they resent each other's tone. Eddie urges them to act like adults. But the captain orders his navigator to put up a curtain between him and his co-pilot. Moe pretends to look for something and then throws up his hands.

"We'll take care of it on the ground," Moonitz says as they start to descend.

But when they land in Kingston's Palisadoes Airport, they have other tasks on their mind. Swifty had asked them to give the rest of the pilots a quick report.

Moonitz and Eddie let the other pilots know that the airport workers are friendly. The Jamaicans believe that the plane is Panamanian.

Volunteering to stay with their plane and wait for the other C-46s, Ike urges his colleagues to go into town for dinner. Eddie refuses to leave his buddy alone. As hospitable as the Jamaicans are, they could be swayed into changing their attitude by the United States or the United Kingdom. It will take another fourteen years before the island, which started weaning itself from colonialism toward the end of World War II, will win full independence from the British.

Moonitz promises to bring back Jamaican food for Ike and Eddie.

"Make mine spicy," Ike says.

"I think that's the only option," Moonitz says.

"Pick me up a local newspaper," Eddie says.

Taking a taxi into town, Moonitz and Moe roll down the windows to let the Caribbean breeze cleanse their lungs and salt their lips. Dropped off at a shack recommended by an airport worker, they breathe in a mix of smoke from small fires set to drive away mosquitos, ganja spliffs lit by Rastafarians, and jerked meat barbequing on the grill.

Over curry goat, green-amaranth callaloo, and bammy flatbread, Moonitz asks Moe about his background. The navigator says that, in retrospect, he realizes how lucky he was that his German guards never knew his religious affiliation. Had they figured it out, they might have sent him to a death camp.

"What was it like to be in prison for a year?"

"Frustrating," Moe says, putting down his Red Stripe. "All I wanted to do was bomb the heck outta them again. Do you think we'll get to drop bombs as part of this operation?"

Initially, Moonitz shakes his head. But, pondering this legitimate question, he shrugs. Who knows? It's enough to give Moe hope.

Moonitz and Moe arrive back at Palisadoes Airport to see that the other four Millville C-46s have landed safely and are being refueled with no suspicion.

Moonitz has forgotten about wanting to put up a cockpit curtain, and Moe doesn't remind him. Also, after they take off for Panama, the navigator waits until they are more than slightly off course before he brings up that they should correct it.

~

The Burbank C-46s make their refueling stop in Mexico City. Four have landed. Sam watches the fifth come in. He's worried about the sixth: Gershon and Bud's. He hasn't heard from them. Flying without a radio operator, they've made little contact with the rest of the group.

On the horizon, he spots a plane that looks like a C-46. Soon, Gershon and Bud land. Instead of rebuking them, Sam offers them the radio operating services of Harold for the leg to Panama. They say that's unnecessary, insisting they're fine flying as just a duo and promise to communicate better.

As the C-46s are refueled, Sam gathers his pilots for a briefing. He tells them that Mexico City is a "hot-and-high" airport, which presents a takeoff challenge.

"Didn't you just recently refuel here with the Cadillac?" Gershon asks.

"Yes, but the Cadillac was not overloaded," Sam says. "And I have a lot of experience with hot-and-high airports. The air is less dense. That weakens the engines and reduces the lift."

The pilots ask him to elaborate on the lift issue.

"The rotors and the wings produce less air," he says.

"Doesn't the long runway compensate for that?" Marty asks.

"Yes," Sam says. "But our planes are overloaded by 10 percent. We're going to need every one of those 12,795 feet and every ounce of our skill and concentration."

The pilots nod. They applaud when Sam announces that, instead of attempting the difficult takeoff at night, they will fly out at dawn. They accept Hank's dinner invitation. Speaking from experience, he warns them about American, British, and Arab spies and operatives.

"If you hit it off with a dame and it all goes too fabulously well, consider her a spy," Hank says. "Fault on the side of caution. Your life—heck, the whole future of this operation—could be on the line."

Instead of sobering them up, however, Hank's words spark some of the aviators' imaginations. Their work suddenly sounds glamorized.

"Don't worry," Harold quips, "I always question the motive of any woman who wants to be with me."

"Well," Hank says, "if she wants to take you to her place after one or two drinks and she's not naming a price, no need to ask, you have your answer."

At dawn the next morning, Sam is the first to take off. He wants to model how to deal with the hot-and-high conditions, but he nearly succumbs to them. Covering every inch of the runway, he climbs out off the edge, kicking up soil and soot. His overloaded C-46 dips before coughing out a feeble ascent.

Next in line, Marty remains composed despite witnessing Sam's close call. He, too, exhausts the runway, and he, too, must muster everything he's got to lift off.

Following Marty is the operation's third-most experienced pilot, Gershon. He races down the runway but fails to gain much altitude. Clawing for any upward trajectory, he dumps the flaps, a highly tricky maneuver that, when executed flawlessly, can counteract the heat's negative effects. But not this time.

The C-46 plunges to the ground, breaking into a hundred pieces, several of which ignite into small fires.

Hal, captain of the next-in-line C-46, jumps out and makes a mad dash to the crash site. He spots Bud's body on a rock a few yards from the nose of the destroyed plane. He looks him in the eyes. They're vacant. He checks Bud's pulse. He finds none.

Hearing belabored breaths, he finds Gershon fighting to live despite suffering what appear to be fatal injuries. Hal, along with other OZ members and Mexican medics, rushes the pilot to the hospital.

On the way, they encourage him like ringside boxing trainers. However, Gershon loses consciousness, which he never regains.

With Hal by his side in the ER, Gershon is pronounced dead at sunset.

~

The two planes that took off—Sam's and Marty's—continue to Panama, stopping to refuel in Managua, Nicaragua. Soldiers point their rifles at them. But the LAPSA markings clear all suspicions.

"We have no political aspirations," Sam tells their commander in Spanish. "We just want to refuel and continue on to our home base in Panama."

When they arrive in Tocumen, they're greeted by saluting soldiers and President Enrique Adolfo Jiménez Brin, who's staged a state ceremony complete with a red carpet and a military brass band. Would-be stewardesses—energetic and shiny—welcome the American aviators with smiles, some simply friendly, some more suggestive. Tuxedoed servers carry trays of *almojábanos* (cheese-filled fried corn dough), *yuca fritas* (Latin fries), *cocadas* (coconut balls), and other local finger foods, along with beer and wine.

Sam, Marty, and their crews and the Millville group members, who arrived the previous day, graciously shake the president's hand, but they're not in a festive mood. They're depressed and distraught about Gershon and Bud's deaths. Harold, in particular, is torn up about losing his mentor and friend.

"I could've been in that plane," Harold says. "Spare parts are replaceable."

The others agree. They're confused and angry about the cause of this mess: Al's insistence on overloading the planes.

To add to the tension, they're worried about the three C-46s that still must clear that hot-and-high Mexico City runway.

All the aviators except Sam, whose managerial duties and close relationship with Al conflict with his loyalty to his pilots, meet after the presidential ceremony behind closed doors. Marty suggests they cease all of the activities—such as training, flying, loading, and unloading—until their demands are met.

"You mean," Moonitz says, "go on strike?"

Marty shrugs—yes, kind of.

"What are we demanding?" Ray asks.

"That they stop overloading the planes," Marty says.

"That they give us more timely, relevant information," Harold says.

"Yeah," Ike says, "stop keeping us in the dark."

"And buy life insurance for each one of us," Marty says. "You know, to take care of our families."

They agree on everything, including keeping this "strike" a secret from the Panamanians but sending Al a stern message.

In Mexico City with Shechtman dealing with the crash aftermath, Al had planned to stay in that country to help Hank free their US Navy and Mexican weapons. But when they hear about the mutiny in Panama, Al and Schechtman hop aboard the last C-46 to take off.

Late that night, as soon as they arrive, Al and Shechtman hold a "Come to Jesus" meeting with their men. The pilots pull no punches, accusing Al of causing their friends' deaths—and putting their lives at unnecessary risk. They list their demands.

Al starts by praising Gershon and Bud for their contribution and sacrifice. "We have lost two good men, two good friends," he says. "May they rest in peace."

Al surprises the aviators by saying he plans to visit Gershon and Bud's widows as soon as he returns to the United States and give them the $10,000 payout from the life insurance policy the operation had taken on each OZ pilot and crew member.

A murmur spreads through the room.

Al surprises his team further by owning up for overloading the C-46s.

"I ordered it, I'm the one to blame," Al says. "But I'd never ask you to do something I wouldn't. I just flew one of the overloaded planes. We took off from Mexico City. It was tough, but we cleared that runway."

The OZ aviators nod. Yes, it was rough. And yes, most of them made it. But so what? Two did not.

"I take full responsibility," Al says. "But I'm not apologizing or changing this policy."

The aviators gasp.

"This is war," Al says, "and we must do everything we can to help the Jews win. That means taking many necessary, calculated risks, like overloading the planes. We have no choice. What should we have done—left behind 10 percent of our precious spare parts and equipment? That's something we'd regret later."

"If we're being asked to share in the risks," Marty says, "shouldn't we also get all the information we need? I understand this is a secret operation—"

"You're right," Al says. "We should, and we will provide more information to you. Here's some info I've shared with many, but perhaps not all: Now that we're out of the States, we can breathe a little better, but we cannot get complacent. The nature of this operation remains the same. The risks are the same. We can lose our lives. We can lose our freedom. Heck, we can even lose our American citizenship."

"Wait, what?" Ike says. He, along with many of his colleagues, did not realize they were risking their citizenship.

"Yes," Marty says, "they can take it away from you." He opens his passport and reads a red stamp that appears in everyone's: "Not valid for travel to a foreign country for purposes of serving in a foreign army."

"I've read that," Ike says. "It doesn't say they can take it away from you."

"It implies it," Marty says.

The aviators groan.

"This is why we have to pretend to work for Panama," Al says. "And so far, for the most part, it's working. We couldn't fool the FBI, but we got out just in time. And the Panamanians believe we're their national airline."

Some of the aviators chuckle.

"As Americans, we don't have to be in the States to break US law," Al says. "We can do that anywhere in the world. We don't have to be in the States to get in trouble, to get arrested, or to get killed. Leaving the US, we didn't lose an enemy; we simply gained several more. The British, the Arabs, God knows who else. So the less we say, the better. The less we play, the better."

The OZ team members exchange impressed looks. They had no idea their somewhat-aloof leader could speak with such passion.

Al finishes by saying this is the reality of racing against the clock to prevent a second Destruction.

No one has said it yet, but the strike is over.

Shechtman follows with a rousing speech of his own. He describes the existing Jewish air force as a collection of useless small planes flown by inexperienced pilots with little direction or purpose.

"The war has already begun, and we're losing," Shechtman says. "Once the British leave and the Arabs officially invade, we won't last more than a few days without your help. You are the key to our survival. You're bringing us arms, a real air force, cargo planes, fighter planes, and great hope."

A natural-born orator who played chess for years with his Russian immigrant father, Shechtman anticipates his audience's reactions.

"That's a lot of pressure, I know," he says.

Some of the aviators nod; others shrug. They've grown immune to pressure. For several, it has become the fuel of life.

"This is the kind of pressure you are uniquely qualified to handle," Shechtman says. "In fact, you thrive in it. You already beat the Nazis and the Japanese during the greatest war. Now you're fighting to give a safe home to the hundreds of thousands of Jewish refugees stuck in Europe with no other place to go."

The OZ aviators project renewed determination. They're ready to do whatever it takes. Shechtman goes for the jugular.

"In Palestine, we're dying," he says. "Without you, we have nothing. We're gone."

Marty shakes Shechtman's hand. Harold follows.

Harold looks for Al, but he's gone.

~

Al prepares to knock on Mrs. Gershon's door. He takes a deep breath. He reminds himself that she's already received the death notice; he's here to deliver some good news. Still, when he signed up his men for life insurance, he never imagined collecting so soon.

Al knocks. A slender woman opens the door, two young children at her feet. They have red eyes and puffy cheeks. Al places a hand over his heart.

When he introduces himself, the widow frowns. When he hands her the $10,000 check, she throws it back at him.

"Keep your blood money," she says. "You are a murderer!"

She slams the door in his face. He picks up the check. He knocks again. No answer. He slides the money under the door. He turns to walk away.

The door opens. He turns back. Mrs. Gershon spits in his face.

Al had planned to visit Bud's widow next. But after this experience, he asks the late mechanic's friend, Templeton, to do it.

Al sticks the check in T's shirt pocket before the mechanic can answer.

Bud's widow had not heard the news. When she realizes why a sullen T is at her door, she collapses in his arms.

~

Staying in Tocumen but spending much of their time twenty minutes away in Panama City, the OZ members let loose. During the days, they take care of LAPSA business and train—the pilots with Sam, the navigators with Moe, and the radio operators with Harold. At night, they go out, expand their palates, meet women from around the world, mambo and merengue, and gamble at state-run casinos.

Moonitz, Kurtz, and Harold, in particular, take it all in. With a pile of balboa they won at a casino on a hot-hand night, they buy a 1936 Buick Phaeton and a marmoset. Driving with the top down and the radio volume up, they act like teenagers who've just gotten their license. The other ATC members roll their eyes but come along for the free rides in the back seat.

This is one way to get over the deaths of their teammates and deal with the anxiety of their own uncertain future. But there's a problem: The Panamanians expect a fully functional airline.

Al shows up, instructing his men to make official LAPSA flights.

"What kind?" Moonitz jumps to ask, startling the monkey on his shoulder.

"I don't know," Al says. "Go up and fly around. Be visible."

Al tells LAPSA's Panamanian point person that they're starting to conduct route-survey flights.

"When will you fly passengers?" the point person asks.

"We're not quite ready for that," Al says. "What else have you got?"

"Well," the point person says, "we have a lot of cattle in this country."

Moonitz, Ike, Eddie, and Moe make the first official LAPSA transport, flying fifteen heads of cattle from a farm on the eastern part of Panama to a slaughterhouse on the western side.

When Moonitz gets into the cattle-packed C-46, his marmoset shrieks. He's unsure whether it's because of the sight or smell. But the monkey refuses to share a ride with the stinky cows. It stays with Ray.

Moonitz, Ike, Eddie, and Moe deliver the cattle on time. For the next few days, the LAPSA crews transport cows, chickens, pigs, and agricultural supplies.

It's a grimy affair, but it does satisfy the Panamanians—for now.

Sensing that they've solidified their position as Panama's national airline, Al prepares his men for the main event—flying to Zebra. He and Sam wish they could take the North Atlantic Tracks, which would speed and simplify the journey. But they know the US authorities would never give them access to the flight routes established by the North Atlantic Organized Track System (NAT-OTS).

As far as the State Department is concerned, the LAPSA planes are smuggled US property that must be returned at once. So Al maps out the planes' long, complicated routes, starting in the Southern Hemisphere and making their way carefully, selectively, to Zebra. To ease the journey, he sends Harold to fetch airplane radio licenses from the Panama Transit Authority (PTA).

The PTA official has no idea that his country has a national airline. Harold shows him a copy of the LAPSA incorporation paper. He's assured that it's legit, but he still has no airplane radio licenses to issue.

"I deal in ships," the official says.

"Well, now you're dealing in airplanes," Harold says. "So give us what we need, *por favor.*"

The official motions that he'll be right back. He disappears for a long time. Harold sweats, thinking, *I'm in trouble. He's going to check around and find out that this is a scam.*

But he returns with ten airplane radio licenses—one for the Connie and nine for the C-46s. Harold thanks him and leaves before the official can ask any questions about this so-called LAPSA airline.

~

Sam planned to return to the United States with pilots and crew members to fly out the remaining two Connies, but Al has determined that doing so would only lead to their arrest. The Feds have frozen any OZ asset they could get their hands on and have grounded the planes.

Saddened by this not unexpected development, Sam focuses on the one Connie he managed to get out. He compares it to spending his energy on raising his lone surviving child after losing two to a freak accident. Without consulting anyone—not even Al—the chief pilot decides to fly to Czechoslovakia right away. This trip will allow him to accomplish two vital goals:

- Blaze a trail for the C-46s' refueling stops around the globe. The layovers that he, Al, and their colleagues have set up in conjunction with the Jewish underground are, at this point, merely theoretical. The

chief pilot wants to test them, as well as meet the Haganah representatives who are supposed to greet them at each location.
• Deliver the Czech weapons to the Jews in Palestine ahead of schedule.

To the Palestinian Jews, who are engaged in intensifying fighting with deficient war instruments and dwindling ammunition, even an immediate, magical materialization of foreign weapons would not be too early. So Sam heads out of Panama with several crew members, including Ernie, the Connie mechanic who's fluent in Czech. The OZ chief pilot asks Harold to stay in Panama to head up communications.

Things go smoothly for Sam and his team until they land in Catania, Sicily. Against the backdrop of the volcanic Mount Etna, the Vincenzo Bellini Airport guards point their rifles at the LAPSA crew like hunters surrounding beasts.

"It's a good thing we're clearing the path," Sam says to his crew. "I wouldn't want our less experienced pilots dealing with this situation."

Sam never flinches when an arm-waving airport official fires accusatory questions at him. He gives one answer: Meyer Lansky.

The official leaves to check with his boss in the small terminal of an airport named after a nineteenth-century opera composer. He soon returns, apologizing to Sam and directing his staff to "refuel the plane and the pilots."

Using the Bellini Airport radio facility, Sam lets Al know that he can send the rest of the OZ planes. Walking to the cafeteria, he smells the zesty scent of a nearby lemon tree grove, then the garlicky aroma of old-fashioned Italian cooking. He joins his crew for a meal highlighted by a local favorite: *melanzane* (eggplant). The shareable dishes, which cover the table, include grilled *melanzane* and squid, pork-filled *melanzane*, and smoked *melanzane* drizzled with olive oil on crusty focaccia.

"I hope you like eggplant," Sam tells his crew.

"I usually can't stand it," Ernie says as he refills his plate with every type of *melanzane*.

When they return to the Bellini Airport, Ernie, a restless feller who always has something to do, takes a nap among the crates in the belly of the Connie.

~

Receiving the go-ahead from Sam, the OZ members prepare to leave Tocumen. To expunge the livestock stench, they fumigate and scrub their planes. To have enough fuel to cross the Atlantic Ocean, they equip their C-46s with ferry tanks and full oil drums. To stay faithful to their mission, they again overload the Commandos by about 10 percent, leaving little behind. Moonitz and Kurtz want to take the monkey with them, but they know it'd be unfair, so they leave him with one of their Panamanian friends.

The monkey cries when they leave. Some spot tears in Moonitz's eyes, too.

To slip away without raising immediate suspicion, the OZ pilots tell their point person that they plan to make a final route-survey flight the following morning. They mention that this will be a major undertaking involving all nine C-46s.

The point person is excited. Having noticed the frantic activities around the planes in recent days, he figures the LAPSA crews are preparing to start flying passengers. He plans to be the first one.

The next morning, he watches the C-46s take off—never to return.

Embarking on the trail blazed by Sam, the C-46s make their first refueling stop in Paramaribo, Suriname (Dutch Guiana). So far, the LAPSA cover works well. Without asking questions, the Zanderij Airfield workers prepare the planes for their next leg to Natal, Brazil.

Here, in the South American airport nearest to Africa, the Panamanian pretense pays even more dividends. South American Airways employees offer assistance to the new airline, giving the LAPSA aviators access to a radio facility, on-site lodging, and a repair shop.

The timing's impeccable. Leo and Harold's C-46 started coughing as it came in for a landing in Natal. Willie and Robert stay behind with the pilots and crew to fix it as the other eight planes hop across the Pond.

When they reach Dakar, Senegal, many of the aviators go into the beautiful fifteenth-century French colonial city for some *yassa* (chicken with mustard, garlic, lemon, and onions over rice) and *maafe* (beef-and-peanut stew). Moonitz, Ike, Eddie, and Moe stay at the airport to watch the planes. They plan to have their fun at the next stop: Casablanca, French Morocco. But when they land at the Nouasseur Air Base, formerly the US military's Berrechid Airfield, they're greeted by chants of "Kill the Jews!" They know the protest, which is taking place on the tarmac, isn't directed at them or anyone present. It's aimed at an entity more than 3,000 miles away—the Yishuv. But the men still feel uneasy.

The Nouasseur Air Base manager who welcomes them apologizes, but only because he worries that the demonstration is a nuisance. He has no idea that the protestors could quench their bloodthirst right there and then. Three of the LAPSA aviators— Moonitz, Ike, and Moe—are Jewish and, according to the sign-carriers, should, therefore, be killed.

They're eager to depart Casablanca, but the refueling and mechanical checkup take several hours.

"An air force buddy of mine who served here said Moroccan food makes Egypt's seem bland," Ike says, recalling the spicy Middle Eastern cuisine he savored in Cairo.

They ask the manager whether he knows anyone trustworthy enough to guard the C-46 while they go into town. He points at the protestors.

"Are you sure?" Moonitz asks.

"Yes," the manager says. "They work here."

Several of the protestors put down their antisemitic signs to guard the Jewish plane. They also recommend a small restaurant in Casablanca's Sour Jdid neighborhood.

Sitting at an outside table across from the world's tallest minaret, the Hassan II Mosque's, Moonitz, Ike, Eddie, and Moe feast on couscous, *tagine* (meat and carrots simmered in a pointy clay pot), olive-oil-and-tahini-topped hummus, and mint tea so sweet it gives them a sugar rush.

But as much as the hummus, which is also sprinkled with parsley and pine nuts, takes him back to his relatively simple days in Cairo, Ike can't relax. He's worried about the plane. His teammates, who enjoy his stories about running around Egypt with Steve and Harold, are also anxious.

Without Steve or Harold there to stop him, Ike tells Moonitz, Eddie, and Moe about his conversations with the British fighter pilots.

"The Brits would never fight us," Moonitz says. "We're their best friends."

"Are you talking about Jews or Americans?" Eddie asks.

"Americans," Moonitz says.

Ike would usually argue—stressing that he knows what he heard and pointing out that their operation has recruited pilots from around the world, including the Yishuv—but his mind is elsewhere. He's uneasy about the protestors-turned-guards. What if they peer inside the C-46 and see the weapons?

What if the LAPSA plane piques the interest of members of the US Air Force Strategic Air Command stationed at the Nouasseur Air Base?

Ike tries mentally to shelve his concerns to enjoy this meal. After all, it could be his last.

~

Although Sam's Cadillac could easily handle a direct flight from Catania to its final Czech destination, Žatec, it makes a stop in Brno, Czechoslovakia, mainly to continue paving the way for the C-46s.

Greeting Sam and his crew in Brno—a town dotted by medieval buildings such as the thirteenth-century Špilberk Castle, which the occupying Nazis turned into a prison during World War II and the Czech army now uses as its regional headquarters—is Dr. Otto Felix, forty.

Dr. Felix, an attorney, left his Hebrew name (Uriel Doron) in Palestine when he returned to Czechoslovakia to use his connections to help the Haganah make an arms deal. His Charles University (Prague) classmates now play important roles in the military and government. They include Bedřich Reicin, a communist and a member of the Czech army's Main Staff, and Dr. Pavel Tomek, one of the two managers of the Brno-based gun-manufacturer Česká Zbrojovka Uherský Brod.

Concerned about Operation Zebra's slow progress, Dr. Felix is thrilled to see the LAPSA Connie land in Brno. He becomes even more excited to speak with Sam and the crew and learn that their journey went relatively smoothly. He flies with them to Zebra, where he checks them into their Czech home—the Stalingrad Hotel.

"*Stalin*-grad?" Sam says. "Oh, the FBI's going to love this."

The British and the US State Department have increasingly painted the Yishuv as a communist entity. Although a ridiculous notion, it has gained traction. Spun to fortify domestic and foreign policies opposed by such pro-Jewish state leaders as Eleanor Roosevelt, it twists and decontextualizes such observations as:

- The Yishuv was founded and is run by Eastern European socialists.
- Key components of the Yishuv, such as the kibbutzim, function in an economically communist manner.
- Many Palestinian Jews and Holocaust survivors come from countries that are now part of the Soviet bloc, such as Poland.

- The Soviet Union has been the biggest proponent of the creation of a Jewish state.

It is the last point, in particular, that the British and US State Department have been hammering home. The facts that the burgeoning Jewish state has no communist ties or aspirations, that it is emerging as the Middle East's only democracy, and that its ideals resemble America's wash away when the prospect of an alliance between the Soviets and the Jews rears its peculiar head.

Unlike the other points about the Yishuv's communist tendency, this one has merit. The Jews need a powerful ally. It's not going to be the United States or the United Kingdom. What's left in the post-WWII world? The Soviet Union. Sam wonders whether Ben-Gurion would partner with Stalin. He can't imagine it. He doesn't want to, anyway. All he can do is worry about what he needs to do. At this moment, he wants to start loading the Connie, but he needs to take care of his crew members, who are spent from the long trip.

Sam invites Dr. Felix to join them for dinner in town, but the Haganah emissary is flying to Prague to join the organization's European arms procurement chief, Ehud Avriel, in meeting with Czech government officials.

"I thought the deal is done and signed," Sam says.

"It never hurts to remind them of it," Dr. Felix says. He neglects to mention that he and Ehud are negotiating the purchase of additional fighter planes.

Sam and his crew step out of the Stalingrad Hotel and onto the cobblestones of the former Hitler Plaza. But they find no trace of the Nazi occupation. The Czechs have cleared away all local reminders of the Third Reich except for the Messerschmitt factory, which now produces Avia S-199 parts not for the Germans but for the Jews.

What Sam and his crew do not know is that, as part of the postwar purge, the Czechs expelled the three million ethnic Germans who for generations made up the majority of this region, the Sudetenland, of which Žatec (Saaz in German) is a part.

Sam and his crew have heard that Žatec grows some of the world's best hops. They're eager to try the local pilsner, which they order at a plaza bar that, like the rest of the town, strikes them as a bit strange. Examining their surroundings, it hits them: it's the first place they've been on this journey where they have little to worry about. There are no secret agents in sight. No other foreigners, for that matter. Besides them, everyone's local, and they mind their own business. Even Ernie's American-accented Czech solicits no probing.

Drinking pilsner on tap—which the waitress brings out with *utopenci* (pickled, spicy sausages)—they compare it to other beers they've sampled around the world. Sam says it reminds him of Stella Artois. He's right. Saaz Noble Hops give the ubiquitous Belgian pilsner its edge. It's a nice change of pace from their typical conversations about flight routes and safety procedures.

Although it's their first time in Zebra, Sam and the crew members feel at home. As tuba and accordion players give rise to a spontaneous polka on the cobblestones, the OZ members relax so much that when the chief pilot says it's time to go start loading the Connie, they look at him like he's crazy.

∼

Moonitz, Ike, Eddie, and Moe return to the Nouasseur Air Base to find their C-46 just as they left it. The guards never peeked inside. The US Air Force personnel never noticed it. The protest has dispersed. However, the OZ aviators realize that they should have never put their trust in adversaries who could've blown their cover. They vow never again to leave their plane alone.

Refueled, the C-46 heads to the island of Sicily. Moonitz, Ike, Eddie, and Moe breathe a sigh of relief at trading a potentially hostile environment for what they've been told is the friendliest of places.

"Sam said get ready to be treated like kings," Ike says.

Instead, they chance upon a Sicilian schism of sorts. Unaware of their mafia connections, the Bellini Airport official who greets the OZ members insists on checking their cargo. When he discovers the arms, he impounds the plane. As Moonitz and Ike scramble to get an abort-mission message to the other Catania-bound C-46s and get in touch with Al, a second LAPSA plane lands. Although the Sicilians find it free of weapons, they seize it, too.

Local journalists swoop on the airport. They snap photos of the C-46s and bombard the LAPSA aviators and Bellini official with who-what-where-when-how-and-why questions.

Moonitz, Ike, Eddie, and Moe ignore the questions. The airport official fills the information gap with uneducated guesses, rash observations, and wild theories. But the reporters' line of inquiry makes him wonder whether the weapons are meant for Palestine.

"We have enough problems of our own," the official says. "We don't need to get involved in that conflict."

Eddie reaches the other LAPSA planes flying toward the Mediterranean island. He passes along Al's instructions to refuel in "Jockstrap"—Ajaccio, Corsica—a stop he's set up for the upcoming trek from Zebra to Palestine.

"The Corsicans aren't expecting us for several more days," Al told Eddie. "But that's all right. Tell the pilots to just say we're ahead of schedule."

"Of all our stories," Eddie said, "that may be the hardest to believe."

Eddie relays another Al message, this one to the pilots and crews of the two impounded C-46s: keep their mouths shut and maintain a low profile while he works to free their planes.

In the next twenty-four hours, Al makes considerable progress toward releasing the C-46s—that is, until the *La Sicilia* article about "munitions aboard planes registered to Panama going to the Jews in Palestine" hits the wires. The unwelcome press coverage—a first for OZ—complicates matters for him and other ATC operatives.

In Natal, the South American Airways employees lending a hand to Leo, Harold, Willie, and Robert read this story with great interest.

"Those impounded planes in Sicily wouldn't be yours, would they?" they ask Harold.

Harold denies it. But the story specifically mentions Lineas Aereas de Panama. In a preemptive move, Leo tells the South American Airways employees that they'll fly out that night. Willie and Robert rush to complete the repairs.

In Sicily, the Mediterranean air, which blurs the line between sea and land, prompts Ike and Eddie to stop sitting around waiting and start exploring. They hike the mountains, play backgammon on the beaches, listen to a cellist and a flutist perform Bach's *Siciliano* (from Sonata no. 2 in E-flat Major), watch street acrobats risk life and limb for a livelihood, and frequent a downtown bar. On the way, they sample so many foods from sidewalk vendors—*arancini di riso* (fried mozzarella-filled rice balls), fried sardines, homemade gelato—that they leave little room for beer by the time they get there.

Soon after they sit at an outside table, a muscular regular towers over them.

"You guys got me worried," he says, his gravelly voice doing his thick neck justice.

"What do you mean?" Ike says. "We're just having a beer."

"No, you don't understand," the regular says. "You come, you go. We don't know where, we don't know when."

Another, even bigger mafioso joins them, cracking his knuckles. Ike looks at Eddie, who nods. They might as well just tell them.

"We're on a mission," Ike says.

"What sort of a mission?"

"To help our Jewish brothers and sisters in Palestine," Eddie says.

"Oh, mamma mia!" the regular says. "Why didn't you say so in the first place? Is there anything I can do for you guys?"

"Well," Ike says, "we can use some Thompson submachine guns."

The next day, Ike receives a crate containing eight new Tommy guns, along with rounds of ammunition, all Cosmoline coated to prevent corrosion. Running to tell his teammates the good news, Ike hears that their planes are free to go. Letting Moonitz know he'll be right back, Ike catches a taxi into town to thank the bar regular.

"What you did is beautiful," Ike tells him. "They're in good hands now."

"It's nothing," the regular says. "What you're going to do with them, now that's beautiful."

Ike returns to the airport as Moonitz taxis to the runway. He jumps onboard and takes the right seat but not before making sure the Tommy guns crate is safe and secure next to the other weapons in the plane's full belly.

Now the one C-46 to not be overloaded (due to its lighter cargo of arms instead of engines and equipment) contains more than it should carry.

∼

After purchasing twenty Norsemen, the Haganah brings in more aviators to fly them to Palestine. They hail from the United States—including Collie and Phil, who has experience delivering aircraft to distant locations—the United Kingdom (Hugh Curtiss and Joe Sunderland), France (Gino Narboni), and the Netherlands (Victor Abraham "Appi" Wijnberg).

Buzz, Leonard, and Giddy test-fly the first Norseman to arrive from Germany. Arazi asks them to stay in Rome and continue making sure every plane is ready for the trip to Palestine. The Canadian and Briton would rather go to Czechoslovakia, but they're up for doing what's needed. The American likes the idea of extending his stay in Rome. He's making the most of his visit to the City of the Seven Hills. Too much, in the judgment of the Haganah representative, who keeps telling the aviators to be careful in dark alleys and halls at night, and with overly friendly women at all hours, especially twilight, when they sweep out across the bars like bats flying out of their caves for their daily feast.

Arazi, who promoted Phil to Norseman chief pilot, considers giving Giddy the second-in-command role. But Buzz insists that his new best— some would say *only*—friend continue to test the planes with him in Rome. The Haganah representative wants to keep the Jewish air force's Canadian ace happy. So Arazi deputizes Lou instead.

The next morning, Phil, Collie, and Lou lead seven Norsemen out of the city's small airport, L'aeroporto di Roma-Urbe. Their flight to Palestine proves even more difficult than expected—dizzyingly long, dangerously boring, and deceptively uneventful.

"Imagine watching a propeller go round and round and round," Lou later tells Eddy Cohen, Ezer, and Modi.

The Norsemen pilots, who have no food or parachutes, encounter bad weather almost from the start. But their biggest challenge is maintaining enough fuel to make it to the Aqir Airport outside Tel Aviv, one of the few British military assets the Jews have seized, which they'll soon rename Ekron.

As they close in on Palestine, the Norsemen fly on fumes. The first to land in Aqir—Collie—fires a red flare to warn the next pilot to watch out for a bulldozer on the runway. Taking it as a signal to avoid landing here altogether, Lou does so anyway.

"I was out of fuel thirty miles ago," Lou says. "I would've landed on top of a church steeple if I had to."

Of the seven Norsemen, only four reach Aqir. Lack of fuel forces three to make emergency landings in Egypt's Sinai Desert.

Appi, Hugh, and three Americans—Robert Daniel Fine, William Malpine, and Albert Trop—become OZ's first prisoners of war. They spend the 1948–1949 Arab-Israeli War in Cairo's Mazeh prison, where they and seven female Haganah members are subjected to the elements in flimsy huts but receive better treatment than the tortured, starved POWs at the nearby Abbasia prison.

The fact that the aviators escape such abuses as "mock executions," during which blindfolded Jews face bluffing firing squads, shows the Egyptians' reverence for pilots.

The Norsemen pilots who make it to Palestine know how lucky they are.

"It's like Chanukah all over again," Lou says. "Our oil lasted a lot longer than it should. I don't know how we made it. I really don't."

Lou, Phil, and Collie have no time to dwell on the possibility of a modern-day Festival of Lights miracle. They're eager to return to Rome to make up for their failure to deliver all the planes and to cope with their guilt and concern for their captured colleagues. They leave some of the other aviators in Palestine to start transporting supplies to secluded Jewish communities on the four Norsemen.

Despite the disappointing outcome, Arazi is relieved to welcome back Lou, Phil, and Collie. He's determined to get all the remaining thirteen Norsemen safely to Aqir. But he sends the fighter pilot to Czechoslovakia to train on the Messerschmitt.

Since arriving in Rome, Arazi has felt like the pilots' old man. He keeps warning them about this and that. Giving Cohen, Ezer, Lou, Milt, and Modi their new identities and passports, he instructs Lou to keep his mouth shut until they arrive at České Budějovice, the Czech air base where they'll train, because his Hungarian accent could draw attention.

After bidding farewell to the other pilots from Palestine, who are scheduled to join them as soon as their documentations are in order, Lou pretends to be a monk who's taken a vow of silence. It should be relatively easy, with Giddy not there to badger him.

Lou stays silent on the flight to Geneva, the train ride to Zurich, and the flight to Prague. He continues saying nothing during their overnight stay in the City of a Hundred Spires and on the Czech military flight to České Budějovice.

Given Luftwaffe flight jackets upon their arrival, the OZ aviators are horrified to see that they still feature a swastika emblem.

Finally allowed to speak, Lou is speechless.

Lou removes the swastika and dons the jacket, which fits him to a T. The others do the same.

OZ fighter pilot Gideon "Giddy" Lichtman during his WWII days with the US Army Air Forces in the Pacific.

Credit: Gideon Lichtman collection

OZ transport pilot Marty Ribakoff flies C-46s over the Hump in China during World War II.

Credit: David Ribakoff collection

OZ chief pilot Sam Lewis is known for his ability to fly any transport plane under any condition.

Credit: Sandra Brown collection

OZ radio operator Harold Livingston during his post-WWII days of setting up communications stations in the Middle East.

Credit: Harold Livingston collection

During World War II, future OZ fighter pilot Leon Frankel serves as a US Navy torpedo pilot in the Pacific. He receives a Navy Cross for sinking a Japanese cruiser.
Credit: Leon Frankel collection, courtesy of *A Wing and a Prayer*

United Nations General Assembly members discuss what to do about Palestine in a former ice rink in Flushing Meadows, Queens, in 1947.
Credit: United Nations Archives

United Nations General Assembly members debate the idea of a Jewish state in a former ice rink in Flushing Meadows, Queens, in 1947.

In 1948, Operation Zebra chief pilot Sam Lewis, leader Adolph "Al" Schwimmer, and chief mechanic William "Willie" Sosnow in front of one of their three Connies at their Service Airways headquarters at the Lockheed Air Terminal in Burbank, California.

Operation Zebra's three Connies at the Service Airways headquarters at the Lockheed Air Terminal in Burbank, California, in 1948.
Credit: Sandra Brown collection

Operation Zebra chief pilot Sam Lewis helps to fix his favorite Connie at the Lockheed Air Terminal in Burbank, California, in 1948.
Credit: Sandra Brown collection

One of Operation Zebra's three Connies at the Service Airways headquarters at the Lockheed Air Terminal in Burbank, California, in 1948.

Credit: Sandra Brown collection

In 1948, Operation Zebra leader Al Schwimmer (third from left) discusses logistical challenges with chief mechanic Willie Sosnow (fourth from left) at their Service Airways headquarters at the Lockheed Air Terminal in Burbank, California.

Credit: Al Schwimmer collection, courtesy of *A Wing and a Prayer*

The author's grandparents, Holocaust survivors Rivka and Ozer Grundman, in Israel after the 1948–1949 war.
Credit: Boaz Dvir collection, courtesy of *A Wing and a Prayer*

Hyman Shechtman (third from left) becomes the Haganah's liaison with Operation Zebra in 1948.
Credit: Israel Government Press Office

OZ mechanics prepare chief pilot Sam Lewis's favorite Connie, with its Lineas Aereas de Panama registration number (RX-121), for flight in 1948.
Credit: Sandra Brown collection

The Millville Airport in New Jersey serves as Operation Zebra's second base in the United States, along with Burbank, California.
Credit: Betty Ann Hickman

OZ mechanics work on one of the nine remaining Curtiss-Wright C-46 Commandos in Panama in 1948. At that point, the operation's planes were part of that country's national airlines, Lineas Aereas de Panama.
Credit: Al Schwimmer collection, courtesy of *A Wing and a Prayer*

A 1948 postcard of Panama's international airport, Tocumen. It includes a photo (middle right) of the Lineas Aereas de Panama Connie. The planes and airport are real, but Panama's national airline is fake, a cover created to shield Operation Zebra.
Credit: Al Schwimmer collection, courtesy of *A Wing and a Prayer*

Two C-46 crews. Left to right, Ed Styrak, the author, Harry Schwartz, Al Raisin, Cyril Steinberg, Ed Chinsky, Gordon Levett, Sheldon Eichel (in shadow) Jack Goldstein, Len Dichek Al Dobrowitz, Eli Cohen Ajaccio, Corsica, June, 1948

Eddie Styrak, Harold Livingston, Irwin "Steve" Schwartz, Al Raisin, Cyril Steinberg, Ed Chinsky, Gordon Levett, Sheldon "Ike" Eichel, Jack Goldstein, Len Dichek, Al Dorowitz, and Eli Cohen in front of a Lineas Aereas de Panama C-46 in Ajaccio, Corsica, in 1948.

Credit: Harold Livingston collection

Harold Livingston secures airplane radio licenses from the Panama Transit Authority for Lineas Aereas de Panama's identification card.

Credit: Harold Livingston collection

Operation Zebra mechanics work on one of the nine remaining Curtiss-Wright C-46 Commandos in Dakar, Senegal, on their way to Zebra in 1948.

Credit: Al Schwimmer collection, courtesy of *A Wing and a Prayer*

During their time in Zebra, the OZ members—including their chief pilot, Sam Lewis—
ventured into Prague a few times to take a break from the intensity of their mission.
Credit: Sandra Brown collection

When the United Nations decides to split Palestine between the Arabs and the Jews
in November 1947, the former reject the Partition Plan, and the latter accept it but
are ill prepared to defend their new homeland. They lack the weapons to be ready
for the war, which officially begins six months later but in reality starts in November
1947.
Credit: Israel Government Press Office

On the eve of the 1948–1949 Arab-Israeli War, Tel Aviv is a bustling city, unprepared for the daily air raids that are about to shake it to its core.
Credit: Al Schwimmer collection, courtesy of *A Wing and a Prayer*

In May 1948, Egyptian Spitfires strafe civilians at Tel Aviv's Central Bus Station, killing forty-one and injuring sixty.
Credit: Israel Government Press Office

In the first few weeks of the 1948–1949 Arab-Israeli War, the Egyptian and Syrian air forces had complete control of the skies and often used it to bomb civilian populations such as kibbutzim and city centers.
Credit: Israeli Air Force

An OZ C-46 flies over Israel in 1948. The operation members used the Commandos to transport weapons, fighter planes, fighter pilots, supplies, troops, and military and political leaders.
Credit: Ralph Lowenstein collection, courtesy of *A Wing and a Prayer*

A paratrooper jumps out of an OZ C-46 over Israel in 1948. The operation members washed away the Panamanian flag from the plane's tail and replaced it with a Jewish star on the side.

Credit: Ralph Lowenstein collection, courtesy of *A Wing and a Prayer*

A downed Israeli Air Force Messerschmitt in 1948. Of the twenty-five Avia S-199s OZ brought in, only four were operational at any given time. The Czech version of the famous German fighter plane proved fatally inferior.

Credit: Israeli Air Force

Coming in for a landing in Ekron, Israel, in May 1948, Norman Moonitz and Sheldon "Ike" Eichel crash their C-46, which carries half a Messerschmitt.

Credit: Sheldon Eichel collection, courtesy of *A Wing and a Prayer*

OZ navigator Moses "Moe" Rosenbaum's body lies in front of the C-46 that crashed upon trying to land in Israel in May 1948. Moe, imprisoned for more than a year by the Germans during World War II, is twenty-eight when he dies on what would have been his first visit to the Jewish state.

Credit: Sheldon Eichel collection, courtesy of *A Wing and a Prayer*

OZ captain Norman Moonitz, co-pilot Sheldon "Ike" Eichel, and radio operator Eddie Styrak recover at Kibbutz Givat Brenner in Central Israel after crashing their C-46 in May 1948.

The nucleus of the Israeli Air Force's first fighter pilot squadron—101—in front of one of its Messerschmitts in 1948.

Operation Zebra leader Al Schwimmer (fourth from left) and chief pilot Sam Lewis (second from left) in Tel Aviv in 1948.

Credit: Al Schwimmer collection, courtesy of *A Wing and a Prayer*

Some of the Mauser rifles OZ smuggled in from Czechoslovakia featured German eagles clutching swastikas in the talons.

Credit: Boaz Dvir

An Herzliya air base mechanic installs a camera into one of the fifty-nine Spitfires that Israel bought from the Czechs.
Credit: Israeli Air Force

An Israeli Air Force officer keeps score of the fighter pilots' dogfights and air battles in 1948.
Credit: Israeli Air Force

One of the three B-17s Al Schwimmer buys in the United States and smuggles into Israel drops bombs on the Egyptian army in the Negev Desert in 1948.
Credit: Israeli Air Force

One of the three B-17s destroys Egyptian Army positions in the Negev Desert in 1948. The Flying Fortresses add a major military dimension to the Israeli Air Force.
Credit: Israeli Air Force

Sheldon "Ike" Eichel, a US Army Air Forces B-24 bomber pilot in Europe during World War II, becomes an Operation Zebra transport pilot in 1948.
Credit: Sheldon Eichel collection, courtesy of *A Wing and a Prayer*

OZ chief pilot Sam Lewis participates in smuggling Spitfire fighter planes from Czechoslovakia to Israel via Yugoslavia in 1948.
Credit: Sandra Brown collection

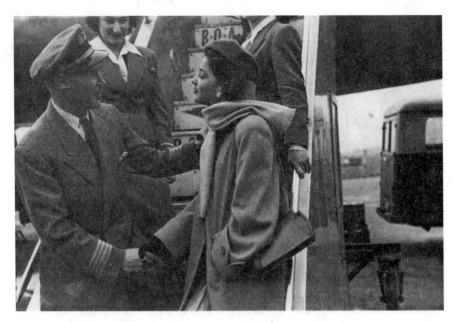

OZ chief pilot Sam Lewis becomes El Al's first captain in 1949.
Credit: Sandra Brown collection

After leading Operation Zebra from 1947 to 1949 and being tried for arms smuggling in 1950–1951, Al Schwimmer starts an aviation firm in Burbank, California.
Credit: Israel Government Press Office

El Al workers refuel a Lockheed Constellation in 1951. Al Schwimmer's planes and men launch Israel's national airlines.
Credit: Sandra Brown collection

After accepting a direct offer from Prime Minister David Ben-Gurion, Al Schwimmer creates Israel Aircraft Industries in the early 1950s.
Credit: Al Schwimmer collection, courtesy of *A Wing and a Prayer*

In 1959, Israel Aircraft Industries founding CEO Al Schwimmer (third from left) shows the country's founding prime minister, David Ben-Gurion (white-haired, center), the first jet built in the Jewish state: the Fouga CM.170 Magister, a French trainer.

Credit: Al Schwimmer collection, courtesy of *A Wing and a Prayer*

Israel Aircraft Industries (IAI) founding CEO Al Schwimmer (third from left), who led OZ from 1947 to 1949, leads Prime Minister Golda Meir (fourth from left), who raised $50 million in the United States to fund OZ and the weapons it airlifted, and other political and military leaders on a tour of IAI in 1970.

Credit: Milner Moshe, Israel Government Press Office

Israel Aircraft Industries founding CEO Al Schwimmer joins Prime Minister Yitzhak Rabin and Defense Minister Shimon Peres in unveiling the Kfir (Lion Cub) fighter plane designed and built by IAI.

Credit: Israel Government Press Office

III

MAY 1948–JANUARY 1949

13

May

A<small>L</small> <small>ARRIVES IN</small> Z<small>EBRA TO FIND THE</small> J<small>EWISH</small> ATC <small>HUMMING.</small> A<small>LL THE</small>
C-46s—except for Moonitz's and Leo's, which are due in today and tomor-
row, respectively—have made it. A C-54 that the Haganah has purchased for
Al—where and how, he's unsure—is here, too. The mechanics are repairing
and maintaining the planes. The crews are starting to load them. Here, no one
has to pretend to work for Panama's national airline. The OZ boss jokes that
maybe the operation runs better when he's not around.

Al welcomes several new recruits, including Gordon Levett, twenty-seven,
a transport pilot who served as an RAF instructor during World War II.

"I'm sorry you had to go through that," Al says, referring to the intensive
due diligence, including several interrogation-like interviews, Gordon endured
joining OZ. They included questions about his motivation (he overheard his
employer, a London laundromat owner, criticize the United Kingdom's mis-
treatment of Holocaust survivors), dishonorable discharge from the RAF (he
neglected to put in for a leave he took while in Burma), and flight skills (he
claims instructional, operational, and combat experience).

"If I were you, I'd also be suspicious of a non-Jewish Briton joining a
group trying to undermine his government's foreign policy," Gordon says in
his Cockney accent. "I'd also wonder if he's a spy."

"Well, I'm glad you're here," Al says. "I understand you can fly transports
and fighters?"

Gordon nods. This is the only lie he's told. He realizes that if operation
members find out that he's only dreamed about flying fighter planes, they'll
again suspect that he's an MI5 agent. For now, he has to focus on quickly

learning how to fly the C-46s, the last of which—flown by Moonitz and Ike—has just landed on Zebra's grass runway.

After everyone checks into the Stalingrad, the whole gang gathers at the square. Al asks about their journey. Their stories sound familiar—he's heard bits and pieces for various reasons, sometimes because his assistance was needed, other times because the pilots wanted to vent.

Al brings up the Messerschmitts, noting they'd need to refuel several times to make it to Palestine.

"They don't have the range to fly direct. Not even close," Al says. "We would have to make several refueling stops. Doing that with fighter planes is so risky, it's practically idiotic."

Instead, he says, the OZ crews, working hand-in-hand with the Czechs, will take apart the Messerschmitts, stuff the different sections into the C-46s, fly them to the Aqir airport, and reassemble them in Palestine.

Now it's Al, not Sam, who gets "are you crazy?" looks.

"What's the big deal?" he says. "We'll put the wings in one Dodge and the fuselage and engine in another."

"Easy!" Ike says.

"Piece of cake!" Kurtz says.

"Actually, two pieces," Moonitz says. "I'll take a fuselage."

"Great," Al says. "Who wants the wings?"

"I've ferried fighters this way," Gordon says. "I'm happy to help get them in and out of the Dodges."

The looks of gratitude he receives initially make Gordon feel good. But as the conversation turns to other matters—including lineup changes and Aqir landing procedures—he slips away to start playing with the C-46 controls.

In a festive mood, Al tells the waitress to keep the pilsners and pickled sausages coming and to mix in other Czech dishes. She brings out classics such as *vepřové* (sauerkraut-covered pork), *hovězí guláš* (onion-and-pepper-topped goulash), and *svíčková na smetaně* (roast beef in cream with carrots and cranberries). The hungry aviators eat so much so fast that the chef can barely keep up.

~

Embracing their new reality—beating Nazi swords into Jewish arms—the five fighter pilots emerge from their barracks sporting Luftwaffe jumpsuits.

"This fart sack makes me want to vomit," Milt says, only half joking.

The instructors, who flew for the RAF during World War II, show them the basics of flying the Czech version of the Luftwaffe trainer Arado Ar 96 on the first day of what they call a "conversion course."

After getting into his Avia C-21, Lou scratches his head at the absence of a proper runway. The grass field doesn't bother him. He's taken off and landed from all sorts of runways. It's the lack of any markings on the ground. He'd be happy with natural guideposts like trees. But this is a big, empty space.

Spotting a cloud floating by, Lou heads toward it, maintaining equidistance between the hangars on one side and a row of Messerschmitts on the other. He suddenly realizes that he's closing in on a fence.

Lou yanks back the stick, sending the plane up just enough to clear the fence and land on the other side. He keeps going and finally takes off. Once he reaches altitude, however, he enjoys the flight. *This plane isn't bad*, he thinks.

A couple of days later, the instructors take the pilots up in two-seater Messerschmitts (Avia CS-199s). This is when Lou and the others start to suspect that something is wrong. But they're too focused on learning how to fly these planes to notice what, exactly. They zero in on the problems the day they fly solo.

The Czech version of the Messerschmitt, they realize, is known as the "Mule" for a reason. It suffers numerous issues. It's missing a rudder trim, making it difficult for Lou to control. The engine hum sounds off, too. He notices that it lacks the power and oomph to lift and land properly.

The Czech factory that produced the right Messerschmitt engines burned down, so the Czechs switched to Junkers Jumo 211Fs, which the Germans installed in bombers. They weigh down, yet underpower, the Avia S-199 by nearly three hundred units of horsepower. It's the worst of both worlds.

Lou tries to put down the flaps, but the wheel that controls them proves hard to handle. He has to crank it several times to release the flaps. He feels like he's finally fighting the Nazis—flying this German plane is a battle.

One by one, Milt, Ezer, Modi, and Eddy Cohen take off in their Messerschmitts, which bear little resemblance to the Bf 109s that the Luftwaffe flew and prove more dangerous to fly than the overloaded C-46s.

Soon, the OZ fighter pilots discover that the Avia S-199 may have little value in war: Instead of a four-prong fighter plane propeller, the Czechs installed a three-prong Heinkel He 111H bomber propeller, which sometimes falls out of synch with the two machine guns that fire through it.

Over pilsners that night, the fighter pilots hold nothing back from Al, who's visiting them.

"My biggest accomplishment today was to not flip over when I landed," Lou says.

"If you think landing here was bad," Cohen says, "wait 'til we land them back home."

When Al asks why, Cohen explains that the Messerschmitts were made to land on grass, not concrete or sand.

"I'm less worried about landing or even taking off," Milt says, "than I am about going up against Spitfires in these 'Lesser-schmitts.'"

The Arabs may have better fighter planes, Al says, but the Jewish state has better fighter pilots.

Lou asks Al to do everything he can to get them better planes. The OZ boss mentions that he has not given up on buying P-51s and/or P-47s. The fighter pilots' eyes widen. They urge him to go to Mexico and make it happen. He promises to do his best.

They drink to that.

$\sim$

Sam flies to Palestine a week before the Big Day: May 14. Mystery shrouds the creation of the Jewish state. No one knows what it might be called—Ben-Gurion is rumored to be considering Zion—or if it will even happen. No one's certain that the Yishuv leader will go through with it knowing his troops lack the weapons to win a war.

The war, Sam thinks, will happen no matter what. As soon as the British leave, the neighboring countries will invade, with or without the Jewish state's creation. They've been revving up for—indeed, waging—war for months. A technicality such as the delay of a declaration of independence will mean little to them. Their biggest concern—European refugees flooding Palestine as soon as the Royal Navy lifts its blockade—will occur regardless.

Coming in for a night landing in Aqir, where the Jews light the runway just long enough for the Connie to find its way, Sam gets goosebumps. When the Haganah soldiers unload the Czech weapons with silent reverence, he tears up.

A Jeep drives up to the Connie. Out jumps Ben-Gurion. Seeing the machine guns strengthens his stance. He shakes Sam's hand. The OZ chief pilot assures him that, unlike the *Nora* and the commercial C-54, the Connie signifies the beginning of a major arms airlift.

Indeed, a few days later, the first C-46 arrives in Aqir. Its radio equipment malfunctions, making it impossible for its pilot, Arnold, to notify the Haganah to turn on the runway lights. So he lands in darkness.

When Arnold mentions this incident to Sam later, the chief pilot rebukes him. He could have crashed the C-46.

"Well, I didn't," Arnold says. "Besides, if you don't want us to land in the dark, why did you teach us how to do it?"

"I also taught you how to bail out," Sam says. "They're called last-resort measures for a reason."

A few days later, when Kurtz's C-46 arrives, the Haganah is ready for it, lights and all.

In Zebra, the OZ crews and the Czechs start the process of taking apart a Messerschmitt. It proves to be tricky.

～

Against the advice of his political allies and consultants, as well as many Jewish leaders, Ben-Gurion decides to move forward with the creation of a Jewish state on May 14.

But first, Ben-Gurion, who grew up in a Zionist home in Poland, must convince his provisional government's administrative leadership. Several of the ten members who are able to make the May 12 meeting in Tel Aviv express concern that their new country would be unable to defend itself. They advocate accepting US Secretary of State Marshall's truce proposal, which would indefinitely postpone the Jewish state's creation.

But after hearing Ben-Gurion's impassioned plea, the administrative leaders give him the green light by a six-to-four vote. They also accept his recommendation to call the new state Israel.

Two days later, at 4 p.m., Ben-Gurion declares, "Eretz-Israel [the land of Israel] was the birthplace of the Jewish people. . . . After being forcibly exiled from their land, the people . . . never ceased to pray and hope for their return to it. . . . The Catastrophe which recently befell the Jewish people—the massacre of millions of Jews in Europe—was another clear demonstration of the urgency of solving the problem of its homelessness by re-establishing in Eretz-Israel the Jewish state."

When Ben-Gurion concludes by saying, "We appeal to the Jewish people throughout the Diaspora to rally round the Jews of Eretz-Israel," the OZ members feel he's talking directly to them.

To a large extent, he is. Involved in every major military decision, Ben-Gurion receives a daily briefing on the OZ progress. He becomes obsessed with the deliveries from Czechoslovakia.

Much like they did in the hours after the United Nations voted to partition Palestine, Ben-Gurion and Al avoid joining the celebrations. They know that declaring and winning independence may be two sides of the same coin, but that coin is up in the air. Where it will land will depend, to a large extent, on OZ.

Eleven minutes after Ben-Gurion declares independence, Israel and OZ receive a surprise boost. President Truman shocks the world—and his State Department—by recognizing the new state.

For Pat, this is just another sign that he's losing this fight. The OZ planes, pilots, and crews are gone. His main suspects, including Al and Hank, are nowhere to be found. But he continues to build a legal case against them. Did Truman just undermine it?

Although Truman's recognition is informal—de facto, not de jure—it gives the new state immediate credibility. It's real. It may not survive its first war, but it's real. The American president's stroke of a pen is so important that it forever leaves the impression that the United States stood firmly behind Israel's creation. Many believe it was America, not the Soviet Union and the United Nations, that made it possible.

Truman's rebellious recognition also fortifies the OZ members' new status. They are no longer gun runners for factitious entities but arms transporters for a legitimate country. This, of course, is just semantics. The fact remains that the United States and the United Kingdom still consider them renegades, and even the United Nations has recently issued its own version of an arms embargo.

"It's like a midwife helping a mother give birth but trying to keep her from feeding her baby," Ike tells Eddie when the latter mentions the UN embargo.

Nonetheless, the OZ members find reasons for optimism on the diplomatic front. A couple of days after Israel incarnates, the Soviet Union becomes the first country to recognize it formally. Other Soviet bloc countries, including Czechoslovakia and Poland, soon do the same.

Things are looking up for the Israelis—if they can hold on.

~

Just after midnight, the first official Israeli ATC landing takes place at Aqir, which the new country has renamed Ekron. Leo and Harold sandwich their arrival between the Declaration of Independence eight hours earlier and the expected Arab invasion a few hours later.

The scent of the nearby orange groves fills the air. Recalling Al mentioning that this is what he remembers most about his visit to Palestine, Leo and Harold watch the Israelis unload the weapons with efficient urgency.

"Shalom," one of the Israelis says.

"Shalom," Leo and Harold say.

"You're Americans?"

"Yes, we're Americans."

As the Israeli returns to unloading the weapons, Harold turns to Leo to say, "I feel a sense of accomplishment. For once in my life."

Leo chokes back tears. The combination of finally shipping the arms, doing it just as the war is about to start, and setting foot for the first time in Israel overwhelms him. Knowing they have to get out before sunrise to avoid being shot down by enemy planes or anti-aircraft artillery gives weight to every moment.

All OZ transport aviators have been instructed to follow this procedure and get in and out of Israel under cover of darkness. Leo and Harold fly back to Zebra at predawn. They get out just in time. Within hours, Egyptian Spitfires strike Ekron. They make daily passes over this vital airport, dropping bombs on the runway and hangars and strafing aviators and mechanics.

They do the same to Tel Aviv, turning it into a practice range during daylight. For now, the Egyptians have free reign of the skies. They believe they'll easily maintain it through the rest of the war, which they expect to last a couple of weeks. Lacking anti-aircraft artillery, all the Israelis can do is blast their sirens at the sight of approaching Spitfires and Douglas C-47 Dakotas.

The Israelis, the vast majority of whom have no idea that their government bought Messerschmitts, also pester the Egyptian planes with machine gun fire. A mostly symbolic act, it achieves little more than alleviating some of the defending troops' frustrations. And yet, on the first day of the war, a volunteer from the United Kingdom, Sam Rose, hits a Spitfire as it attacks the Sde Dov airfield.

The Spitfire crashes on Herzliya Beach, north of Tel Aviv. The Israelis quickly grab it. Who knows, maybe they can restore it.

The Israeli downing of the Spitfire, however, does little to deter the Egyptians, who see it for what it is: a lucky shot. They remain fixated on ripping out Israel's heart—Tel Aviv. They base their strategy on simple logic: Although its extremities, such as Jewish military outposts in the Galilee and the Negev Desert, as well as its largest community, Jerusalem, may continue to function a bit longer, the new state would be brain dead.

Ben-Gurion declared Jerusalem—the Jews' holiest city and home to 100,000 Israelis—the capital but continues to run the country from Tel Aviv. This vibrant city houses the country's political, military, and business leadership, as well as its media.

Besides fighter planes and bombers, the Egyptians send an expeditionary force of two brigades totaling 10,000 infantry, artillery, and armored troops to squash Israeli resistance from Beersheba to Tel Aviv.

The expeditionary force's leader, Major General Ahmed Ali al-Muwawi, leads one of the brigades directly toward Tel Aviv. Under the protection of the Royal Egyptian Air Force, he picks his battles along the way. The fifty-one-year-old Southern Sector commander scores one of the war's biggest Arab victories when he captures the Yad Mordechai kibbutz after five days of fighting. But he avoids most other confrontations to try to make a beeline for Tel Aviv.

Although it eventually fell, the Yad Mordechai kibbutz, named after the Warsaw Ghetto Uprising leader, took pride in delaying the Egyptian march on Tel Aviv. But Muwawi remains confident about achieving his objective. Who's going to stop him?

~

In a Rome bar, Buzz, Giddy, and Leonard have drinks with a WWII Italian fighter pilot. The Canadian ace had shot down the Regia Aeronautica officer's Macchi 202 Folgore over Malta. They reminisce about their dogfight as if recalling a soccer game.

Buzz describes coming upon this pilot's Italian-made Folgore (Thunderbolt) at the end of a long, fruitless day.

"In the beginning," Buzz says, "I underestimated the Thunderbolts."

"You didn't think the Italians could build a good fighter plane, did you?" the Italian asks.

The Canadian nods. The Italian indicates that he gets that a lot.

By the time he ran into this Italian pilot's Thunderbolt, Buzz knew better. "I learned the hard way just how sneaky and swift they can be."

The Italian pilot kisses his fingertips to gesture *sono eccellenti* (they're excellent)!

The skirmish lasted several long minutes. Every time Buzz had the Folgore in his Sight, it broke away. The Falcon almost gave up and returned to base, but then, Buzz says, he "got lucky." He found himself dead on the Italian's tail. He fired a confident burst. In those circumstances, he rarely misses.

The Italian bailed a split second before his plane blew up.

As was his custom, Buzz went after the parachuting pilot.

"I know! You tried to kill me," the Italian says. "Why did you do that?"

"I didn't want you to come back and get me the next time," Buzz says.

"You had nothing to worry about," the Italian says. "I never flew again."

Giddy wants to ask how they figured out their mutual history, but an attractive blonde winks at him from across the bar. He joins her. She buys him a drink. Leonard slashes his hand across his neck, trying to tell his friend to "abort mission" because she's likely a British secret agent.

Giddy continues flirting.

Leonard's signals become more overt, until finally Giddy acknowledges him—but continues bantering with the supposed spy.

Giddy knows he's scheduled to test-fly a Norseman with Buzz in the morning, but he figures he can sleep with this woman and still get enough z's to be alert. So when she invites him up, he follows her with no hesitation.

As they approach her room, however, he hears a strange sound. She pretends not to notice it. When she opens her door, Giddy spots the shadow of a man.

Saying he has a toothache, Giddy disappears.

He returns to the bar. Buzz, Leonard, and the Italian pilot are gone. Giddy picks up an Italian woman and takes her to his room.

~

The OZ pilots are getting better at wrangling the unruly Messerschmitts. They have a long way to go and need a great deal more practice to overcome the Avia S-199's numerous flaws, but they're making steady progress—and getting antsy. They ache to take on the Arab air forces.

The Israelis may have declared independence, but they control only the earth beneath their feet. The air above them still belongs to foreign nations.

In Tel Aviv, the aerial attacks have become part of the daily routine. The sun rises, businesses open, children walk to school, soldiers go off to battle, generals strategize, political leaders tackle crises, and Egyptian Spitfires and Dakotas drop bombs.

"What are we doing here?" Milt says, pointing at the red, white, and blue Czech flag flying above their barracks. "We should be in Israel, fighting."

"I'm with you," Lou says. "But none of us is ready."

Nonetheless, the OZ fighter pilots plot their first attack. They know that most of the Egyptian onslaughts originate from El Arish, just south of the Gaza Strip. Using some of their light planes, the Israelis have photographed this air base. It shows Spitfires resting uncovered and unprotected outside the hangars.

"They're not worried," Lou says, "because they don't know that we have an air force."

This sets a plan in motion: attack the Spitfires while they're on the ground.

"If we make this our debut mission," Lou says, "they won't know what hit them."

"We can destroy most of their Spitfires in one fell swoop," Cohen says.

"A predawn sneak attack," Lou concurs.

"The element of surprise to the tenth degree," Ezer says.

"All right," Modi says. "What are we waiting for?"

Lou, the group's informal and soon-to-be-official leader, speaks with the Czech instructors about concluding the training as soon as possible. "Maybe even today."

The Czech trainers urge the pilots to stay at least one more week.

"What good is the element of surprise if you can't execute on it?" they ask. "You don't want to go all the way to El Arish and find out that you don't know how to hit your target."

Lou consults with Al, who agrees they should get to Israel as soon as possible, but notes that they may as well continue honing their skills in České Budějovice while the Czech technicians reassemble the Messerschmitts in Israel.

"It's gonna take them a few more days," Al says.

Lou passes this recommendation to the other fighter pilots, who agree.

"We need two, three months," Modi says. "Let's get at least two or three more days. Surprised or not, the Egyptians will still shoot at us. We have to be prepared."

~

Early the next morning, Giddy, who doesn't want his night with the Italian woman to end, zips down the hallway to ask Buzz whether he can skip this test flight. The Canadian ace says no pilot should ever fly hungover and spent.

"What are you talking about?" Giddy says. "I'm fine."

"That's exactly my point," Buzz says. "You're delusional."

"I'll test-fly the next one," Giddy says.

Giddy goes back to bed. Buzz heads to Rome Urbe Airport, where he test-flies the Norseman with Leonard. As he always does, the Canadian ace climbs into the cockpit clutching a Bible.

Giddy will wonder whether Buzz ever got to say a last prayer. As it levels off over Rome, the Norseman explodes.

Arazi later tells Giddy that he's received an intelligence report implicating the British.

"I don't get it," Giddy says. "Buzz and Leonard were RAF."

"Right," Arazi says. "They killed two of their own."

Feeling guilty, Giddy says it should've been him up there.

Arazi debates whether to keep Giddy in Rome or send him to Czechoslovakia. The fatal sabotage has thrown everyone off their game.

Giddy stops going out. He grounds himself in his room, silhouetting air attacks and angles on a backlit sheet.

~

In Zebra, Moonitz and Kurtz compete to see which C-46 will take off first with half a Messerschmitt. With the Avia S-199 wings snuggled in the back of his plane, the former policeman has the lead. The former fireman hurries his crew to complete fitting in the fuselage and engine.

Kurtz's C-46 leaves before Moonitz and his crew members finish loading their plane. He radios back, "Boys, the runway's clear," referencing the FBI agents and T-Men who tried to block their departure from Burbank and Millville.

Moonitz refuses to give up.

"We can catch up in the air," he tells his crew.

Although they never come close to catching Kurtz, Moonitz milks this contest for as long as he could. It's a transparent tactic to infuse his crew with a renewed sense of teamwork. He's never gotten along with Ike, but until they got stuck in Catania, he had a decent relationship with Eddie and Moe. In the long days they spent on the Italian island and in Zebra, the radio operator has drawn closer to the co-pilot, drifting away from the captain, and the navigator has become a bit lost.

Moe is the kind of guy who has to stay busy. Unlike most of the other OZ aviators, the former Eagle Scout avoids going out, drinking, chasing women, and getting into any sort of trouble. He prefers to work. Sitting around waiting drives him crazy. He's had little to do between flights.

Back in the air, Moe's in his element. He's fired up, knowing the airlift means nearly nonstop work. He expertly navigates the plane to its layover in Jockstrap. This time, everything goes as planned. The C-46 needs no repairs, and the Corsicans refuel it quickly without asking about the cargo. Moonitz and Ike take off into the Mediterranean skies with gusto.

When they start to descend in Israel, Moonitz and Ike cannot believe they made it without a hitch. Their flight has been so smooth, it's making them a little nervous. They look back at the half Messerschmitt. It's still there. They glance at Eddie and Moe. They're wide awake.

Lighting a cigarette, Moonitz offers one to Ike, who waves it off.

"I quit," Ike says.

Moonitz gives him a questioning look.

"I was smoking a pack a day," Ike says. "I hated the way it stunk up my clothes and yellowed my teeth."

Moonitz puts out his own cigarette. But, as his anxiousness returns, he lights another.

~

Arazi visits the OZ team in Zebra. He tells them that things look bleak in Israel. "Our worst fears are materializing; our greatest hopes are fading."

The Egyptian division advances toward Tel Aviv. Although it's days behind schedule, it remains on track to choke the city that the Yishuv created on sand dunes four decades earlier.

Little do the Egyptians realize, these days will make a crucial difference. And little do the OZ pilots realize, the Messerschmitts they've been tirelessly delivering one half at a time will directly impact the enemy division's progress.

Besides the Messerschmitt parts, the C-46s bring in the Czech mechanics to reassemble them. As they work inside the Ekron hangars, they hear Egyptian Spitfires buzzing by.

Looking up, Al and Sam see a Spitfire head straight toward them and then make an abrupt turn and fly toward Tel Aviv. They breathe a sigh of relief.

"I feel guilty," Sam says. "He's probably going to mow down civilians instead."

The next visitors to Ekron—the Israeli Air Force's new commander and his deputy—also spark mixed feelings in Al and Sam. They've never met or even heard of the commander, Aharon Remez, twenty-nine, born and raised in Tel Aviv in a Zionist home adjacent to Ben-Gurion's. Aharon's father, Minister of Transportation David Remez, had chaired the Yishuv's executive branch, signed the Declaration of Independence, and has consulted his next-door neighbor for years.

Although he flew for the RAF during World War II after training in New Jersey and heading the Shrut Avir, Aharon Remez projects the demeanor and mind-set of a bureaucrat. He's the stiffest Israeli and the blandest aviator Al and Sam have ever met. He immediately strikes them as the wrong man for the job.

Yet his deputy elicits an even stronger reaction. Al and Sam are upset to see that they've lost their most vital and effective liaison, Shechtman, who, like the team player that he is, never thought about turning down this appointment, even if it means trading the coolest boss in the world—Arazi—for Remez. But the good news is that he continues to work with Al, Sam, and the rest of the OZ aviators. In fact, he may even spend more time with them now. After all, they are the Israeli Air Force.

~

Despite being engulfed in a thick fog, Moonitz and Ike home in on the Ekron airport.

Moe calls out their altitude: "One thousand feet."

Ike stresses to Moonitz that these are just estimates; they cannot fully count on them, especially during low visibility. Ike recommends they make at least one pass over the runway prior to landing so "I can look straight down and time how long it takes to get to the end of the runway at our current speed, plus thirty seconds."

"120 miles per hour," Moonitz says.

"Make a ninety-degree turn, fly for thirty seconds, make another ninety-degree turn, and fly the same time the last pass took, plus thirty seconds," Ike says. "I'll tell you when to turn."

"Got it," Moonitz says. "Let's establish the base leg."

"Don't get below five hundred feet," Ike says.

They time the runway, plus thirty seconds, and do the ninety-degree turn.

"Four hundred feet," Moe says.

"Norm!" Ike yells. "Get her up!"

For a reason Ike will never understand, Moonitz ignores him. The co-pilot taps the altimeter. No reaction. He considers pushing back the stick but fears it would prompt the captain to push forward instinctively.

The wingtip catches the ground. The plane crashes into a hill.

A fire erupts. The C-46 slides down the hill. Ike bangs his head. A flame shoots up between his legs. His nose hairs burn.

Recalling his WWII trainer telling him that breathing during a fire can "burn your interior tissue and drown your internal organs in your own fluid," Ike holds his breath.

When the C-46 comes to a stop at the bottom of the hill, Ike pushes back his seat to escape the flames, snaps open his seatbelt, looks around, sees death and destruction, opens his window, and bails out.

With his hands on his knees as he sucks the oxygen out of the air, he hears moaning. He hesitates, takes a deep breath, and jumps back into the burning plane, which has split in two. He glares at Eddie, who lies face down and motionless on a broken seat, his belt strapped around his back.

Concluding that the radio operator's dead, Ike turns his attention to Moonitz.

He's alive!

Ike kicks open Moonitz's window and yells at him to evacuate. But the captain's strapped. The co-pilot undoes Moonitz's seatbelt and pushes him out the window.

Following Moonitz out of the plane, Ike hears Eddie yelling, "I'm burning, I'm burning." Again, the co-pilot hesitates. He looks to Moonitz, but the captain is walking away. He examines the plane's broken tail. He spots Moe's legs and arms sticking out from underneath the Messerschmitt engine, which had rolled on top of him.

Ike jumps back into the front of the plane and tries to repeat the drill, unstrapping and trying to push Eddie out the open window. But this time, he faces two major obstacles: the radio operator is too big, and Ike's skin starts falling off like shawarma cut from a spinning rotisserie.

Ike summons Moonitz: "Norm! Norm!"

Moonitz stops, turns, and rushes toward them. The former fireman pulls Eddie out as if uncorking a bottle of champagne.

Having badly injured his leg, Eddie cannot walk. So Ike and Moonitz carry him toward the runway they measured while airborne.

Harold runs toward them, saying, "Where have you been? We've been waiting for you."

Ike points at the fire behind them.

Harold and other OZ members take the three injured aviators to the hangar, where they give them morphine, clean their wounds, and bandage them up like mummies. They place them on stretchers and rush them to the nearby Kibbutz Givat Brenner, which has one of the country's few sanatoriums.

Although they all need to stay in the sanatorium for at least a few days, only Eddie has suffered serious injuries and remains unconscious for a while.

Ike wakes up twelve hours later as he's being examined. The doctor instructs the nurse to "give the wounded soldier a cigarette." Hearing a match being struck, the pilot tries to protest, "I don't smoke anymore."

What comes out of his mouth, however, is *"mumble, mumble, mumble."*

As the lit cig dangles off his half-numb bottom lip, Ike thinks, *I almost died*, and he takes a drag.

Soon, he smokes two packs a day.

When Moonitz sees him bum a Dubek cigarette from Kurtz, he ribs Ike: "You refuse an American smoke from me but take an Israeli stinker from him?"

Ike replies, "Now I smoke anything that burns."

~

Lou tells his fellow OZ fighter pilots that it's time to go. One of their Czech trainers overhears him.

"You're not ready," the Czech trainer says.

"If we wait 'til we're ready," Lou says, "there won't be any battles left to fight."

Any reservations Lou may have had about cutting short their Messerschmitt training evaporate when he hears that Egyptian Spitfires attacked civilians at Tel Aviv's Central Bus Station during rush hour. Strafing Israelis as they ran for their lives and blowing up a double-decker bus, they killed forty-one and injured sixty.

Infuriated, Lou meets with the Czech commander, saying, "We have to leave."

"How can you do that?" the Czech commander says. "You haven't practiced firing, you haven't dropped bombs, you haven't done formation flying."

"We have no alternative," Lou says. "We can't just sit here with flyable airplanes while Israel gets bombed daily with not even an anti-aircraft gun."

"Well," the Czech commander says, "what are you going to do?"

"I know we have a problem," Lou says. "The Egyptians have forty new Spitfires that the beautiful British government sold them."

"Yes, brand-new, postwar manufacture. G model," the Czech commander says. "Your air force is made up of four mediocre airplanes."

"If they're mediocre, what happens in a shabby plane?" Lou says. "Instant death?"

The commander chuckles. He likes Lou's straight-shooting doggedness.

"I think the only chance we have is to destroy the Egyptian planes on the ground at El Arish," Lou says. "As soon as our planes are reassembled, we take off at dark and strike at first light."

Lou, who's been named the commander of Israel's first fighter-pilot squadron, makes the decision—they're cutting short their training and going to Israel today.

They arrive in Zebra a few hours later to fly to Israel in Collie's C-46, which is packed with weapons. He and Lou become instant, lifelong friends.

As Collie prepares to taxi the C-46 to the runway, Lou jumps out. He returns a few moments later with wildflowers. He says he plans to give them to the first woman he sees after they land in Israel.

"Just hope that she's not married and that her husband isn't there to check out one of the guns we're bringing," Collie says.

During the flight, Lou has to make a tough decision. Who among the five pilots should he leave out of the squadron's first mission?

The OZ transport planes have thus far brought in only four Messerschmitts. Lou, of course, must lead the attack, so he has to pick three pilots from among the other four. Milt is the most experienced. Ezer, Modi, and Cohen have flown over Israel, so they know the topography and can help navigate.

He decides to leave out the American, for two main reasons: first, Milt can lead the second mission, whatever that may be; second, the three Israelis should participate in their country's first air assault.

Milt is miffed until it sinks in that he'll lead the second mission. He starts contemplating potential targets.

Collie's C-46 lands in Israel on schedule. As soon as he jumps out, Lou spots a young Israeli female soldier sorting through the Mausers. He hands her the wildflowers. Taken aback at first, she accepts them with a smile, puts them by her side, and continues organizing the weapons into bins.

Lou, meanwhile, insists on going to the hangar in which the Czech technicians are reassembling the Messerschmitts. The other fighter pilots join him. They're happy to see the mechanics working overnight.

"They've been going nonstop," Al tells them.

Al introduces them to the lead Israeli mechanic, Binyamin "Benny" Peled, nineteen, who was born and raised in Tel Aviv and will one day become IAF commander. For now, he's focused on helping the Czechs breathe life into the Messerschmitts, which, he tells the OZ pilots, are easier to take apart than put back together.

Lou asks how long it will take. Benny says a few more days. He stresses that they're just reattaching these planes, not improving them.

"They're still junk," Benny says. "Anybody who sits in them deserves a medal."

Lou consults Al on whether they should test each Messerschmitt as soon as it's assembled. They decide against it. The Egyptians fly over Ekron every day. If·they spot the Messerschmitts, at best, they'll know that Israel has fighter planes and the element of surprise will vanish; at worst, they'll do to them what the OZ pilots plan to do to the Spitfires in El Arish.

All the OZ fighter pilots can do is wait for the Messerschmitts to be reassembled and then gamble that they actually work. The prospect of sitting around doing nothing for several days upsets them as much as the inability to test their planes.

"I told you we should've stayed longer in Czechoslovakia," Milt says.

"You're welcome to go back," Lou says.

Milt is not taking a chance on missing out on leading Israel's second air assault. If his colleagues are wiping out the Spitfires at El Arish, what should he do? He seeks information and insight from the Israelis. He meets with an intelligence officer, Lee Silverman.

"Wait a second," Milt says, "weren't you a point guard at UCLA?"

Lee's dumbfounded—he's the one who's supposed to be in the know.

"I'm trying to put together an Israeli Air Force basketball team," Lee says. "Do you play?"

Shaking his head, Milt, who's still standing, points at his short stature. Lee stands up. He's also five feet, five inches. The fighter pilot tips an imaginary hat. That's impressive—playing for UCLA at that height.

"You must be a devil of a dribbler," Milt says.

"I run between their legs," Lee says, smiling.

Milt asks about potential targets for his upcoming aerial assault. Lee mentions a couple, starting with the Egyptian division making its way to Tel Aviv.

"Do we have the ground forces to stop them?" Milt asks.

"I don't think so," Lee says. "And even if we did, they'd need aerial support." Milt likes it.

"If this indeed becomes your first assignment," Lee says, "it will require joint operation planning."

"Will we have time?" Milt asks.

Lee nods, noting, "The Egyptians are moving slowly."

The second target, Lee says, consists of an Iraqi division of a similar size and makeup that appears to aim to split Israel.

"They're on a westward trajectory from their base in Tulkarm," Lee says, "heading straight toward Netanya."

Milt has never heard of Netanya. Lee says it's a twenty-year-old coastal town nestled between Tel Aviv and Haifa. The fighter pilot also had no idea that Iraqis had joined the invasion. "I thought it was the Egyptians, Palestinian Arabs, and Syrians," he says.

"Also the Lebanese, Transjordanians, and Saudis," Lee states. "And the Iraqis."

The Iraqis are about a quarter of the way on their forty-six-mile march to Netanya, named after Macy's co-owner Nathan Straus for his support for the Yishuv's most vulnerable residents. Although Israel could handle the loss of this coastal town, it would struggle with being split in two. The north, which includes Haifa and the Galilee, would practically have no chance of survival.

Milt leaves feeling even more restless than before. He asks Al whether he can participate in the arms airlifts while waiting. The OZ boss says that's fine with him, but Milt must check with his squadron commanding officer.

Lou ponders the proposal. It's risky either way—Milt could crash flying a C-46 or the C-54, but he could also become overly anxious sitting around waiting. The squadron CO approves it—just one flight for now. The Czech mechanics have completed assembling two Messerschmitts and are moving fast on the other two.

Before Milt takes off, Lou gathers the team to name their squadron. Cohen suggests "101," to make it sound like the just officially formed Israeli Air Force has a slew of squadrons.

The four thumbs up Cohen receives make it official: the 101 Squadron is launched.

∼

Inside one of the Ekron hangars, the Czech and Israeli technicians drop like discarded puppets. Although it's only eighteen hundred hours (6 p.m.), they could fall asleep right on the greasy floor. They've finally crossed the Messerschmitt marathon finish line. The 101 Squadron—including Milt, who just returned from Zebra with a C-46 full of rifles and bullets—stand back in awe of the four Avia S-199s' resurrection. The German-Czech-Israeli planes are ready for flight and fight, their fuel tanks full, their cannon and machine guns ammoed, their two 150-pound bombs strapped in like paratroopers, and their sides painted with blue and white Jewish stars.

For the first time since it launched a year earlier, Operation Zebra shows off its true colors. No more fake names, fraudulent registration numbers, false flags, or residual swastikas.

Always more practical than sentimental, Modi cuts short the pilots' rare moment of reverent quiescence, asking Lou, "What's zero hour?"

"Zero five hundred hours," Lou says. "Report for duty at this hangar at zero four thirty hours."

Even Ezer, for whom a night in tends to be out of the question, plans to go straight to bed tonight. Like the other pilots, he's aware that every move he makes in the morning will be scrutinized and recorded for posterity.

Lou itches to go to their temporary home at Tel Aviv's Park Hotel. The previous day, he barely escaped an Egyptian air raid that caught Ekron by surprise. Having just arrived at the airport, he jumped into a ditch to take cover. An air traffic controller walking to the tower leaped in after him, saving the OZ pilot's life but losing his own to a barrage of shrapnel. The Spitfires injured several others—some severely—and razed the second, empty hangar.

Whether by missed calculation or shots, the Egyptian Spitfire pilots left the hangar that houses the four Messerschmitts standing.

"I don't want to jinx it, and I don't even believe in God, but I think someone upstairs is watching over us," Lou told Modi when the Israeli pilot yanked him out of the ditch.

Stepping out of the hangar the following day, Lou finds himself again thinking about invisible powers. He doesn't pray; he just hopes his lucky streak, which he believes started when he joined the Marines, continues for at least another twelve hours.

Snapping him out of his thoughts, a Jeep bursts onto the tarmac, braking at his feet. Out jumps Givati brigade commander Shimon Avidan, thirty-seven, a no-nonsense leader who reminds Lou of the best Marines. Born Siegbert Koch in Germany, the Galilee kibbutznik is one of Israel's sharpest military minds and one of its few card-carrying communists.

Avidan implores the OZ pilots to attack the Egyptian division—which has reached the Palestinian Arab town of Isdud, nineteen miles south of Tel Aviv—*right now*.

Earlier that day, Givati soldiers blew up the Lachish River bridge that the Egyptians need to cross. Avidan initially sent in two mules with 650 pounds of explosives. But the donkey-horse hybrids, who are smarter than their jackass fathers, ran away. So he reluctantly assigned the job to human beings. They knocked down the bridge and returned unharmed. However, their successful effort has done little more than slow down the invaders.

Avidan expects the Egyptians to complete putting up a truss bridge over the Lachish River by nightfall.

"If we don't stop them," Avidan says, "they'll be in Tel Aviv tomorrow night."

Overhearing him, Remez, the Israeli Air Force commander, interrupts, saying the 101 Squadron already has its debut mission—destroying the Egyptian Spitfires on the ground at El Arish.

"We get to play the surprise card only once," Remez says.

"If we don't attack Isdud with our fighter planes right now," Avidan says, "nothing else will matter."

"Our entire air force could be ambushed and annihilated during or right after attacking Isdud," Remez says. However, a successful demolishing of El Arish will make many of the Israeli military's objectives much more attainable.

"We won't have any more objectives," Avidan says, exasperated. "If the Egyptians take Tel Aviv, the war is over. We're finished."

~

The OZ transport pilots have turned the Zebra-Ekron airlift into an armament assembly line, freeing Al to worry about other aspects of the operation—and Israel's long-term survival. Although he believes that the Czech rifles, machine guns, and bullets will sustain the Jewish soldiers for the foreseeable future, he worries about the Messerschmitts' inferiority and the lack of bombers.

Hearing it's imminent, Al makes a last-ditch effort to stop Israel's purchase of fifteen more Messerschmitts from Czechoslovakia.

"Cancel it," Al tells Arazi.

"This has come from the very top," Arazi says.

"From someone who's probably never seen a Messerschmitt," Al says.

Actually, Ben-Gurion has visited Ekron to see the reassembled Messerschmitts. He understands their downside. But he's pragmatic. The Israelis need fighter planes in the sky above Israel, not on a piece of paper in a briefcase. He's seen nothing from Mexico and plenty from Czechoslovakia to convince him which is a pipe dream and which is helping to make the Zionist dream come true.

Still, Al believes Ben-Gurion is making a huge mistake.

"It's obscene enough to overpay by millions," Al tells Arazi as they drive out of the Ekron airport. "But it's downright criminal to stick the few fighter pilots we have in these death traps."

"What's the alternative?" Arazi shoots back. "And don't say the Mexican Mustangs."

"Why not?" Al says. "They want to make a deal."

"I'm sure they'll take our money," Arazi says, referencing the fact that Hank's weapons remain locked up. "I'm equally certain it will be extremely difficult, if not downright impossible, to actually get the P-51s from them."

"I thought money was not an issue," Al says.

"It is when we get taken to the cleaners," Arazi says.

About to call the Czech deal "runway robbery," Al senses that they're stuck and heads in a different direction, asking, "Are you working on any deals anywhere to buy bombers?"

Arazi shakes his head sadly.

"If I buy bombers," Al says, drawing an instinctive eyebrow arch from Arazi, "will I have to put up with the same nonsense?"

"Even if you pull off the greatest Jewish feat since Moses parted the Red Sea," Arazi says, "how would you ever get the bombers here?"

"That'd be my problem," Al says.

"Your problems are everyone's," Arazi states.

Al gives Arazi a frustrated look.

"Fine, I'll support you," Arazi says. "I'll make sure our whole apparatus supports you. Where are you thinking about going?"

"The States."

Arazi bursts out laughing.

"This is from a man who bought an aircraft carrier," Al says.

"We've grown wiser since then," Arazi says. "And so have the T-Men, the British, the FBI, the Arabs, and everyone else trying to make sure we never, ever get a bomber."

Al returns to North America. He's not delusional. He knows perfectly well that his chances of getting arrested are much higher than smuggling out bombers. But after spending a few days in the Jewish state, he feels he must go to the ends of the Earth to try to add this key element to the Israelis' survival kit.

The OZ recruiting has been going well enough to allow him to disappear for a while. Recent additions include pilots such as William "Blackie" Bradshaw, a Royal Canadian Air Force veteran, and Percy (Pesach) "Pussy" Tolchinsky, who flew Douglas DC-3 transports in the Pacific; navigators such as Canadian Benjamin "Red" Sturrey and South African Cyril Steinberg; and mechanics such as Californian Fred Dahms, a former Flying Tiger, and New Jerseyite Al Pozzoli, whose immigrant parents bestowed on him fluency in Italian. In fact, the lineup has solidified enough to allow Al to take Leo and Willie with him.

"It has fallen on us to build this air force," Al tells them. "So let's build a good one."

~

As Remez and Avidan squabble, Lou leads the squadron back into the hangar. He asks the mechanics to prepare the Messerschmitts for immediate takeoff and then gives Cohen, Ezer, and Modi a set of instructions:

- Forget El Arish for now and focus on stopping the Egyptian division. Avidan is right. It's now or never. "Let's go save Tel Aviv."
- Fly in wall formation. In the air, line each Messerschmitt abreast with Lou's. "Otherwise, the anti-aircraft gunners will aim at No. 1 and hit No. 4. That was my experience in the Pacific. So do not hang back."
- Start the Messerschmitts in the hangar. This violates aviation safety rules, but it may be less risky than exposing the planes for longer than is necessary to enemy bombardment.

Cohen, Ezer, and Modi, who had nodded their heads in agreement to the first two points, express concern about the third.

"We could blow up the whole Israeli Air Force," Modi says.

"You'd be able to hear that explosion and see that fire from Cairo," Ezer states.

"We have only one truck to pull the Messerschmitts to the runway," Lou says. "We can't go way down there and come back four times. We might as well send the Egyptians a printed invitation."

Lou, Cohen, Ezer, and Modi open the hangar doors and hop into their Messerschmitts. They rev up the engines. None sparks an inferno. The IAF remains intact. Although they still have no idea whether their guns will respond when they pull the triggers or if their bombs will drop when they press the levers, the pilots know they can at least take off.

Racing down the runway, Lou climbs up first, heading west.

In the nearby Givat Brenner, Ike hears shots. He dashes out of his sickbed to see kibbutz members firing Czech Mausers at two fighter planes. Grabbing binoculars, he yells at the trigger-happy kibbutzniks, "Stop, they're ours."

By the time his words register, the kibbutzniks have wasted hundreds of bullets, none of which came close to the long-gone Messerschmitts.

Leveling off at 6,000 feet, Lou looks around for his pilots. He sees only Modi, who, as instructed, flies at his commander's wing. Ezer and Cohen take off too late to directly join them.

Realizing he has only a rough idea of Isdud's location, Lou looks to Modi, who points south.

Lou turns and, within a couple of minutes, sees the Egyptian division spread out like fire ants at a picnic. Uttering the only prayer he knows, "*Shema Yisrael* . . . Hear, O Israel: the Lord is One," he dives toward the town's center, which is packed with military vehicles and personnel.

He releases a bomb.

It hits the town's mosque, which serves as Muwawi's headquarters.

Lou drops his second bomb.

It blasts a fuel tanker, kicking up a fireball and spreading panic among the Egyptian officers and soldiers.

Having been led to believe that the Jews have no fighter planes, the stunned Egyptians need a moment to crank up their anti-aircraft artillery. But once they do, they fill the sky with enough flak to destroy several squadrons.

Trying to ignore the ballistics popping around him like firecrackers, Modi drops his bombs on the armored vehicles that line up at the truss bridge.

Zipping in from the opposite direction, Ezer turns loose one of his bombs on the division's tail, which stretches south of Isdud. He saves his other bomb for his second pass.

Before it could get into the action, Cohen's Messerschmitt gets hit on its first pass. Aching to continue fighting but aiming to avoid losing a quarter of the IAF, he heads back. Instead of flying to Ekron, though, he makes his way to the Hatzor air base, which the Israelis took over from the RAF a couple of weeks earlier.

Unaware of Cohen's troubles, Lou makes his second pass parallel to Ezer's first. The former Marine fighter pilot strafes the Egyptians with his cannon. Executing a maneuver he picked up in the Pacific—a cloverleaf, which weds a barrel roll to a loop—he dives deep and then sharply levels to skim the top of the division, firing at tanks, tents, and trucks.

Lou's cannon jams just as he reaches the truss bridge.

Crisscrossing Lou's Messerschmitt, Modi empties his cannon shells at any and all targets in sight.

Ezer's second bomb ends up on an empty field north of the river. He beats himself up for holding on to it for too long.

Spewing thick black smoke, Cohen's Messerschmitt crash-lands a mile and a half from Hatzor. Egyptian ground forces snatch him—dead or alive, no one will ever know. He will never again be seen or heard from. He will be dearly missed.

The IAF is down to three Messerschmitts and four fighter pilots.

On their third and final pass, Lou and Modi strafe the Egyptians with their combined four machine guns. Their guns soon jam or run out of ammunition.

Lou waits for Modi and Ezer to clear out and then follows them to Ekron. No Egyptian Spitfire chases after them.

The first to land, Modi deals with a malfunctioning brake by rotating the Messerschmitt horizontally, blowing the left tire and sticking the left wing in the ground.

The IAF is down to two functioning Messerschmitts.

Lou and Ezer land. They taxi into the hangar.

About to pepper them with questions, Milt, Remez, and Shechtman bite their tongues on seeing how spent Lou, Ezer, and Modi are.

The pilots ask about Cohen. Remez says that he crashed near Hatzor, and it appears that the Egyptians got to him first.

Modi, Lou, and Ezer collapse to the floor. They sit there, dazed. Milt, Remez, and Shechtman join them in a circle. Composing himself, the squadron CO debriefs the group: "I doubt we caused any meaningful damage. We destroyed, what, a dozen military vehicles?"

Modi and Ezer nod. That sounds about right.

"We killed, how many, eighty to ninety soldiers?"

They nod again.

"They have hundreds of vehicles and thousands of soldiers," Lou says.

The raid appears to have wreaked greater havoc on the Israelis than the Egyptians.

"Right now, they have no idea how big our air force is," Lou says. "They don't know if we have four, ten, or twenty Messerschmitts."

However, the Egyptians may start to suspect that the lone Ekron hangar may house some of those Messerschmitts. Modi suggests they move them to another airport.

Halved of its precious content and drained of its do-or-die adrenaline, the Ekron hangar reflects the pilots' sense of failure—and predicament. It is a depressing sight.

"If we attack the Egyptians again," Modi says, "they'll know we only have two fighter planes."

"We may not have a choice," Remez says.

"True," Lou says. "Let's get a good night's sleep and decide in the morning."

None of them can sleep. They stay up waiting for the intelligence report.

Coming out in the middle of the night, the report—which, like all IAF communications, is in English—includes a translation of an urgent message radioed by the Egyptians during the raid: "We're coming under a heavy attack by enemy aircraft. We're scattering."

The report indicates that, although the raid inflicted insignificant physical damage, it psychologically scarred the Egyptians. They were unprepared for such an onslaught.

Meeting with Avidan, Remez, Shechtman, and several intelligence officers, they come up with a new game plan:

- Over the following days, Givati will bombard the Egyptians, send platoons to destroy specific targets, and determine the best time to launch a full ground attack.
- If the Givati soldiers see signs of a renewed advance toward Tel Aviv, they will immediately alert the fighter pilots.
- Givati will aim to drive the division back (and maybe even conquer Isdud).

- The fighter pilots will meanwhile tackle the similar threat posed by the Iraqi division threatening to bisect Israel.

Everyone agrees that the IAF may inflict more damage on the Egyptians at this point by waiting to attack. The element of uncertainty will continue to cloud the Egyptians' judgment.

Also, Remez points out, Lou, Ezer, and Modi may wish to delay taking on the Spitfires, which are sure to challenge them next time, until more Messerschmitts are assembled.

The conversation turns to the next mission. To pick his wingman, Milt uses simple logic: Since he's flying Lou's Messerschmitt, he chooses the pilot of the only remaining functioning Israeli fighter plane—Ezer.

"Don't tell me zero hour's still zero five hundred hours," Ezer says. "That's in just a few hours."

"Fine," Milt says. "Zero five thirty hours."

∼

Al, Leo, and Willie's first North American stop is Mexico. They aim to hasten the weapon delivery. They have seen how valuable each machine gun is and how prized each round of ammunition is. It frustrates them to think that they have weapons just sitting in an overseas warehouse.

Hank is thrilled to see them. He's on the verge of a breakthrough, but he's too caught up in the intricacies of the situation to realize it.

Al, Leo, and Willie provide a much-needed fresh perspective. They help Hank sort out the details:

- The US government has been pressuring the Mexicans to prevent all weapons, even if they're already paid for, from going to Israel.
- For months, Hank has been saying that the *Kefalos* (code-named *Dromit*) will head from Port of Tampico on the Pánuco River (which it's expected to reach any day now) to China.
- The media and the US authorities publish articles and issue memos debunking this claim. Regardless, Hank has stuck to his story like a non-swimmer clinging to a life raft in the middle of shark-infested waters.

This, Al says, is the ticket. If they can "prove" that the weapons are, indeed, going to China, they should give the Mexicans enough "ammunition" to free their weapons.

"Just like we made our planes officially Panamanian to get them out of the States," Al says, "we should make these weapons officially China bound to get them out of Mexico."

"But you actually took the planes to Panama," Hank reminds them. "We are not going anywhere near China."

"That might not matter once the *Dromit* leaves the Port of Tampico," Leo says.

"It probably will," Hank says.

"We can worry about that then," Al says. "First, let's get the arms out on the ocean."

Hank proposes a crazy idea: asking the Chinese to give them an official letter accepting the arms. Everyone agrees it's not a bad approach.

Knowing how well he worked with Hank in Hawaii, Al leaves Willie with him and flies to the United States with Leo. Time to look for bombers.

At the same time, *Kefalos* captain Adolph S. Oko Jr., forty-four, sails to Tampico believing the weapons are already there, waiting for him. He is in for a rude awakening when all he'll find are hundreds of sugar sacks purchased by Hank as a literal cover.

~

The Iraqis have reached Kfar Yona, a Jewish pioneer town four miles east of Netanya. They have yet to hear from the Egyptians that Israel possesses fighter planes. So they're caught by surprise at the sudden appearance of two IAF Messerschmitts.

Milt dives low to strafe the Iraqis. Just like the Egyptians at Isdud, it takes the Iraqis a moment to fire their anti-aircraft guns. In those precious seconds, the Messerschmitt shoots at four British-made tanks. But as it pulls away, it loses its left wing to anti-aircraft artillery.

Ezer goes through a similar pattern. After firing at Iraqi soldiers—he has no idea how many, if any, he kills—he takes hits to his wings.

Ezer and Milt try to return to Ekron. The former succeeds. The latter runs into an Egyptian Spitfire that follows the black smoke spewing from the Messerschmitt's left wing.

Milt breaks abruptly in the opposite direction. He climbs just high enough (1,200 feet) to jump out and ditch his Messerschmitt in the Mediterranean.

The IAF is down to zero functioning fighter planes.

Landing in the sea with only a partially opened parachute, Milt breaks several ribs and batters his privates. Struggling to swim to shore, he realizes after two strenuous hours that the water level is low enough to traverse by foot.

Standing up, however, exposes Milt to the armed farmers who have stormed the beach believing he's an enemy pilot. The members of Kfar Vitkin, a farmers' co-op north of Netanya, shoot to kill.

Dodging the bullets, Milt waves his arms and yells the only Jewish words he knows, "Gefilte fish! Shabbos!"

The secular, socialist farmers, who share resources and provide each co-op member an equal plot of land, have little connection to gefilte fish, a traditional dish served during ritual meals, or Shabbos (the holy Sabbath). But as Milt keeps insisting, in his way, that he's one of them, they lower their guns, bring him ashore, and rush him to a small Netanya hospital.

Released a few hours later, Milt joins the other fighter pilots for a beer at Tel Aviv's Yarden Hotel. His onset of post-traumatic stress disorder (PTSD), which neither he nor anyone else recognizes as such, is swift and debilitating.

He joins the pilots in toasting an intelligence report that mirrors yesterday's—in lieu of major, actual harm, the raid has exacted profound psychological impact. The Israelis plan to attack the Iraqis on the ground soon. They believe they can stop them and prevent the splitting of their country.

But the celebration fails to make Milt feel any better.

A couple of days later, he returns to the United States.

The IAF is down to three fighter pilots.

Then two, as Ezer breaks his left hand in a motorcycle accident.

To make matters worse, the Egyptian Spitfires attack Ekron every day. It's only a matter of time before they finally destroy the hangar in which the mechanics race to fix the IAF's only two, badly damaged Messerschmitts.

~

In the days and nights since the Messerschmitt raid on Isdud, Avidan has ordered his troops to bombard the Egyptians, lay mines around the town, and attack specific targets. At the same time, he's tried to determine the best opportunity to launch a full assault. With less than half the number of troops—he has 1,150 while Muwawi has about 3,000—the Givati commander knows he must time the attack perfectly. Once it starts, there's no turning back.

Avidan sees the good and bad in the Egyptians staying put in Isdud and taking no offensive measures. Although that has been good news for Tel Aviv, it means that his soldiers will take on a division that has dug in its heels and is prepared to defend its turf.

Initially, Avidan picks June 1 for the Isdud assault. But when he finds out that a cease-fire is expected for June 1–2, he changes his attack plan to June 3.

Meanwhile, the *Kefalos* arrives in Tampico. Hank and Willie welcome Captain Oko and his Spanish crew with a feast of pork, chicken, and beef enchiladas, tacos and burritos, and a vow to get the weapons to the port in "coming days."

Hank and Willie go to the Chinese embassy to speak with a junior official. During the meeting, they get the sense that this young man lacks the authority to solve their problem. So on their way out, they pretend to leave, sneak back, and steal stationery.

They craft a note from China thanking Mexico for the weapons. Hank hand delivers it to his contacts. Now all he can do is wait.

He hates waiting.

~

Back in the United States, Leo and Al (who now answers only to Ervin L. Johnson) act like strangers in their own country. To pursue their illegal objectives, avert harassment, and escape arrest, they must plot, conceal, obscure, claim false identities, reveal information on a need-to-know basis, zigzag, and run. On a personal level, they find postwar America more hostile than war-torn Israel and Soviet-encroached Czechoslovakia.

Although it takes its toll, having to constantly evade the US authorities rarely slows down Al. Much like the bombers he chases, he comes in, hits his targets, and gets out. In a whirlwind ten days in the United States, the groundwork for which he laid in advance, he's purchased four B-17s. For a sham Italian importer, he bought two Flying Fortresses from the USAAF and two from Miami-based produce exporter Charles "Charlie" Thompson Winters, thirty-five.

Al immediately connects with Charlie, who was raised in Boston by Irish immigrants. Although they only talk about some of it—and then only in passing—they have a great deal in common. They grew up in poor Northeast households during the Great Depression. Childhood traumas—in Charlie's case, polio—left them limping. They fell in love with aviation the moment they saw a plane. They can handle flight duties—even serve as co-pilots—if needed but focus almost exclusively on running their operations. And they appear to be rigorously pragmatic while basing many of their decisions on idealistic beliefs.

Charlie takes Al into his B-17s to prove that, although demilitarized, they still possess functioning bomb bay doors.

Al senses that Charlie may be willing to venture beyond just selling them the bombers, for which he's asked and received a very reasonable price of $30,000 each. So the OZ boss reveals his hand, stressing that Israel could lose the war without bombers. The Caribbean produce transporter, who was disqualified from serving during World War II due to polio complications, jumps at the chance to make a contribution to what he views as the "righteous" side in the conflict.

Al—who has a more balanced perspective, understanding that the Arabs have legitimate grievances and that many Israelis are far from saintly—avoids getting into a political discussion with Charlie. Instead, he happily accepts his selfless offer to let the OZ group use his export license for all four B-17s.

Afterward, Leo tells Al that it "sounds too good to be true." In response, the OZ boss repeats Charlie's catchphrase: "Keep the faith."

An atheist since his bar mitzvah, Leo lets out a nervous laugh. Although equally secular, if not quite as certain about God's absence, Al smiles. He agrees that it's silly, maybe even dangerous to incorporate the notion of divine intervention into their strategic thinking. But if it nets them an otherwise extremely elusive export license, why not roll with it?

Al and Leo need around a dozen crew members, including three to four pilots, for each B-17. They bring in aviators just for this mission, never disclosing its nature. They plan to send most of the hired hands back to the States after they land in Zebra and then give the controls to OZ members such as Katz, Kurtz, and Moonitz, who mastered the complex B-17 during World War II.

The word quickly gets around that Charlie, a well-known and respected figure in Florida and Caribbean aviation, is offering large sums—$1,000 for each pilot, $500 for each crew member—for a straightforward gig: flying demilitarized bombers from Miami to Europe. This allows Al and Leo to be selective. Knowing that the US military requires a minimum 3,000 flying hours to pilot this bomber, they consider only B-17-certified candidates.

"I don't care if they carpet-bombed Germany," Al tells Leo. "If it wasn't in a B-17, we don't want to waste our time talking to them."

But these blinders keep Al and Leo from checking other important factors. They hire three heavy drinkers to fly the heavy bombers. Fortunately, several of the other pilots—including Ron Conway, Norman Novak, and Harold Rothstein—are goody two-shoes who balance out the team.

Al picks captains based on names, preferring that they sound non-Jewish. In choosing John Doe for the first B-17, he gets the bonus of having a former USAAF lieutenant colonel crown the roster.

Little does Al know that one of his other hires—a co-pilot with the most Jewish of names—will have to take over for John and become the de facto captain mid-flight. David Goldberg, twenty-eight, who flew B-17s and B-24s for the USAAF in Europe through World War II, may be the most battle-tested of the new team; yet he never complains about his co-pilot role.

"I've always wondered what it's like in the right-hand seat," he tells Katz, who, like Novick and a few other OZ members, has had to be summoned from Zebra to round out the B-17 crews.

Seeing that they could still use another hand, Charlie volunteers to co-pilot one of the B-17s.

Meanwhile, in Israel, after unloading the Czech arms, Zebra-bound C-46s turn into temporary bombers. OZ pilots fill their emptied planes with bombs, which their crew members chuck on enemy positions.

14

June

THE ANTICIPATED ARAB-ISRAELI CEASE-FIRE NEVER TAKES PLACE. THE MAJOR Givati offensive on Isdud begins at 6 p.m. on June 2 with Modi strafing and bombing the Egyptians using one of the IAF's two functioning Messerschmitts. Remez has grounded and demoted Lou, who's been acting strange since the first raid. Despite the positive outcome, as indicated by the intelligence report, he's been unable to shake off the feeling of failure. He's shell-shocked and confused. Milt's abrupt departure, Ezer's motorcycle injury, and, especially, Eddy Cohen's death have all shaken the former Marine pilot.

Lou feels guilty about his inability to lead a casualty-free, decisively victorious mission. He's lost his grip. He's in a daze. He needs a few more days before anyone can even think about sending him back up to fight.

The IAF is down to one fighter pilot.

Promoted by Remez to squadron CO, Modi aims to put on an exemplary display above Isdud, but he can only do so much with the Messerschmitt. After dropping his two bombs on military vehicles that have retreated from the bridge and line the main road, he fires his machine guns and cannon at the Egyptian positions on the north side of town, where everyone expects Givati to attack.

Modi's guns and cannon soon jam. He manages to once again evade the anti-aircraft fire, a noteworthy achievement considering that it appears to be twice as thick as what he encountered the first time. He returns unharmed to Ekron.

A few hours after Modi's raid, Givati strikes. Their two-pronged onslaught resembles the fighter pilots': It achieves little tangible results, costs severely in terms of lives, and yet accomplishes its main goal.

After a two-day battle, the Egyptians abandon their march on Tel Aviv. Although a small force stays in Isdud, which the Givati failed to conquer, most of the division heads to Jerusalem to bolster Transjordan's Arab Legion.

The Israelis name the bridge (which they will rebuild later that year) Ad Halom—Hebrew for "Up to Here."

The Egyptian division's departure allows the IAF to recover. The OZ transport pilots have continued bringing in Messerschmitts, and the Czech and Israeli mechanics have continued to assemble them, as well as fix the existing ones. Soon enough, the 101 Squadron again possesses four functional Messerschmitts—and it's about to have more than enough pilots to fly them.

~

Twenty-three hours after his solo attack on Isdud, Modi again flies alone, this time over Tel Aviv. He runs into an Egyptian quartet—two Spitfires and two Dakotas. Attacking from the east to blind the enemy pilots with the setting sun, he tailgates one of the Dakota bombers, which reverses course and heads back to El Arish.

Scores of Tel Avivians, who normally run for cover at the sight of military planes, gather on balconies, rooftops, and sidewalks to witness what to them appears to be the birth of their air force. Modi fires once, twice, and thrice. One shot pierces the Dakota's fuel tank, turning it into a fireball above Jaffa. The city erupts in cheers.

Encouraged by his first kill and/or swept up by the crowd, Modi searches for the second Dakota. He sees one of the Spitfires stealing his sun trick. He averts his eyes, cuts away, dives under the Egyptian pilot, escapes, and locates the second bomber up ahead.

Modi chases after the No. 2 Dakota, prepared to finally visit El Arish if he has to. But he catches up to it—and shoots it down—south of Rehovot.

Flying back to base, Modi asks himself three questions:

- Did the Dakota pilots and crews survive?
- How much longer will the 101 Squadron stay in Ekron, considering the Egyptians just severely damaged two Messerschmitts on the ground?
- How much longer will he have to fly solo?

The first Dakota's pilot and crew are believed to have been killed and the second's to have survived. No one knows for sure. Modi and Ezer will find a new, more secure airfield in the next few days. And Modi will have to fly alone for just a little longer.

Ezer and Lou need a little more time to recover. The second group of five České Budějovice trainees—Israelis Ben-Chaim, Ben-Porat, Hennenson, Kenner, and Me'iri—have all washed out. Some of them crash-landed their Messerschmitts. They're returning to their homeland to play other roles in the air force.

The third group of five trainees, all Americans, are set to arrive in České Budějovice in the coming days. Modi hopes they have what it takes.

~

With the Norsemen all sent to Israel, Giddy can finally train on the Messerschmitt in České Budějovice. Seeing him off in Rome, Arazi gives the fighter pilot Nescafé to bring to their Czechoslovakia contact person, Dr. Felix.

"Dr. Felix will meet you at the airport and take you through visa check," Arazi tells Giddy. "To thank him, give him this Nescafé. He loves it."

Giddy is immediately annoyed. There's something about the whole thing that rubs him the wrong way. He thinks, *What's with this feller, Dr. Felix?* But he takes the Nescafé on his circuitous route to Prague.

Everywhere Giddy goes, the Nescafé goes.

Joining Giddy on the journey to České Budějovice are two other recruits who have just arrived in Rome. Brooklynite Aaron Leo "Red" Finkel, twenty-eight, and Bostonian Syd Antin, also twenty-eight, sat by each other on their TWA flight from New York but exchanged no more than pleasantries. Now they realize they're on the same secret, illegal team. Their paths may have also crossed during World War II: They flew USAAF P-47s in the China-Burma-India Theater (CBI).

When they land in Prague, Red and Syd—whose passports and visas are in order—clear immigration. But Giddy, who lacks the official paperwork to get in and has been told Dr. Felix would whisk him through, gets held up.

Dr. Felix is nowhere to be found. While Red and Syd wait in the terminal, the Czech police interrogate Giddy. He gives them nothing, which makes them even more suspicious.

After a few long hours, Dr. Felix shows up. Although he releases Giddy in minutes, he never apologies, introduces himself, or welcomes the American pilots to Czechoslovakia. The first thing he says is "Give me my Nescafé."

Giddy hands it to him, thinking, *I hope you choke on it.*

Driving to the air base, however, Dr. Felix finally shows some interest in something other than Nescafé. But even now, he irks the three pilots, assuming they're out of practice.

"It must be, what, three years since you've flown a fighter plane?" Dr. Felix says in an accusatory tone, as if it's these pilots' fault.

"Actually, I've joined the Army Air Corps Reserves," Giddy says. "So once a month, I get to fly the latest, best planes."

"Not anymore," Dr. Felix.

Giddy has no idea just how right Dr. Felix is. Arazi has made sure that the new crop of trainees heard nothing from the original five about the Messerschmitts' flaws.

Arriving in České Budějovice, Giddy, Red, and Syd are eager to jump into a Messerschmitt. Soon, they'll be eager to get out. In the meanwhile, they meet the other American trainees in their group, former UCLA art students Vickman and Stan.

When Giddy finds out that neither is a fighter pilot, he cautions them.

"I respect what you did during the war," Giddy says. "But I have to tell you, it did not prepare you for this."

"I flew bombers for almost four years," Stan says.

"Flying fighters requires completely different expertise than flying a bomber," Giddy says. "In a bomber, you're a truck driver; in a fighter, you're all over the sky."

Pretending to pull down a truck's horn harness while bellowing a corresponding honking din, a new member of the OZ team joins the pilots.

"Watch out, another trucker coming down the pike," says Leon Frankel, twenty-four, who grew up in a working-class Jewish section of St. Paul, Minnesota, and opened a used-car dealership after World War II.

Giddy, Red, Stan, Syd, and Vickman are surprised to hear that Leon is not part of their training group. He's the first member of the next cohort to arrive in České Budějovice.

"Why did you show up so early?" Red asks.

Leon says that after going through the painful task of informing his mother, who refused to accept the news, he could not linger in the United States. He had to ship out.

"She fell apart," Leon recalls. "I mean, she threw herself on the floor and was crying, and I was crying. I started out that door knowing that if I turned around, I would never go."

"We can't blame our parents for trying to stop us," Vickman says.

"My mom had just gotten her son back from three years of war," Leon says, "and all of a sudden I'm taking off again into the wild blue yonder."

"What are you going to do for the next two weeks?" Stan asks.

"Two weeks?" Leon says. "We start in two days."

Giddy, Red, Syd, Stan, and Vickman are shocked. They had no idea that the Czechs, at the Israelis' request, have substantially condensed the training.

The Czech trainers have in fact done a 180. They've gone from trying to keep the first training for several weeks to agreeing to push through the next cohorts. They've come to realize that they have no choice—České Budějovice must keep up with Žatec. The OZ transport planes continuously ferrying Messerschmitts must also consistently carry fighter pilots to fly them.

Imagining what Buzz would say—probably "Start practicing right now"—Giddy slips away to familiarize himself with the Messerschmitts.

With Giddy gone, Stan can finally ask Leon what kind of bombers he flew without inviting a snide remark.

"Torpedo bombers," Leon says.

"Where?" Syd asks.

"The Pacific."

"Did you ever sink a Japanese ship?" Red asks.

"Yeah," Leon says, "the *Yahagi*, a cruiser."

Leon never mentions that he won a Navy Cross for this accomplishment. But he does wonder what Giddy would have to say about that.

～

After just a couple of days of training, the Czechs certify the second group. This worries Giddy, who's used to getting a hundred hours of training on each new plane.

"They're out of their minds," Giddy tells the other pilots, "certifying us after only thirty-five minutes in the air."

Flying to Israel out of Zebra, Giddy, Stan, and Vickman board one C-46, while Red and Syd board another. For the first Commando, everything goes smoothly. But the second runs into mechanical problems and makes an emergency landing in Treviso, where the Italians search the plane, find the Czech munitions, and throw everyone onboard in jail for three days.

If Modi, Ezer, and Lou—who's back in fighting shape but not as CO—are disappointed to see only three of their new teammates arrive, they never show it. They shower Giddy, Stan, and Vickman with the same kind of warm attention they'd give their favorite relatives.

They take them to their new air base—Herzliya. They picked this Band-Aid airstrip because the Arabs have never bombed it, which means the Arabs most likely have no idea this tiny military base exists. The Israeli Air Force pilots plan to stay here for as long as the Egyptian and Syrian pilots continue to mistake it for a paved patch of the orange groves that surround it.

Vickman and Stan ride in one Jeep with Lou while Giddy drives in the other with Ezer and Modi, who tell him about a mysterious plane that appears to be gathering intelligence about the Israeli military. Since the start of the war, they've been wondering about the source of the midday contrails streaking across the sky at around 9,000–11,000 meters. Borrowing an RAF term for reconnaissance aircraft, they call it the Shufti (Arabic for "look") Kite (British lingo for "bird" or "plane").

Since it appears to travel from north to south every day, Modi believes the Shufti Kite takes off from Syria. Ezer pins it on Iraq.

"I'd love to go up there and find out," Giddy says.

The shifty reconnaissance plane, they say, flies beyond the reach of the Messerschmitts or any other IAF plane.

Giddy asks them to convert "9,000–11,000 meters" to feet. It takes Ezer a split second: "30,000–36,000." Noting that the Messerschmitts run purely on the metric system, the American asks the Israelis to teach him the basics.

"It drives me crazy in the cockpit," Giddy says. "I can't read the temperature, speed, or anything else."

Modi and Ezer call out estimates of the outside temperature, the Jeep's speed, and other proximate examples in the metric and imperial systems. By the time they reach Herzliya an hour later, the international way to measure no longer gives Giddy the heebie-jeebies. Instead, the Shufti Kite does. What is that thing? Where does it come from?

Meanwhile, in the other Jeep, Lou asks Vickman and Stan to draw up an insignia for the 101 Squadron. "Sure," they say, "of what?" About to tell them a flying scorpion—Modi's idea—he instead suggests the angel of death.

When Stan and Vickman present their drawing—a red and black helmet-topped skull with wings—Modi likes it so much that he forgets about the scorpion.

After Red is released from the Italian jail and arrives in Israel, he mails a copy of the insignia design to his sister in New York. She turns it into wool badges, which she embroiders into red baseball caps and sends back to her brother in the Holy Land.

Soon, the 101 becomes known as the Red Squadron.

~

As the door shuts behind him, Giddy crashes on his Park Hotel bed believing he's about to get a good night's sleep. The fighter pilot doesn't have to report for duty at Herzliya until zero six thirty hours, and he's been told that the Arabs launch airstrikes only during daylight. So, with Buzz's advice to always take care of himself ringing in his head, he trades painting the town with Stan and Vickman for some REMs.

As he's about to fall asleep, Giddy hears a knock at the door. Before he can get up to open it, Modi barges in. As they rush to Herzliya, the 101 CO tells the new arrival that IAF intelligence is reporting that two Egyptian Spitfires are heading to Tel Aviv for their first night raid.

At Herzliya, Giddy takes off on a reassembled Messerschmitt. He follows Modi to Tel Aviv. He sweats. He may be a bit nervous, but it's mostly the Middle Eastern heat. Wiping his brow, he notices the 101 CO signaling something. He's not sure of what the signal means.

Then he sees them: two Egyptian Spitfires.

Modi stops motioning and starts shooting. But he misses and finds himself being chased by one of the Spitfires.

The other goes after Giddy. As if flexing his muscles and showing his teeth, the Egyptian pilot puts on an acrobatic display, rolling on his back, diving straight down and appearing to bounce off the ground, and turning this way and that.

For applause, Giddy fires his machine guns.

The curtain closes on the Egyptian acrobat. His Spitfire crashes into the Mediterranean.

Giddy rushes back to Herzliya. He lands on his last drop of fuel.

Modi greets him. When Giddy mentions that he shot down one of the Spitfires—a kill later confirmed by IAF intelligence—the 101 CO gives him a hug.

"You just became the first Israeli Air Force pilot to win a dogfight," Modi says.

"Wasn't much of a fight," Giddy says. "It was almost too easy."

Modi smiles, saying, "You can't argue with history."

~

In the weeks since he joined OZ, Gordon has earned his teammates' full respect. Flying back and forth from Zebra to Ekron, the cargo captain has flown dangerously low and slow to allow his crew members to chuck bombs on enemy targets, expertly dodged flak, lent a hand in loading and unloading arms when he could've been resting, trained new pilots, and politely reminded airport workers to turn on the runway lights. Yet the operation members continue to ask about his background. They're not suspicious; they're just intrigued.

His religion and nationality, by themselves, are far from unusual. A good portion of the operation and even the IAF is Christian, and several of his countrymen—such as Cyril Horowitz, Maurice Mann, and Baron Weisberg—serve as OZ pilots and crew members. But the combination makes him stand out. He's the only non-Jewish Briton in the Israeli Air Force.

Hundreds of British non-Jews participate in the Egyptian, Transjordanian, and Iraqi war efforts. They include Arab Legion leader John Bagot Glubb, who some believe played a role in convincing Transjordan's King Abdullah I to break the understanding he reached with Golda in a clandestine-yet-famous 1947 meeting.

Gordon has gotten used to strange questions. But the inquiry he receives today is so peculiar that, to answer it, he needs a great deal more information and time to figure out a response. Shechtman, who's changed his last name to Shamir, asks how he feels about carrying out an official IAF mission that involves bombing a Jewish ship.

Taken aback, Gordon demands details. A lot more details. Shamir reluctantly says an Irgun ship filled with French weapons left Port-de-Bouc a few days earlier bound for Israel. The extremist organization agreed a few days earlier to become part of the just-formed Israel Defense Forces (IDF) in coming weeks. But its latest action contradicts its stated intentions and throws a monkey wrench into the solidification of the country's military structure.

The SS *Altalena*, Shamir stresses, represents a fierce foe. Led by Peter Bergson, who threw Eddie and the rest of the *Ben Hecht* crew a party upon their arrival in New York from the British prison in Acre, the 6,000-ton ship threatens Israel's unity and stability.

The aerial bombing that Gordon is asked to carry out would aim to stop, not destroy, the *Altalena*, which carries nearly 1,000 crew members and new Irgun recruits, more than 5,000 guns, and five million rounds of ammunition. Israel, Shamir says, could certainly use those fighters and weapons. The goal would be to convince the Irgun to deliver them to the IDF.

Since discussions with the Irgun about the *Altalena* have yielded no results so far, it's time to utilize another method to convince them to do the right thing.

Gordon wonders why Shamir is not going through Al and whether he's asked other pilots to execute this mission.

Shamir answers both questions with one blunt explanation: He cannot ask Jews to kill Jews.

This makes sense to Gordon. He has no problem using whatever he's got—even his religious affiliation—to advance the cause for which he's fighting. He's just unsure about firing the first shots in what could quickly escalate into a civil war.

To Shamir's chagrin, Gordon says he needs to sleep on it.

Well, he never quite falls asleep. The pros and cons of accepting this assignment keep him awake. On one hand, he's here to save Jews, not kill them. On the other, he's here to help give them a safe home. Maybe attacking the *Altalena* will *prevent* a civil war?

Maybe he doesn't need to kill anyone to accomplish this. Perhaps a few bomb drops *around* the *Altalena* will accomplish the same goal?

The next morning, Gordon tells Shamir he's willing to do it. But it's too late—the *Altalena* has just arrived in Israel, dropping its anchor in the same spot where Milt ditched his Messerschmitt: Kfar Vitkin. Much like the fighter pilot's reception, the ship's crew members receive a hostile welcome—in their case, from the IDF soldiers waiting on the beach. But initially successful negotiations between the government and the Irgun lead to the overnight unloading of nearly half the weapons and most of the volunteers.

It appears a civil war has been averted until Bergson—who returns to using his real name, Hillel—and Irgun leader Menachem Begin insist on dictating where the other half of the arms should go: their troops in Jerusalem.

Hillel returns to the *Altalena*, taking Begin with him. A gunfight ensues, killing six Irgun fighters and two IDF soldiers and injuring two dozen Jews.

The *Altalena* sails south.

~

Ike and Moonitz have a hard time leaving Givat Brenner. Sure, they'll pine for the nurses and the field-to-table fruits and vegetables, but mainly they'll miss Eddie, who needs a few more weeks to recover. Although he'd rather go with them, he makes the most of his time, tearing into books, newspapers, and magazines like a toddler tearing up boxes of tissues.

On their way to Ekron to check on the incoming C-46 they're scheduled to fly back to Zebra before dawn, Ike and Moonitz stop at a Tel Aviv bar for a celebratory drink. They find it swarming with journalists from around the world. An American reporter approaches them. When they ignore his questions about what they're doing in Israel, he pitches them a deal: baseball scores for a story.

As much as Ike would love to hear how his beloved Dodgers are doing, he finds the offer insulting, telling the reporter to "buzz off."

Walking away, Ike leans into Moonitz to say, "Baseball scores? We're warriors."

After they finish toasting their return to the warfront, the Dodgers, Eddie, and their fresh start as captain and co-pilot, Ike and Moonitz arrive at Ekron as the C-46 lands, bringing in, besides the weapons, a new recruit who's just completed his Messerschmitt training in Czechoslovakia—Leon.

"You wouldn't happen to have the baseball scores, would you?" Moonitz asks.

"My hometown only has a minor league team," Leon says, "and they stink."

Moonitz and Ike laugh. They like this feller already. They warn him that foreign journalists may try to interview him.

"The only story they'll get outta me is that I'm a used-car salesman, and they shouldn't believe a word I say," Leon says. "Unless, of course, they're in the market for a smooth ride with low miles."

Leon heads to the Park Hotel in Tel Aviv. After making sure that the C-46 is in good hands in terms of refueling and minor repairs, Ike tells Moonitz they should also go there to get a good night's sleep.

"What's the point?" Moonitz asks. "I'm just going to sleep here."

Ike indicates he's leaving.

"If you're not here by zero four hundred hours," Moonitz says, "I'm leaving without you."

So much for a new start.

When Ike enters the Park Hotel, he runs into Leon, who just took a shower, got dressed, and is ready to hit the town.

"Where's Giddy? Bob? Stan?" Leon asks.

Ike shrugs. He shrugs again when Leon invites him for a drink. Why not? They hear gunshots and screaming. Stepping out of the hotel, they get nearly run over by an IDF truck.

They run down the street toward to the source of the noise. They see a ship pulling in as a crowd gathers on the beach.

It's the *Altalena*.

The military truck fires mortars over Ike and Leon's heads. They return to the Park Hotel and race to the rooftop, from which they watch the IDF battle the Irgun.

They never see Begin, who three decades later becomes Israel's prime minister, wave the white flag. Neither do the IDF soldiers, who continue shooting at the Irgun members even after they jump off the burning *Altalena* and try to swim to shore. Tel Avivians risk their lives to fish out the injured.

"Now he's got his story," a shaken-up Ike says, referring to the journalist who had approached him at the bar a few hours earlier.

By the time the battle subsides, the new country pays a heavy price for its inner squabble, losing nineteen soldiers: thirteen Irguniks, three IDF troops, and three *Altalena* passengers—young volunteers who planned to fight in Israel's War of Independence.

The Kfar Vitkin and Tel Aviv battles may also cost Israel its air transport command and Red Squadron.

~

His shirt soaked in sweat from the sticky Miami air and his sunglasses screwed on against the scorching sun, Al inspects his B-17s like a general reviewing his troops. A debate rages in his mind: Should he send the three bombers lined up in front of him on their 5,000-mile journey to Zebra, or wait for the fourth Flying Fortress?

He discusses the pros and cons with Leo and Charlie. On the one hand, simple logic dictates that the threesome take off now. It may be a while before the USAAF base in Tulsa releases the fourth B-17. The US military accepted Al's payment and issued a purchase order but has yet to set a pickup date. The delay could be due to a bureaucratic hang-up or an FBI request to investigate.

On the other hand, it may make just as much sense to wait for the Tulsa B-17. If the first three leave without it, they could expose its true destination simply by going there and make the real Oklahoma, not Israel (code-named "Oklahoma"), the bomber's permanent home.

Then again, risking three to save one doesn't add up.

Three birds in hand, Al, Leo, and Charlie agree, are worth more than four in the bush.

Al and Leo—who planned to serve as a flight engineer and a co-pilot, respectively, on one of the B-17s—decide to send the three Flying Fortresses on their way and stay in the United States to try to extradite the fourth.

Scary scenarios spinning in their heads, Al and Leo anxiously watch the B-17s take off one by one into a South Florida sky painted blood red and screaming orange by a fading sun.

Traveling eastward, the B-17s hasten nightfall for their pilots and crews.

In the lead bomber, Novick, who's never flown a B-17, takes copious mental notes, observing John, David, and the crew handle their duties with surprising harmony, considering that this is their first flight together. He notices that, lacking the proper equipment, the navigator charts their course by reading the stars. He asks Eli Cohen (not to be confused with the Israeli spy of the same name) about stargazing's level of accuracy.

"In terms of getting us where we need to go—my raison d'être—100 percent," Eli says. "Otherwise, my job would be to guess, not navigate."

His confidence will soon vanish, for a reason no one could ever guess. It will be part of a series of challenges that the B-17 crew members will face during their transatlantic crossing.

As they finish refueling in San Juan and prepare for their final stop before Zebra—Santa Maria in the Azores, a string of Portuguese islands in the Atlantic, west of Africa—they glare at their captain in disbelief. John had joined the other two heavy drinking pilots at the San Juan airport bar for a round of shots and returned smashed.

David and Novick throw John in the back of the plane. David takes over as captain. Katz steps into the right seat. Novick remains in the cockpit as an apprentice and a backup.

Soon after they take off, mechanical problems cause one of the other B-17s to make a U-turn and return to San Juan. Soon, David and Katz hear strange sounds from their own plane. Fearing it might be a similar issue, they send Novick to check.

~

The morning after the *Altalena* battle, Gordon wonders whether he could have prevented Israel's self-inflicted Waterloo had he made his decision faster and stopped the Irgun ship from entering the Tel Aviv harbor. Guilt torments him as he joins fifty other OZ members at the IAF headquarters in Tel Aviv's Yarden Hotel.

They plan to speak in a unified voice. They didn't need to discuss this in advance. They know in their bones that all of them—Jews and non-Jews, North Americans and South Africans, transport and fighter pilots—feel the same way: They will never participate in a civil war.

Their mere presence shows that they mean business. Remez and Shamir are fully aware that Ike and Moonitz have put their flight to Zebra on an indefinite hold and that Leon has delayed his Herzliya check-in. If the OZ members do not get what they want, the decorated WWII torpedo bomber may sell used cars in North Dakota instead of flying Messerschmitts in Israel.

With Al in the United States and Sam in Zebra, it falls to Marty and Lou to represent OZ. Having landed in Ekron with half a Messerschmitt less than an hour earlier, the transport pilot has forgone his post-flight meal, shower, and sleep. He'll have plenty of time to rest if Remez and Shamir fail to meet their demands.

For Lou, showing up at IAF headquarters to issue a complaint would've posed a dilemma if it meant skipping a squadron assignment. As a former

Marine, he's built to put his military duties above all else. But as luck would have it, the Israelis agreed to a UN-brokered cease-fire with the Arabs a few days earlier. Although neither side has been keeping the truce religiously, it frees up the fighter pilot who played a pivotal role in stopping the Egyptian advance on Tel Aviv to join the sit-in.

"Did you agree to a cease-fire with the Arabs so you can start a new war with the Jews?" Lou asks the leaders of the Israeli Air Force.

"The main reason the IDF signed this truce," Remez says, "is to allow you to airlift the Czech weapons."

"We fly them in no matter what," Ike states.

"Apparently not," Shamir says, pointing at the fifty members surrounding him and Remez.

"Let's get back on track," Marty says, motioning to Ike to let him and Lou do the talking.

They do not mince their words.

"We are not here to serve as your pawns in a sick game," Marty says. "I'm sick to my stomach thinking that the weapons we brought in have been used to shoot Jews. For all we know, they're still out there killing our brothers, maybe also our sisters."

"We didn't come here to fight in a Jewish civil war," Lou states.

"A house divided against itself cannot stand," Marty says.

He quickly regrets this statement, as Remez and Shamir seize on the American Civil War reference to outline their case. This is painful, but it must be done, they say. They go as far as saying that the OZ air transport command and 101 Squadron may be called upon to "help stabilize our military structure."

Marty and Lou counter that unless the IDF ends its fight with the Irgun, they're out.

In the end, they reach a compromise. The OZ members agree to stay regardless of the outcome of the IDF-Irgun fight, as long as they never have to participate in it on any level.

~

It takes Novick a few moments to find the source of the noise on the B-17 flying over the Atlantic Ocean. It takes another moment or two for it to register. Having stepped on it with perhaps too much force, Eli, the stargazing navigator, has broken and fallen through the plywood that has replaced the

Plexiglas. Now he's hanging for dear life, his legs swinging in the fierce wind, his arms striving to keep his whole body from being sucked out.

Novick resists his first idea—to pull up Eli by himself—and rushes to summon assistance. David and Katz slow down the B-17 to the minimum speed possible without stalling, activate autopilot, and join their backup to show their navigator the way home.

Pulling him up proves a more painful process than they may have imagined. Leftover Plexiglas fragments around the edge of the opening puncture David's skin as he slowly, steadily lifts Eli while Novick and Katz form a human chain behind him.

When they finally stick Eli on the floor of the plane, they all fall on top of each other. Shell-shocked, the navigator remains horizontal the rest of the flight, seeing stars but unable to read them.

Novick assumes the navigator role. David returns to the left-hand seat. But having awakened due to the commotion, John reclaims it.

David returns to the right-hand seat.

As they start to descend, the clouds follow. The "low ceiling measurement," as aviators call a low-hanging cloud cover, reduces visibility to the point that John refuses to land at the airport, which is located on the other side of the volcanic mountains ahead.

The captain orders his crew to prepare to land on the shore instead. This would mean losing the B-17.

David has had enough. After trying unsuccessfully to politely talk the captain out of this "nonsense," the co-pilot offers to take over the landing. John sneers.

David gets up, picks up a Kent Copper & Brass fire extinguisher, and, suspending it over John's head, threatens to "crush your skull if you don't get out of your seat."

John slithers away, David hops back into the left-hand seat, and he, Katz, and Novick land the plane at the Santa Maria Airport.

~

The fifty Operation Zebra members walk out of IAF headquarters with a clear understanding—they'll continue doing their jobs exactly as they have been, with no involvement in any internal Israeli strife—but diverse feelings. Harold declares victory. Lou urges everyone to give the IDF time to digest and act on the OZ message. Marty remains sick to his stomach. Gordon fails to shake off his guilt. And Leon goes to check in at the Herzliya air base harboring doubts about his place in this wacky war.

Moonitz and Ike drive to Givat Brenner to speak with Eddie. Who better than their resident Irgun expert to give them insight?

Having been following the story of the *Altalena* since the BBC reported it after the ship departed Port-de-Bouc for Israel, Eddie extols the OZ members for taking a strong stance.

"Looks like we have to save Israel from its enemies," Eddie says, "and from itself."

However, Eddie also shines a light on the IDF's aggressive actions. The Irgun, he says, has proven again and again to be untrustworthy and a liability. A couple of months earlier, as the Yishuv geared up for independence and war, the extremist organization begged the Haganah for weapons to protect its members in a besieged part of Jerusalem.

The Haganah reluctantly handed scarce guns and rounds of ammunition to the Irgun members, who used them to massacre more than 150 innocent Arabs in Deir Yassin, a village outside the holy city.

They shot children, raped women, and knifed unarmed old men.

They also gave Israel's enemies an eternal rallying cry: "Deir Yassin."

The story disturbs Ike and Moonitz, who leave with a better grasp of the reasons for the IDF-Irgun conflict.

"Israel won't survive if the Irgun does," Ike says.

That night, they take off to Zebra from Ekron. They return the next night, just after the IDF and the Irgun agree to a cease-fire, which, after a few days, turns into a de facto peace treaty.

The Irgun's former US representative, Hillel, survives the battles but ends up spending two months in an Israeli prison. Escaping the FBI for years in the United States, he's always had the feeling that he'd one day be incarcerated. He just never thought it would be in the Jewish state.

Within a few weeks, the Irgun dissolves. But the Arabs continue to cry out, "Deir Yassin!"

~

Coming to terms with the likelihood that the USAAF will never release the fourth B-17, Al tells Leo they should "go get it."

"You mean steal it?" Leo asks.

"You can't steal something you own," Al says.

They ask around to see whether someone they know might know someone who works at the Tulsa air base. As luck would have it, an old WWII friend of Al's—a Jewish mechanic—works there. They ask for his assistance.

"We bought it so we can scrap it," Al says.

The mechanic, a Zionist who senses that the B-17 may serve a different purpose, agrees to become OZ's Trojan Horse.

Al asks the mechanic for three favors: find out the bomber's location, let them know whether the USAAF moves it at any point, and top off its fuel tank.

The mechanic grants all three wishes. Al and Leo wonder why they neglected to recruit him for the operation. Then it hits them—had they done that, they wouldn't have an inside man in Tulsa.

Donning USAAF uniforms, they fly to the Tulsa Municipal Airport, long past its status as the world's busiest a decade earlier. A rainstorm greets them. They hail a taxi to the air base. The gate guard asks whether they're going to "the party."

Party? What party? they think, but answer, "Of course."

"Well," the gate guard says, pointing toward the base interior, "it's over there."

Driving by the restricted area where their friend said they'd find the B-17, Al asks the taxi driver to let them spend a "few nostalgic moments with the plane we flew during the war."

The taxi enters the area. Sure enough, the B-17 sits there like a child waiting to be picked up by her parents.

Al blocks the taxi driver's view of a big, yellow "Seized by the US Government" sticker on the side of the B-17. He pays for the ride, tipping generously. He says they'll just walk to the Oklahoma Air National Guard party when they're done.

The taxi drives off.

Using a flashlight, Al and Leo—neither of whom had ever flown a B-17—survey the bomber. It appears to be in good shape. They figure out the basic controls, crank up the plane, and taxi with the lights off to the runway.

Al and Leo position the B-17 on the runway.

The air traffic controller screams, "Stop!"

~

Since joining OZ, Kurtz has had little time for himself or by himself. After Al asked him to oversee the remilitarization and delivery to Ekron of the three B-17s that are coming in for a landing in Zebra, he finds that operating solo has its pluses and minuses. He loves the assignment—what could be better than putting his WWII experience to such good use?—and the challenges of securing the needed parts and arranging the logistics. But he misses seeing the Israelis' grateful faces and spending time with his buddies. He's tapped Moonitz to captain one of the Flying Fortresses, but it will be a while before they're ready.

Having been stripped after World War II, the B-17s arrive in Zebra as castrated bulls. They retain almost no trace of their intrinsic ferociousness. Kurtz sets out to restore them to their fiery glory.

He searches for Norden Sights, used by all B-17s, but settles for Nazi-surplus Zeiss Lotfernrohr 7Ds. He soon discovers that the Lotfe 7s, with their easy-to-use knobs, are actually better. Just as gyroscopically stabilized as their American counterparts, they also show targets up ahead.

Sometimes, Kurtz learns, a perceived failure can breed a surprising success.

He works with the Czechs to restore the bomb bays and install shackles and racks to hold and drop the bombs, as well as set up three gunning stations. He'd love the M2 machine guns that defend most B-17s but feels satisfied with the reliable Czech ZB-53s. Also, he secures such "luxuries" as oxygen supplies and masks.

"To maximize these babies' striking capabilities," Kurtz tells Al, "we must be able to conduct high-altitude bombings."

That, they both know too well, takes oxygen.

Kurtz works with Al and Sam to come up with the lineup for each bomber. They can no longer get away with crews of two or even three or four. Besides the two pilots, radio operator, and navigator, they need a bombardier and at least one gunner for each plane.

They have plenty of pilots, radio operators, and navigators. Besides Moonitz, Kurtz plans to call on Katz and Al Raisin, twenty-eight, who flew several types of planes for the USAAF during World War II, including B-17s.

Katz—the experienced pilot who, together with David and Novick, saved Eli's life when the navigator dangled out of the B-17 they were flying from Miami—is so excited about the bombers' rebirth that he spends every free moment between his C-46 and C-54 flights checking on them.

Kurtz has heard that Katz has voiced concerns about "lack of progress" and has implied that he'd do a much better job.

Indeed, Katz views Kurtz as something of a sober version of John, the B-17 captain he and David replaced after they took off from San Juan. He'd love to step in. The remilitarization should take days, not weeks. Alas, all he can do is stand by.

Kurtz, meanwhile, has bigger personnel issues. He needs bombardiers and gunners. After checking with Sam, Kurtz asks Jules to switch from a transport navigator and bomb chucker to a bona fide bombardier.

Jules gives Kurtz a thank-you hug. He's been waiting for this.

Sam calls Steve to recruit B-17 bombardiers and gunners. As always, the Brooklynite delivers, adding several new members to the team, such as John Harris, twenty-seven, a Briton who served as a bombardier on RAF Mosquitos during World War II.

Harris quits his job flying seaplanes for British Overseas Airways Corporation and arrives in Zebra in time to join Jules in advising Kurtz on what type of bombs to get and how to best position them on the plane.

Kurtz is alone no more.

～

Al and Leo race down the Tulsa runway and take off. In bumpy bravura, they gain altitude and rescue their fourth B-17.

A few hours later, they land at the Westchester County Airport in New York. Swifty, who also has no experience flying B-17s, greets them. As the OZ mechanics do some basic maintenance, he receives his instructions: fly to Zebra via the Azores.

An incoming storm would usually delay his takeoff, but not today, not with the FBI looking for the B-17. He and his crew take off into relentless rain and wind.

Trying to navigate through the storm with faulty equipment, however, Swifty is forced to land in Halifax, Canada.

When the Royal Canadian Mounted Police Customs and Excise agents search the plane, they find ammunition and European and Middle Eastern maps, which Swifty had brought onboard. The Canucks make a deal with him: fly right back to where you came from and we won't arrest you and your crew.

He promptly and with theatrical flair agrees to their terms. The Royal Canadian Mounted Police Customs and Excise agents siphon his fuel to ensure that he has only enough for a one-way flight to New York. What they don't know is that Swifty would say anything to get out of jail, especially if it means continuing on to his intended destination, and that he'd never attempt to cross the ocean without extra oil drums, which they somehow missed during their search.

Heading to the Azores, Swifty stays below the radar. Flying this low for this long overheats his engines. One dies. So he makes it to the Santa Maria Airport on three.

Not bad for a pilot who doubted whether he could handle this bomber with all four engines.

At the Santa Maria Airport, US agents arrest Swifty, impound the B-17, and fly the crew back to the United States.

~

On a cool Sunday morning, Al drives a borrowed 1948 Lincoln Convertible Coupe up the Pacific Coast Highway with the top down. Traveling from Santa Monica, where he spent the night at the car lender's home atop the Cliffs, he heads to Ventura to meet with an arms dealer.

The ocean breeze blows against his receding hairline, threatening to accelerate his balding. The purring V-12 engine and nearly empty road tempt him to zip by the lone car up ahead. He looks around. Sure enough, he spots a California Highway Patrol (CHP) car in his rearview mirror. He lifts his foot off the pedal, slowing down to WWII's 35 mph Victory Speed Limit, enacted to preserve America's resources.

He accelerates back to the new speed limit—45 mph—to avoid drawing any attention from the policeman. From this point on, he locks in on the precise speed limit as if operating the recently invented but yet-to-be-released cruise control.

The policeman tailgates Al.

For a nerve-racking minute, Al reminds himself that he's Ervin Johnson, an LA textile importer, driving a friend's car to Santa Barbara.

Finally, the policeman passes, tipping his CHP hat. Al nods and breathes a sigh of relief. Seeing an old sign marked "Roosevelt Highway," he recalls that this road (like OZ itself) stretches from Canada to Mexico. He thinks about Buzz—may the Canadian ace rest in peace—and the Mexican weapons—may they soon wage war in Israel.

Earlier this morning, Al received encouraging news. The government officials with whom Hank has been dealing have accepted the Chinese letter and are set to deliver all the weapons to the *Kefalos*, which is docked at the Port of Tampico.

This allows Al to focus on his next acquisition—his most audacious yet. He's on his own on this one. He hasn't discussed it with anyone, not even Arazi, fearing that he would nip it in the bud. It's the kind of deal that the Israeli leadership has discouraged—acquiring fighter planes in North America.

Al figures that if he fails, no one needs to know about it, and if he succeeds, no one will complain. He can make this deal on his own—he has access to millions of dollars in a Swiss bank account. Since the war started, no one has asked him about his expenditures. The biweekly meetings at the Hotel Fourteen with Arazi and/or Nahum are history.

Al wishes Leo was still here. But needing someone who can directly represent him on the ground, he's had to send Leo back to Zebra.

Arriving an hour early in Ventura, Al goes to the designated diner to have breakfast and collect his thoughts at a corner booth. Just as a waitress places a cup of coffee on his table, a short, unassuming man approaches.

"Ervin Johnson?" the man asks.

Al examines him. Seeing a small scar on the side of his neck, the OZ boss nods. The arms dealer never reveals his name, works strictly in cash, and refuses to put anything in writing. He says he has four P-51Ds for sale.

"Best fighter plane in the world," the arms dealer says.

"I think that honor belongs to the P-47," Al says, putting the negotiating skills he's developed in the past year to use.

"The P-51 has a better range," the arms dealer says. "Regardless, it's the best fighter plane you can get."

Al buys all four. He has them taken apart and placed in crates marked "agricultural equipment." To boost their chances of getting to Israel, he sends them onboard two ships.

~

An increasing number of Israelis view the OZ members as pampered bad boys. They fail to see the humor in the aviators stealing automobiles, filling Tel Aviv bars with Wild West clichés—fist fights, gunslinging arguments, furniture-smashing brawls—and, in general, behaving like they rent the place.

Contributing to OZ's declining image, the transport pilots dress like sloppy civilians, favoring jeans and baseball caps, speak not a word of Hebrew, and come and go in the middle of the night like thieves.

It irks Al, who's returned to Israel to address a long list of serious issues, to deal with what he views as a juvenile distraction. When Remez brings it up in a tone even more somber than usual, the OZ boss waves him off.

Feeling disrespected, Remez suggests the C-46 pilots and crews wear IAF uniforms, perhaps even become part of the Israeli military.

Al refuses to even discuss this notion. He defends his men, arguing they may have the most dangerous jobs in the IAF. He notes that they risk their lives every time they take to the sky, whether to chuck bombs or to airlift Czech arms.

Al relays a conversation he just had with Novick, who flew him back from Zebra, where Al spent a couple of days on his way from the United States.

"Novick told me that what's keeping our pilots alive is pure luck."

Al notes that the transport crews fly beaten-down planes in often-turbulent weather without oxygen masks. Crossing the Alps on their way to and from their main refueling stop in Corsica, they risk hypoxia.

"Fly low to attain access to oxygen, and you crash into the mountains," Al says. "Fly too high, and you lose consciousness from lack of oxygen and still crash into the mountains."

What he and Al don't know is that the OZ transport pilots will soon have to navigate through and around one of the Cold War's first showdowns—the Berlin Airlift.

After the Soviets cut off Berlin by restricting all ground transportation to and from the city sections controlled by the West, the Americans, the British, and the French will launch the mother of all supply missions. The Air Bridge, as the West Berliners will call it, will crowd out smaller operations like OZ.

Annoyed at being talked to like a child, Remez tells Al he'll make his decision and get back to him. In other words, the discussion is over.

"Are we not on right on schedule?" Al asks.

Remez gestures that they are.

"Are the fighter pilots and planes we're bringing in not gaining control of the skies?"

The IAF commander motions that they are.

"Then what's the problem?"

"The problem," Remez says, "is that this is a military, and it's time for everyone to act accordingly."

The next day, Remez announces the formation of three new IAF squadrons:

- 35: the handful of Norsemen that have survived the journey to Israel and their war missions;
- 103: the three Dakotas that have just arrived to supply the Negev; and
- 106: the C-54, Connie, and nine C-46s.

When Remez informs him, Al shrugs. He refrains from giving the IAF commander the satisfaction of asking why he chose 106.

"You can call it whatever you want," Al says. "I'm going to run my operation however I want."

Remez goes back to the drawing board. A couple of hours later he comes up with something that finally truly rattles Al: He names someone else 106 Squadron CO.

Al would be furious no matter who he picked—even Leo or Sam. But when Al learns that he's being replaced by an old-school Haganah fighter with zero aviation experience, he goes over Remez's head.

Al calls Arazi, who's shocked to hear that his Haganah buddy, Munya Mardor, is the new head of the operation.

Munya is known for a long string of covert operations, including the sinking of two ships: the SS *Lino* and the SS *Patria*.

A month before Ben-Gurion declared independence, Munya led three Haganah navy seals to the Yugoslav port of Molfetta, where they disappeared underwater to blow a hole in the *Lino* hull. Within minutes, the Syria-bound ship and its 6,000 Czech guns and eight million Czech bullets rested on the sea floor.

Eight years earlier, Munya "achieved" one of Aliyah Bet's most dubious "victories" when he indirectly forced the United Kingdom to allow more than

1,500 European Jews into Palestine. The British succumbed to global pressure to make an exception to their draconian immigration policy after a bomb sunk the ship that carried these refugees. Two hundred sixty-seven men, women, and children drowned; 172 suffered injuries, many of them critical.

The Haganah member who placed the bomb on the SS *Patria* was Munya. He expected a far less damaging explosion, aiming to just disable the ship and thus prevent the British from sailing it back to Europe. Nonetheless, he's taken full responsibility inside the Haganah for the incident. Nine years later, he'll own up to it in front of the whole world.

Al asks Arazi to take him to see Ben-Gurion.

"The buck does stop with him," Arazi says, referencing Truman's famous quote.

Ben-Gurion and Al—founding fathers of Israel and the IAF, respectively—hit it off.

Ben-Gurion, who'll become prime minister after Israel's first elections several months later, apologizes for not meeting Al earlier.

Al says he understands that Ben-Gurion may have been a little busy.

Ben-Gurion says he's heard a lot about Al.

"I don't know where we'd be without you," Ben-Gurion says.

When Arazi mentions that Remez is trying to push out Al, Ben-Gurion shakes his head in sadness and frustration. After asking a few questions, HaZaken makes his decision.

The only way he can reposition Munya, he tells them, is to remove Remez. At this point in the war, he cannot do that.

As Al and Arazi pace in his simple home office, Ben-Gurion calls Remez. He says it's a matter of national security—beyond the jurisdiction of the IAF—that Al continue running OZ exactly as he has been. No one, HaZaken says, should ever interfere.

"What about Munya?" Remez asks.

"His top priority as the CO of the 106 Squadron," Ben-Gurion says, "should be to provide Al with the support and resources he needs."

15

July

EXACTLY A MONTH AFTER ARRIVING IN ZEBRA, THE THREE B-17S ARE finally fully remilitarized and ready to fly to and fight for Israel. Shamir arrives from Tel Aviv with orders. The bombers' home in Israel, he tells Kurtz, will be a former RAF air base, Ramat David. Although it has only a small runway carved out of a cornfield, it's the safest location for these large planes, according to IDF intelligence.

Kurtz asks why. Shamir notes that, mistaking it for an Israeli airfield at a time when it still served as a Royal Air Force base, the Arabs have already bombed it. Twice. On the same day.

A few days into the war, Egyptian Spitfires destroyed two British Spitfires, damaged several others, and killed two RAF airmen.

In an act of self-defense, the RAF went after the confused culprits, downing all five attacking Egyptian Spitfires.

The Egyptians have never returned to Ramat David, and Shamir believes they never will.

"Would you?" Shamir asks Kurtz. "If your protectorate was so mad that it knocked your buddies out of the sky one by one like an airborne assassin?"

Although the B-17 landing order makes perfect sense to Kurtz, he finds the next dubious: on the way to Ramat David, from medium-altitude, bomb Cairo and El Arish.

Kurtz has heard about the 101 Squadron's plan to demolish the Egyptian Spitfires on the ground at the El Arish air base. He's always liked this idea and would love to execute it. But Cairo?

"The Egyptians have been bombing Tel Aviv every day since the war started," Shamir says. "It's gotten better since our Messerschmitts have been challenging and sometimes even shooting down their fighters and bombers. But they still attack our civilians. We have to send them a message."

Kurtz accepts this logic but argues against the medium-altitude bombing.

"The flak we've seen so far in the war is nothing compared to what they have in Cairo," Kurtz says. "We're staying at a high altitude. We have the equipment and personnel to hit our target from anywhere."

Shamir grimaces. How can Israel build a bona fide air force when "subordinates" casually dismiss orders? But Kurtz has moved on to the next topic—pilot assignments—and the IAF deputy commander is eager to hear the plan.

Viewing it as the less desirable mission, Kurtz takes Cairo himself and assigns El Arish to the other two captains—Moonitz and Raisin.

After a long internal debate, he's decided against giving Katz his own B-17. Kurtz worries that he would poison the air. So, adhering to the adage of keeping your friends close and your enemies closer, he puts the boisterous busybody on his Cairo-bound bomber.

Katz grumbles. Knowing it's his twenty-ninth birthday, Kurtz gifts him the left-hand seat, with its corresponding captain designation.

"Congratulations, happy birthday, and *zei gezunt* [Yiddish for 'be well']," he says, reminding the birthday boy that Kurtz remains operation commander.

Katz must admit that he admires Kurtz's creative management, which shelves their egos and channels their antagonism into a healthy debate about what exactly to bomb in Cairo. They pick King Farouk's Abdeen Palace.

They agree that the time is right to put their mark on this symbol of Egyptian arrogance. They have no idea that their target represents a measure of geopolitical justice. It was King Farouk who, against his prime minister's recommendation, insisted that Egypt join the Arab war effort against the Jewish state.

~

During the cease-fire, Lou has regained his fighting form. He has no desire to reclaim or even share the CO position. He wants to execute the El Arish plan as soon as the truce is over.

Reluctant to authorize it, Modi succumbs to Lou's daily pressure and assigns him a team: Stan, Vickman, and Bill Pomerantz, twenty-nine, a recent

České Budějovice graduate who, as a USAAF P-47 pilot, shot down four Nazi fighter planes during World War II.

At dawn on the day of the war's official renewal, the four pilots take off in four functional Messerschmitts.

Never mind, make that three. Stan's Messerschmitt sputters as he tries to clear the runway.

Lou circles over the Herzliya air base to make sure Stan's all right. After seeing the artistic pilot emerge from the cockpit a bit shaken up but injury free, the former 101 CO catches up to Vickman and Pomerantz.

On their approach to El Arish, they encounter several Spitfires. Lou orders them to abandon the mission and instead bomb Egyptian military ships along the coast.

The last to drop his bombs, Vickman spots an Egyptian Westland Lysander on his way back to Herzliya. Viewing the ground-support plane as easy prey, he tries to shoot it down, but the Lizzie proves tricky, zigzagging from one cloud to another.

Vickman and the Lizzie gunner fire at the same time. The former misses; the latter does not.

Vickman's body is never found. His best friend, Stan, is never the same.

Lou, who irrationally blames himself for Vickman's death, never flies again.

～

Kurtz and Katz take off from Zebra at 10 a.m. Joining them are Shamir in the cockpit and the other B-17s in formation. They hurdle the Alps, evade flak over communist Albania, overcome Zeus's thunderous fury over Greece, and split off as soon as they reach the Eastern Mediterranean.

On the edge of Cairo, an air traffic controller pipes up, asking Kurtz and Katz to identify themselves. They say they're TWA pilots and request permission to land at the airport, which the controller grants.

Planning to stay at 30,000 feet, Katz and Kurtz descend to half that altitude when their masks suddenly stop pumping oxygen. Shamir smiles. Whatever it takes for these unruly airmen to follow orders.

Over downtown's eastern section, Kurtz orders his bombardier to open the bays and drop half a dozen 500-pounders on Abdeen.

Expecting anti-aircraft fire, Kurtz and Katz instead get hit by searchlights. Having mostly flown daytime bombing missions during World War II, they find these blinding lights just as disconcerting as flak, which soon also covers the sky.

Katz senses that some of the anti-aircraft bullets are hitting the B-17, but he keeps his mouth shut.

Before leaving Cairo, Kurtz and Katz drop their remaining bombs on RAF Fayid, a British air base just northeast of the city.

Meanwhile, Moonitz and Raisin fail to find El Arish. Instead, they bomb the Egyptian-occupied Palestinian Arab towns of Gaza and Rafah.

All three B-17s arrive in Ramat David safely and with several hours of darkness to spare. The mechanics refuel and check the planes, fixing issues such as oxygen supplies. Katz shines a flashlight on the anti-aircraft bullet holes that riddle their Fort. And Kurtz consults with Moonitz and Raisin. Should they try again to bomb El Arish?

"Maybe we can figure out how to find it in the next couple of days," Moonitz says.

"I'm talking about tonight," Kurtz says, "while we still have the element of surprise, while the Arabs still have no idea we have bombers."

Moonitz and Raisin exchange "why not?" looks.

Kurtz leads the three B-17s to El Arish. This time, they locate it.

While he sleeps in his Park Hotel room, Lou's dream comes true as the IAF dodges heavy flak to damage a dozen Spitfires on the ground.

As the B-17s descend toward Ramat David, the sun rises. After they land, Katz counts the number of anti-aircraft bullet holes in the body of his plane.

110.

16

August

THE RECENT STEAM OF RELATIVELY POSITIVE DEVELOPMENTS WORRIES Al. He suspects that he's due for some bad news. The B-17s, which the OZ airmen dub "The Hammers," consistently carry out bombing missions. The Egyptians, fearing another Israeli strike on Cairo, stop bombing Tel Aviv. After three months of continuous flights, the transport planes are closing in on completing the massive Czech airlift. They've also improved their performance as makeshift bombers to the point that the IAF requests that they continue, regardless of the success of a new squadron (69) made up of the Hammers. And the Messerschmitts increasingly ward off the Arab air forces, winning some dogfights and downing several bombers.

To a large extent as an upshot of these advancements, the IDF has been gaining the upper hand in the war. The question is no longer Israel's survival but its size. How much land will it have once the war ends? Will it include the Old City of Jerusalem? The Negev Desert?

Al's heart races when he receives a call from Ike, who, after other transport pilots started flying the B-17s, became captain of the C-54. As a former B-24 pilot, he, too, could've transferred to the new 69 Squadron. But Ike feared he'd end up as Moonitz's co-pilot. So he stayed with the transports. It has paid off. He loves overseeing the four-engine Skymaster, which can fly nonstop from Zebra to Ekron. He's also keen on finishing what he starts. He's in Žatec now to pick up the last batch of weapons that the Jews bought from the Czechs— mostly seventy-pound bombs.

Ike tells Al that as soon as he takes off in the sure-to-be-overloaded C-54, the Czechs will shut down Zebra. This upsets the OZ boss for several reasons:

- The Czechs never notified him.
- He planned to continue buying bombers in North America and remilitarize them in Zebra.
- The Israelis are negotiating to buy dozens of Spitfires from Czechoslovakia.

Does the Zebra shutdown indicate that the Spitfire deal is dead? If not, where will OZ prepare the Spitfires for their journey to their new home? Having a much better range than the Messerschmitts, they do not need to be taken apart and ferried aboard C-46s. They can make it to Israel on their own with a couple of refueling stops. But that means they must be carefully examined, repaired, and maintained in the weeks leading up to their long flight.

Al calls his new main Israeli contact—Ben-Gurion. They've kept in touch since they met. The OZ boss has given the de facto prime minister tours of Ekron and Ramat David and has updated him about key developments. If Al brings up problems, he makes sure to always propose possible solutions. This time, he tells HaZaken that he'll search for another Zebra.

Ben-Gurion asks him to fast-track that process. "We're all waiting for the Spitfires," he says.

What strikes Al about the conversation is Ben-Gurion's lack of surprise. It's almost as if he expected the Czechs to close Zebra. Or did he know?

No one ever figures out for certain why the Czechs did it. The OZ airmen come up with several theories:

- The United States pressured the Czechs into closing an air base run and manned by Americans.
- The Czech bureaucrats figured that once all the contracted weapons and Messerschmitts were sent out, the deal was done, and that included Zebra.
- The British pressured the Czechs into closing an air base that symbolized their post-WWII failures and the decline of their global influence.
- The Soviets told the Czechs to do it.

The Soviet theory intrigues Al. He's heard a rumor that Moscow offered Tel Aviv a strategic alliance. The Russians saw it as their ticket into the Middle East and as a Cold War play against the British. If true, HaZaken may have been tempted for a fleeting moment. After all, the Jewish state has no allies and needs a long-term source of military, economic, and diplomatic assistance.

But still holding out hope for an alliance with the United States, and reluctant to put American Jews in a permanently painful predicament, Ben-Gurion turned down the Soviet overture, the back-fence talk goes. This rejection caused the Russians to retaliate in Czechoslovakia, which they increasingly control.

This theory suffers from several problems, including the absence of any credible evidence and the fact that the Czechs, upon a quick check, confirm that they still wish to make the Spitfire deal with Israel.

As Ike takes off for the last time from Žatec, he hears a strange noise from the cabin. Once he reaches altitude, he puts the C-54 on autopilot and checks. He finds a young, attractive Czech woman crying among the seventy-pound bombs. After hearing about the Zebra closure, the co-pilot—a redheaded Irishman from North Miami Beach—sneaked his girlfriend onboard.

"They better not be looking for her," Ike tells his co-pilot.

Glaring at him, Ike notices that the cross dangling from his necklace features a Jewish star.

"I thought you were Catholic," Ike says.

"In this war," the co-pilot says, "I'm not taking any chances."

"You're taking quite a chance bringing her," Ike says, pointing at the woman, who has joined them in the cockpit.

Glancing lovingly at her, the co-pilot shakes his head. "The risk would've been not to bring her. I would die without her."

Two weeks later, she boards a flight from Tel Aviv to Canada to start a new life without him.

~

Facing a familiar problem—getting the planes the Jews bought out of the country that sold them—Al comes up with a tested solution. He plans to demilitarize the fifty-nine Spitfires that Dr. Felix and Avriel purchased for $23,000 each. This temporary measure accomplishes several objectives:

- It lightens the planes and makes room for additional fuel tanks.
- It cuts the number of needed refueling stops to one.

- It eliminates the main stumbling block to convincing a European country to allow the Spitfires to refuel on its soil.

Al hopes to send his men to Czechoslovakia to transfer the machine guns and cannons from the Spitfires to OZ transport planes. But the Czechs reject his request. So he turns to the Yugoslavs, who've allowed his C-46s to make numerous refueling stops.

For $200 a plane, the Yugoslavs agree.

It's game on. But despite no longer needing to take the fighters apart and fit them into transports, Al quickly realizes that this operation—titled Velvetta after the Israeli body lotion some of the airmen slather on their skin to help ward off jellyfish and other nuisances in case of a sea crash or bailout—poses an array of complications. To hedge his bets, he decides to send the Spitfires in a few rounds, starting with just six.

Al delegates the key tasks to the following personnel:

- Secure a new Zebra in Yugoslavia: IAF bomber pilot Gideon "Geda" Shochat, a former RAF officer whose talents extend way beyond the cockpit
- Set up a Spitfire repair and maintenance way station in Yugoslavia: OZ flight engineer Pomerance, an innovative aviator who earned a bachelor's in aeronautical engineering from NYU
- Equip the Spitfires with additional fuel tanks: Pomerance
- Bring the Spitfires' removed military parts to Israel: Marmelstein, who's emerged as one of OZ's logistical masters
- Put together and lead the Spitfire-flight team: Modi, the 101 Squadron leader who's become the IAF's most beloved commander
- Prepare Messerschmitts to protect the unarmed Spitfires from an Egyptian attack: Lou, who's taken on a tactical role
- Prepare a C-54 and a C-46 as navigation and emergency support aircraft, respectively: Sam, OZ chief pilot

Geda, son of kibbutz movement founder Manya Shochat, chooses the Nikšić's Kapino Polje Airport as their Yugoslav base. Code-naming it "Alabama," he lets out a hearty "yeehaw" when he hears that all the relevant parties—the host country, Al, Remez, and Pomerance—have approved it.

Pomerance gives the Spitfires fueling power. He attaches fuel tanks borrowed from the Messerschmitts to the Spitfires' wings, connects them to the main fuel tanks that stick out of the bottom of the planes like outie bellybuttons, adds cockpit controls to allow the pilots to pump fuel into the main tank, and adjusts their gauges to reflect accurate fuel readings. Simple!

Marmelstein determines that all he needs to carry the entire load of Spitfire machine guns, cannons, ammunition, and spare parts are two Norsemen. When Al asks whether he's sure, the Philadelphian answers, "One would be insufficient, and three would be overkill."

For his deputies, Modi chooses Pomerance, who's not a fighter pilot but has a single-engine flight license and will know this version of the Spitfire better than anyone, and Boris Senior, a South African WWII Spitfire pilot who, along with Ezer, attended London University and joined the Irgun.

Boris has experience bringing in aircraft. A few months earlier, he flew a Beechcraft Bonanza, a light utility plane, from South Africa to Israel.

Proud of his South African heritage, Boris winces when one of his countrymen—fighter pilot Norman "Tuxie" Blau, twenty-eight—neglects to drop his landing gear upon arriving at Nikšić in one of the Spitfires. Requiring extensive repairs, this plane stays behind when, a week later, the other five take off.

The flight goes as planned until Modi and Boris run out of fuel. Instead of refilling their main tank, Pomerance's pumps dump the petrol into the Mediterranean. They make an emergency landing in Rhodes.

It will take them several weeks—and the Spitfires several years—to make it to Israel.

~

Soon after Zebra shuts down, the OZ members receive their next major assignment: supplying besieged Israeli outposts in the Negev Desert.

Tapped to lead this effort, Leo meets with Remez, who expresses skepticism about the ATC's ability to deliver.

Remembering how nasty Remez can be, Leo brings Ike to help deflect the toxicity.

"Haven't we always?" Leo asks.

"This is different," Remez says.

"Yeah," Ike says, "it's easier."

"You Americans are all a bunch of braggarts," Remez says.

To ease Remez's mind—and get him off their backs—Leo and Ike offer to conduct a test airlift. They take off from an expanded Ekron airfield, land in the Galilee, pick up a ton of food, and deliver it to an Israeli position in the northern Negev.

It's enough for Remez to give them the go-ahead.

Additionally tasked with creating an airfield, which they build near Ruhama, the OZ pilots spend the next couple of months flying in more than 2,000 tons of medicine, weapons, food, and other supplies as well as nearly 2,000 soldiers. They also fly out more than 5,000 Israelis, including many physically and mentally beat-up troops.

Remez, who finally gets a close-up view of OZ, admits that they've made it possible to achieve one of Ben-Gurion's main goals—holding on to the Negev.

When he retires a few years later, Ben-Gurion moves to the Negev.

17

September

Besides four B-17s and four P-51s, Al buys another C-46. He gets it to Mexico City, where Hank's contacts shield it from the FBI. But the OZ boss wants to get it to Israel as soon as possible. He asks Sam to send a crew of no more than three to pick it up.

Since their arrival six weeks earlier, the B-17s have poached airmen from the air transport command, forcing Sam to bring in well-paid merchantries—mostly Swiss pilots and crews—to fly the C-46s. He decides to send only two of his pilots to Mexico City. He picks Marty—the second-best cargo captain, who is a born leader, a quick thinker, and a persuasive talker—and Harold, a smooth operator who can handle multiple roles, including radio communications, co-piloting, and, if necessary, negotiating with the likes of customs agents.

Marty and Harold ask Sam whether they can stop in the United States to see their families. The captain wants to talk to his wife, Blanche, about moving their family of five to Israel. The radio operator, who's thrilled to finally have a chance to co-pilot a C-46, needs to spend a little time with his father, who, according to his weekly letters, has lost his ability to sleep because he's so worried about his son.

Sam gives them a week. He tells them to destroy their LAPSA ID cards—the Panamanians shut down their national airline soon after they realized the C-46s would never return from their "route-survey flight." He instructs them to use their fake passports and names and enter the United States through Canada or anywhere except New York.

Doing as he's told, Marty flies to Toronto and hitches rides to his hometown of East St. Louis, Illinois. But Harold takes a TWA commercial flight to New York. It's not that he thinks he can sneak in through Idlewild Airport (which will be renamed JFK after President John F. Kennedy's assassination in 1963)—it's the opposite. He wants US authorities to stop him. He wants to tell them that they should quit criminalizing Americans for helping provide a haven for Holocaust survivors.

Harold's ready to give whoever takes him aside at Idlewild—the FBI, airport security, immigration—a piece of his hyperactive mind. When Eddie urged him to reconsider, he responded, "Let them interrogate me. I'm ready." He figures it will create a scene worthy of including in the book he might write one day. He has been thinking about what to do next. It will take him a few years to realize that he can make a good living as a writer.

At Idlewild, however, Harold faces no obstacles. The immigration official barely glances at him as she stamps his passport—his real passport, with his real name. *Doesn't she know that I'm an arms smuggler?* he thinks. *Isn't she aware that I'm an international operative who should be questioned on the spot?*

Harold will joke about it for years to come, telling Eddie during one of their many reunions, "Those bastards never paid any attention to me." But he never mentions it to his parents. His father tries to convince him to stay in the United States, preferably in their Haverhill home. His medical practice could use someone with Harold's skills.

"Are you flying to see patients?" Harold asks.

"I'm talking about your communication skills," his father says. "If you like, you can just stay home and write."

Halfway through the week, Harold has had enough. He goes to New York and checks into a different hotel every night, to "stay ahead of the FBI," which never chases him.

On his second night in Manhattan, he finds himself having drinks at a hotel bar with a middle-aged Egyptian who says he recognizes him from Cairo. Believing that Harold is a commercial pilot, the Egyptian offers him a gig: assemble a team of aviators and fly a plane from South America to Cairo.

At first, the Egyptian refuses to specify what type of plane. But the drinks, which keep coming, loosen his lips, and he sinks his ship, telling Harold it is a B-24 bomber.

Harold can picture the B-24. He's passed by it at a couple of air bases over the years. It's the ugliest plane he's ever seen, its bulging belly dragging across the tarmac and its nose turned up.

"How much would you pay us to do this?" Harold asks.

The Egyptian offers $10,000. Playing along, Harold demands twice as much, half upfront.

Harold has himself a deal. In theory. Saying he'll think about it, he writes down the contact information for the Egyptian, who says he'll be back in the same place at the same time the next couple of days.

Harold gets in touch with Al, who puts him in touch with Shamir, who happens to be in New York for a few days to take care of a sensitive matter. The IAF deputy commander tells the soon-to-be co-pilot to accept the Egyptian's assignment.

"Tell him you need a couple of weeks to assemble the team," Shamir says, "but otherwise you're all set to go."

Shamir says the Israelis will investigate this Egyptian. If he checks out, Harold will then:

- meet with him again, but this time with Marty, who'll fly in from East St. Louis and be introduced as the captain;
- recruit a navigator, a flight engineer, and a radio operator and, along with Marty, fly to South America;
- take off on the B-24 toward Cairo; and
- kill all the Egyptians onboard and divert the bomber to Israel.

"Did you say kill?"

"You can keep whatever money they give you," Shamir says.

"That's not what I'm asking," Harold says.

"We're at war," Shamir says.

Stuck on "kill," Harold nonetheless meets again with the Egyptian, who, according to Israeli intelligence, does in fact represent the Egyptian military, which has just purchased two B-24s in South America.

The Egyptian is so impressed with Harold's "hand-picked" captain, Marty, that he ups the offer to $25,000.

Afterward, Harold tells Marty he's out.

"I want to help. I really do," Harold says. "But it's just too much. I know we're going back to war, but this feels even riskier, physically and psychologically. Even if we succeed, we may never recover."

Marty agrees and notifies Shamir of their decision.

Shamir is disappointed but thanks them for their efforts.

Marty and Harold venture to Mexico City to pick up the C-46. It goes well. Harold proves to himself and everyone else what he has known all along—he can competently co-pilot a Commando, as well as probably a few other planes.

A couple weeks later, Harold reads in the papers that two Cairo-bound B-24s blew up over the South Atlantic.

~

Driving along the coast to the Port of Haifa reminds Al of his ride up the PCH to meet with the arms dealer in Ventura. The points of connection abound: the open vehicles (a convertible then, a Jeep now), the sea breeze (off the Pacific then, off the Mediterranean now), the anxiety (the FBI and CHP then, the Egyptian air force now), and the mission (buy P-51s then, pick them up now).

At the Haifa port, Al exhorts the stevedores to be careful unloading the large, heavy "agricultural material" crates. They cautiously but efficiently place them on Herzliya-bound trucks.

At the air base, Al takes a deep breath and cracks one of them open. What he sees loosens his chest and puts a smile on his face: the engine of one of the world's best fighter planes.

It takes time to reassemble and adapt the P-51s, but once they get going, they take the IAF to new heights.

In November, when former USAAF fighter pilot Wayne Peake, twenty-eight, gets his turn on the P-51, he uses its high-altitude range to unravel the reconnaissance plane mystery. The "North Carolinian Friendly Fighter Pilot," who earned this nickname for giving a pass to an enemy pilot whose gun jammed, plans to have no mercy on the Shufti Kite.

On this day, the Kite flies at the very low end of its altitude range: about 28,000 feet. Several months of unimpeded skies have given this crew a false sense of security. They figure the Israelis can never get this high.

When Wayne sneaks up on them just south of Haifa, they try to climb above the P-51's maximum altitude of about 30,000 feet, but it's too late. As his oxygen source falters, the Friendly Fighter Pilot instinctively places his finger on the M2 trigger. His vision blurred and his mind foggy, he fires a quick round before diving to suck in oxygen like a free diver coming up for air.

The lack of oxygen doubles Wayne's vision, making him see four engines and leading him to conclude that he's taken on a bomber. Later, he learns that he shot down a two-engine de Havilland Mosquito.

He's dismayed to hear he killed two RAF officers: pilot Eric Reynolds and navigator Angus Love.

No one except Ike had guessed it was a British plane.

The Shufti Kite had been taking off from its RAF air base by the Suez Canal to collect information about the Israelis for the Egyptians.

To Ike, this development provides one piece of the puzzle that shows direct RAF involvement in the war. The other bits of "evidence" come from stories he hears over beer with his 101 colleagues. Most of the time, they describe their opposition as mediocre, unimaginative, inexperienced, and often counterproductively ostentatious. But, on occasion, they marvel at the Egyptian pilots' elegant efficiency and airborne artistry.

The latter group reminds them of WWII pilots, they say.

That's because they are, Ike argues. But the 101s need tangible proof.

The downing of the Mosquito proves little, they say. So the British spy on the Israelis? So what?

What it does prove is that the P-51s give the IAF a new dimension. For instance, while providing air support to a ground offensive in the Negev, the Mustangs shoot down three Egyptian Macchi C.205 Veltro fighter planes.

Buzz, who beat two of Italy's best fighter pilots to knock two Macchis out of the Malta sky, would've been proud.

Speaking of feeling proud—a few days after picking up the P-51s, Al returns to the Port of Haifa to oversee the unloading of nearly 800 tons of weapons from Mexico and Hawaii—as well as the 1,000 tons of sugar covering them—off the SS *Kefalos*.

If only Hank could be here, Al thinks.

18

October

At the Hatzor air base, to which they have relocated after the Herzliya runway proved too hit-or-miss for landings and takeoffs, Ezer and Modi thank Giddy for volunteering to fly the just-reassembled P-51. Unlike the Messerschmitts, on which the 101 Squadron received at least some expert training, the Mustangs only come with a dense manual. The pilots must learn to fly this fighter plane while carrying out military missions.

With as serious an expression as he can muster, the 101 CO looks Giddy straight in the eyes to issue his flight orders: "This is strictly recon. Do not fire on anything, do not engage anyone, just tame this wild horse and take a look at Arab positions here and there."

"Are you positive?" Giddy asks. "This baby's better and faster than anything the Arabs got."

Modi nods. Shrugging, Giddy makes himself comfortable in the P-51—finally, a nonsuffocating cockpit—and takes off into the blue skies. Having always wanted to visit the Paris of the Middle East, he checks out Beirut. At the Bir Hassan Airfield, he spots a row of shiny fighter planes. Tempted to turn them into spare parts, he recalls his CO's words and hesitates.

Had Remez or Shamir given him these orders, Giddy would strafe the Lebanese planes and anyone who dared come near them. But he respects Modi too much. He flies east to Damascus and then south to the Suez Canal. Starting to feel like a tourist, he receives a rude awakening in the form of ferocious Egyptian anti-aircraft fire. Heading back north, he comes upon an Egyptian Hawker Sea Fury. He's never seen one. The British, who hoped to use this fighter plane against the Luftwaffe, finished building it two years after World War II.

Giddy slows down, inviting the Egyptian pilot to attack first and free him from the shackles of Modi's orders.

After a few minutes of examining him like a gamecock, the Fury pilot challenges Giddy.

His efficient, effective maneuvers surprise Giddy, who needs several tries to position his P-51 on the Fury's tail.

About to shoot, Giddy sees the Fury zip away, flying too fast to catch.

Turns out, the Arabs still have better, faster planes.

~

For the 101 Squadron, October marks a turning point. It's exerting control of the skies above the Jewish state and providing air support for Israeli troops. But it's also losing some of its best airmen.

Vickman's death has left Stan a broken man. He never pilots an aircraft again. He becomes the IDF's UN southern liaison. On a cool autumn morning, he boards a Bristol Beaufighter as an observer.

The Beaufighter's mission: bomb the Iraq Suwaydan police fortress, from which the Egyptians have blocked the main artery to the Negev Desert.

"This is what, our fourth, fifth try?" Stan asks the pilot, Leonard Fitchett, twenty-five, who flew fighters for the Royal Canadian Air Force during World War II.

Len wouldn't care if this is the fortieth or fiftieth attempt. He follows a simple motto: never, ever give up.

"Remember our orders—only one pass," says Dov Sugarman, twenty-five, a former RAF navigator whose British wife, Lily, also volunteers with the IAF.

Len rolls his eyes. He heard the orders. The IAF consider a second bombing pass over the heavily fortified Iraq Suwaydan a suicide mission. He likes to reserve judgment.

The first pass proves harmless—to the Beau and the fort. So Len comes around for a second.

The anti-aircraft fire knocks the Beau out of the sky. Stan, Len, and Dov survive the crash—but not the Egyptians, who kill them in the open desert.

A few days later, as they prepare to bomb and strafe the last of the Egyptians evacuating Isdud, Ezer suggests that, afterward, the pilots go out to celebrate this long-anticipated departure. But Modi promised to take his pregnant wife, Mina, to the Sea of Galilee for a romantic night.

Returning from the successful mission, which made the Egyptians feel they made the right decision leaving the area, Modi tries to shake out his stubborn landing gear. But what really concerns Syd, the fighter pilot taking his turn as air traffic controller, is the smoke trailing behind the Messerschmitt.

Syd tries to reach Modi. No answer.

Did Modi's engine overheat? Did his Messerschmitt take a hit when it strafed the Egyptians? Did the smoke knock him out? Or is he just preoccupied with the landing gear, which finally drops—a moment before the plane crashes and burns.

Coming in for a landing, Ezer sees the smoke and cries.

Soon, hundreds of pilots and crew members from every part of the IAF join him.

19

December 1948–January 1949

THE THREE CZECH SPITFIRES THAT MADE IT TO ISRAEL PROVE EXTREMELY useful. They allow the 101 Squadron pilots lucky enough to fly them to concentrate on the military objectives at hand instead of fighting their own planes.

The 101 pilots look forward to receiving the fifty-three other Spitfires that Israel bought from the Czechs. Planning to bring in most of them this month, the OZ members recruit more fighter pilots. They include Chalmers "Slick" Goodlin, twenty-five—a Pennsylvanian who flew Spitfires for Canada during World War II and nearly broke the sound barrier for Bell Aircraft but yielded the historical feat to Chuck Yeager because of contractual disagreements with the US Air Force—and John Frederick McElroy, twenty-eight—an Ontarian who flew with Buzz in Malta and shot down thirteen enemy planes, several of them Messerschmitts.

After managing to deliver only half of the first Spitfire batch, the OZ members express nervousness about attempting to bring in twice as many—a dozen—this time. They panic when the Yugoslavs decline their request to reuse Nikšić.

With a combination of big bribes and desperate diplomacy, Geda and Arazi reconvince the Yugoslavs. Nikšić again serves as New Zebra.

The real problem, however, lies with the fact that the OZ members believe they did things right the first time. It just did not go well. So, after long discussions, they simply repeat their procedures, hoping for a better outcome.

It turns out worse. Much worse.

Due to a storm and technical issues, two of the Spitfires end up back in the original Zebra, though not in their original shape, and one crashes into the Yugoslavian Alps, killing its pilot, Pomerance.

This part of OZ, known as Operation Velvetta, never recovers from the unexpected death of its de facto leader, the pilot most familiar with the rigged version of the plane.

In the end, most of the remaining forty-seven Spitfires are taken apart, placed in crates, and sent to Israel on ships.

This unusual OZ failure embarrasses Al. But he considers admitting defeat and using ships a far better alternative than losing half the planes or any more of his men.

~

The Spitfires play a particularly pivotal—and, some say, peculiar—role on the last day of the fighting with Egypt in January 1949.

As the war's tail-end, the IAF skirmishes with a foe that represents a greater threat than the Arabs—the RAF. After Wayne shoots down the Mosquito, the 101 pilots do their best to avoid confrontations with the British. But on the day a cease-fire with Egypt is to take effect, they find themselves in stupefying dogfights.

It begins when McElroy and Chalmers—who hates the nickname Slick, preferring to be called Chal—fly south to help protect an Israeli column coming under fire from what the IAF assumes are four Egyptian Spitfires.

Seeing the unmarked Spitfires diving to strafe Israeli troops escaping from burning trucks, Chal and McElroy hover above, waiting for the enemy to surface. They regulate their breathing, realizing they're going up against advanced versions of the British fighter: FR18s, which are faster and more robust than their LF9s.

As the enemy Spitfires bounce off their strafing dives, Chal and McElroy attack. They shoot down three of the enemy planes, two of which eject their pilots.

The third downed Spitfire crashes into the sand and explodes with its pilot, Ron Sayers, still in the cockpit.

During the aerial showdown, when all he can do is fight for his life, Chal recognizes the opposition as RAF. He mentions it after they land in Hatzor, but McElroy refuses to believe it. He even dismisses the news that the two ejected enemy pilots, captured by Israeli soldiers, are British officers. How is that possible?

Well, it is. And it's not over. At the same time, Ezer leads four IAF Spitfires in a dogfight against four RAF Spitfires and seven Hawker Tempests, British fighter planes that are even better than the Spitfire FR18s.

The 101 Squadron also wins this round, which turns out to be the last. The IAF's Bill Schroeder, twenty-seven, a US Navy pilot during World War II, shoots down an RAF Tempest, killing its pilot, David Tattersfield.

Ezer and the other two 101 pilots put three additional RAF Tempests out of commission.

But after they land back in Hatzor, the 101 pilots refrain from celebrating. Instead, they prepare for RAF retaliation.

It never comes. Although the United Kingdom threatens a full-fledged war if the IAF continues to antagonize its forces, it never does more than issue statements. Israel releases the British pilots, Schroeder writes a condolence letter to the Tattersfield family, and the 101 Squadron telegrams the RAF a sort of an apology: "Sorry about yesterday, but you were on the wrong side of the fence. Come over and have a drink sometime. You will see many familiar faces."

IAF vs. US Marines

After the war ends in 1949, the IAF basketball team, led by Lee, plays a friendly match with the US Marines who are stationed in Jerusalem.

To avoid inviting quarries about their illegal involvement in the war, the IAF team's three American players pretend not to speak English.

The Israeli Air Force leader, Remez, sits at midcourt next to the Marine commander, a colonel.

Lee dominates the game. But, as he says later, he "pays the price." When he goes in for a layup, the Marines foul him hard. When he stands his ground to defend his turf, they shove him.

Late in the game, with the IAF well ahead, a Marine elbows Lee in the back right in front of Remez and the colonel.

Lee lets fly a series of four-letter words. All in English.

The color drains from Remez's face. The Marines are shocked.

"I went into quite a tirade," Lee will later recall.

After the game, which the IAF wins 42–18 and during which Lee personally outscores the Marines by five points, the colonel tells the Israeli-American point guard, "Not only do I know you're an American, I know you were in the navy."

THE TRIAL

Toward the end of the 1948 war, Al, Leo, Sam, and Willie discover that the US attorney general has put out warrants for their arrest. Over warm, thick pita bread, creamy hummus, and lamb shish kebab at a Tel Aviv hole-in-the-wall, they decide to turn themselves in.

All except for Sam have been planning to return to the United States. Sam has become El Al's first captain. Although he intends to stay with Israel's national airline until retirement, the former OZ chief pilot wants to, as he says, "go back to the States to face the music."

Joined by Hank, Ray, and a few others, the OZ leaders spend a couple of nights in a federal prison in Los Angeles. Although the Jewish Agency has provided them with the 24/7 service of a top law firm, they know the odds are stacked against them. After all, they broke several laws, smuggled weapons, and toyed with the FBI, which has built quite a file against them.

To lower their slim chances of acquittal, the prosecution and the media have portrayed the OZ members as communists in the midst of the Red Scare. They harp on such details as the operation members' work behind the Iron Curtain and their stay at a hotel called Stalingrad.

The OZ members know they cannot fool the judge. Peirson Hall is *the* aviation-law authority in the federal judicial system. Their only hope lies with the jurors. So they implore their attorneys to pick wisely.

As the attorneys impanel the jury on the first day of the trial at the Federal Courthouse in LA, Lee, who's back at UCLA, shows up in the courtroom. He notices a familiar face among the potential jurors. He racks his brain. It comes back to him: This is Michael Chlavin, the Bruin who rebutted their classmate's anti–Jewish state speech a couple of years earlier.

Lee whispers in Leo's ear to advise their attorneys to put Michael on the jury.

They succeed.

At the end of the trial, Michael agrees with the other jurors on the obvious verdict but insists that they stipulate no prison time. Unsure how to handle it, they take the matter to the judge, who initially refuses to even discuss the sentence. But after sending them back for more deliberations, which produce the same results, Hall accepts the guilty verdict's leniency condition.

The only defendant found not guilty is Sam, who charms a female juror. She insists that he was "not part of the conspiracy." The former OZ chief pilot disagrees, but he is in no position to argue.

The other OZ leaders receive $10,000 fines, which the Jewish Agency pays, and lose their civil rights.

"Great," a pregnant Fanya tells her husband, Ray. "The father of my baby is a convicted felon."

"Better than going to federal prison," Ray says.

Fanya is not convinced, saying, "You can't vote, you can't carry a firearm, you can't get a job."

In two other trials, Swifty and Charlie also receive guilty verdicts. The former gets off for time served, while the latter spends eighteen months in prison in Tallahassee, Florida.

Al

After the trial, Al gets used to his routine. He likes sleeping in the same bed every night and going to the same place every morning. Unlike some of his OZ colleagues, he does not miss the intense action, migraine-inducing pressure, breakneck pace, or constant danger.

Al finds working at the original OZ headquarters surreal. He always hesitates before entering the Lockheed Air Terminal in Burbank. This sun-splashed spring morning is no different. As he arrives, he senses his chest tightening and his breathing shortening. He glances over his shoulder. But, as he does every morning, he eases back into his new "normal" existence after seeing that the coast is clear. Although the FBI continues to monitor his activities—and will do so for the next several decades—it now avoids suffocating him, giving him space to restart his life.

He takes full advantage of it. He becomes a legitimate entrepreneur. No more arms smuggling and quasi-legal maneuvers. No more duping governments or overloading transport planes. Running a small cargo and airplane-repair business, Al employs a dozen aviators and mechanics, offers a maintenance service to similar companies, and uses the Connie he's received as a thank-you from Ben-Gurion to transport goods for local clients. In the coming months, he plans to buy another plane.

Everything changes a few hours later, when two unexpected guests show up: Ben-Gurion and his protégé, Shimon Peres, twenty-seven, who represents the Israel Ministry of Defense in the United States. They make Al an offer: move this outfit to Israel, turn it into a government-owned enterprise, increase your budget twentyfold overnight, expand substantially in coming years, and serve a country instead of a county.

To Peres's surprise and Ben-Gurion's delight, Al accepts on the spot. He permanently relocates to the Jewish state to form Bedek Aviation, bringing twenty mechanics from the United States and hiring sixty Israelis.

He switches from worrying about the FBI to butting heads with the IAF. The new commander, Hayim Laskov, and his chief of staff, Dan Tolkowsky, who will take over the top spot a couple of years later, resist the idea of Bedek in general and Al running their maintenance in particular. They argue that the infant Jewish state lacks the means to do more than just basic repairs, which should be done by the Israeli Air Force, not by a separate governmental company.

When they learn that Al's plans include such "crazy" goals as building Israel's first military planes, they wage war against him.

They escalate their attacks once his protector, Ben-Gurion, retires in 1953. Although HaZaken returns as prime minister in 1955, Laskov and Tolkowsky capitalize on his absence to throw bureaucratic and political obstacles in Al's way.

Yet Al feels more at home in Israel than he's ever felt anywhere. If Laskov and Tolkowsky hope to send him packing, they're wasting their time. Although he never learns Hebrew, this American is here for the long haul.

Luckily, Al has Peres, who becomes his lifelong friend and collaborator. Returning from the United States to direct the Ministry of Defense just as Ben-Gurion takes his two-year mental health day, the future president fully backs the former OZ leader. He makes it clear that Al's work continues to be crucial to Israel's survival. The Jewish state still desperately needs arms, particularly advanced weapons and planes.

As Peres forges a strategic cooperation with France based on the two unlikely allies' mutual interests in the Middle East (which include keeping Egypt's regional ambitions in check), Al's value increases. The first major arms deal with the French calls for Israel to build its version of a French jet—the Fouga CM.170 Magister.

When the IAF starts training its pilots with the Fouga—something it will do for the next half century—it shifts its attitude toward Al. He goes from goat to hero.

Less than two decades later, Al leads the government-owned company, now called Israel Aircraft Industries (IAI), in building another Israeli version—Kfir (Hebrew for "lion cub") fighter—of a French plane: Dassault Mirage-5.

This time, he does it with no cooperation from France, which terminates its alliance with the Jewish state in the 1960s.

A couple of years after he unveils the Kfir, Al resigns from IAI under duress. Upon becoming defense minister, Ezer Weizman, who flew the Messerschmitts that OZ brought in alongside pilots the operation recruited, forces Al out. By then, IAI is one of the country's biggest employers and one of the world's most innovative military aviation manufacturers. Among other feats, it becomes one of the first to develop drones.

Al, who stays in Israel for the rest of his life, becomes the government's aviation consultant. In the 1980s, he helps ship US weapons to Iran as part of President Ronald Reagan's Iran-Contra Affair.

In 2001, Al receives a pardon from President Bill Clinton.

Ten years later, Al dies on his ninety-fourth birthday. Although far from anonymous, he never becomes part of Israel's folklore. In fact, few Jews have any idea that he played an absolutely crucial role in the creation of the Jewish state.

Afterword

Yehuda Arazi: After helping to launch and sustain Operation Zebra as the Haganah's representative to the United States, the King of Disguises developed properties and businesses in Central Israel. He died in 1959, a year after Leon Uris published *Exodus*. The best-selling author based the book's protagonist, Ari Ben Canaan, on Arazi.

Hal Auerbach: The OZ all-purpose pilot moved to Carmel, California, and became a financial advisor. He died in 2006.

Nahum Bernstein: OZ's financial point person at the Haganah established a Tel Aviv office for Bernstein, Seawell, Kove, and Maltin to attract US businesses to Israel. He died in 1983.

Sheldon "Ike" Eichel: The OZ transport pilot became a businessman in South Florida. He kept in close touch with several OZ members, including Eddie, Giddy, Harold, and Leon. He remained convinced his whole life that the British flew combat missions against the Israeli Air Force in 1948–1949. He died in 2015.

Leon Frankel: The OZ fighter pilot returned to his used-car dealership in Minot, North Dakota. He retired in Minnetonka, Minnesota. He kept in close contact with several OZ members, including Al, Eddie, Giddy, and Ike. He died in 2015.

Leo Gardner: The OZ transport pilot became El Al's second captain. He spent his professional life flying for Israel. His flights included top-secret missions. In 1958, he was arrested in Algeria with Gordon. Leo retired in Boca Raton, Florida. He died in 2003.

Coleman "Collie" Goldstein: The OZ transport and fighter pilot became a pilot for Israel's national airline. After thirty-five years with El Al, he retired in Philadelphia. He died in 2015.

Chalmers "Slick" Goodlin: The OZ fighter pilot supplied equipment and parts to airlines. In 1960, he took over the Burnelli Company, a controversial aviation-design innovator. He retired in Coral Gables, Florida. He never accomplished what he set out to do after World War II—fly at supersonic speed. He died in 2005.

Hank Greenspun: OZ's lead arms smuggler bought and published the *Las Vegas Sun*. He became the first journalist to take on Senator Joseph McCarthy for his anti-communist tactics. He received a pardon from President John F. Kennedy. He died in 1989.

Lou Lenart: The OZ fighter pilot who led the Israeli Air Force's first aerial assault ran logistics for the IAF, airlifted Jews from Iraq to Israel in the 1950s, flew for El Al, produced films, and managed the Clippers, one of Los Angeles's two NBA teams, in the 1980s. He split his time between Santa Monica and the Israeli city he helped save, Tel Aviv. He died in 2015.

Gordon Levett: The OZ fighter and transport pilot became commander of the 106 Squadron. He retired several years later from the IAF as a lieutenant colonel. He returned to London and flew for several airlines, including El Al. Some of his flights were top-secret Israeli missions. He died in 2000.

Sam Lewis: The OZ chief pilot became El Al's first captain. He divorced his wife Jean to marry a younger Israeli. A decade later, he divorced the Israeli and remarried Jean. In 1992, he received a gift from the Mossad: a pen that could fire bullets. One day, it went off while he played with it. The man who had cheated death for decades died instantly.

Gideon "Giddy" Lichtman: The first Israeli Air Force pilot to shoot down an enemy fighter plane flew combat for the US Air Force in the Korean War. He became a test pilot in Israel in the 1960s. He taught high school math in Miami for a couple of decades. He retired in Pembroke Pines, Florida. He died in 2018.

Harold Livingston: The OZ radio operator and trainer became an author and a Hollywood screenwriter, writing the first *Star Trek* movie in 1979. He received an Academy Award nomination. He wrote many episodes of the *Mission: Impossible* TV show in the 1960s and 1970s. He lives in Los Angeles.

Phil Marmelstein: The OZ transport pilot became an IAF flight instructor. He airlifted more than 10,000 Jews from Yemen, Iraq, and Iran to Israel. He flew for El Al. He returned to Philadelphia to get married and made a living in manufacturing. He died in 2014.

John Frederick McElroy: The OZ fighter pilot rejoined the RCAF as a flight instructor. He retired from the Royal Canadian Air Force in 1964 and became a realtor.

Bill Novick: The OZ transport pilot attended medical school and became an ENT doctor at McGill University's Department of Otolaryngology. He still practices medicine at his private office in Montreal. A tennis player, he's represented Canada in the Jewish Olympics, known as the Maccabiah Games.

Bernarr McFadden "Pat" Ptacek: The FBI's lead investigator of Operation Zebra left the agency in 1954 to run security at the Southern California Edison Company and, later, the San Onofre Nuclear Plant. He retired in Rancho Bernardo, California, in 1974. His son, Edward, graduated from Stanford. Pat died in 2007.

Martin "Marty" Ribakoff: The OZ transport pilot worked for Seaboard Transportation. He quit in the mid-1950s to become a flight instructor. He retired in Winter Park, Florida. He died in 1995.

Milton "Milt" Rubenfeld: The OZ fighter pilot became a businessman in New York and Sarasota, Florida. He was the father of Paul Reubens, also known as Pee-wee Herman. Milt died in 2004.

Irvin "Swifty" Schindler: The OZ transport pilot who made possible two of the operation's three main fake airlines flew for El Al. He returned to the United States a couple of years later to become an antique dealer, a real-estate developer, and a Miami radio talk-show host. He died in 2007.

Reynold "Ray" Selk: The OZ repair shop supervisor's marriage to Fanya and life fell apart. He died heartbroken and poor in 1974.

Boris Senior: The OZ fighter pilot became deputy commander of the IAF. He retired in 1952 as a colonel. He stayed in Israel, living in Kfar Shmaryahu for the rest of his life. He became a filmmaker and Lithuania's honorary consul in the Holy Land. He died in 2004.

Lee Silverman: The American volunteer to the Israeli Air Force became a Maccabi Tel Aviv point guard but had to leave mid-season to take care of his sick mother in Los Angeles. He graduated from UCLA. He moved to Israel in 1984. He's Israel's No. 1 tennis player in his age group. He won two gold medals in the 2009 Maccabiah Games.

William "Willie" Sosnow: The OZ chief mechanic worked in his field in California. He died in 1967.

Eddie Styrak: The OZ radio operator and geopolitical analyst spent his life as a merchant marine. He stopped in Haifa as much as possible to see his old friends. He never married. He retired in San Francisco and died in 2011.

Ezer Weizman: The sabra IAF pilot oversaw operations for the Israeli military. In 1958, he took command of the IAF. He led the destruction, on the ground, of more than three hundred Egyptian planes during the first day of the 1967 Six-Day War. He became minister of defense in Begin's administration in 1977 and president in 1993. He died in 2005.

Charlie Winters: The Irish businessman who sold OZ three B-17 bombers became a chef in Puerto Rico. He died in 1984. He's buried in Israel. He received a posthumous pardon from President George W. Bush.

Time Line

1947

February
- The British declare their intention to end their Mandate of Palestine.
- The British ask the United Nations to study the Palestine issue and make recommendations.

March
- Sam Lewis becomes TWA's first Jewish captain.
- Radio operator Eddie Styrak gets thrown into a British prison in Palestine for trying to bring in illegal immigrants.
- President Harry S. Truman uses FBI agent Bernarr McFadden "Pat" Ptacek's work in crafting the Loyalty Act.

April
- TWA flight engineer Adolph "Al" Schwimmer goes to the Haganah office in New York with his idea to bypass the British blockade of Palestine by flying in the Holocaust survivors.
- Eddie helps the Irgun prepare for its daring Acre Prison escape.
- Truman reactivates the 1930s Neutrality Act.
- The FBI assigns Pat to investigate the Palestinian Jews' arms procurement in the United States.
- Eddie is released from prison and returns to the United States.

May
- The Soviet Union's UN representative, Andrei Gromyko, shocks the world by proposing splitting Palestine between the Arabs and the Jews.

- The UN forms the Special Committee on Palestine.
- Pat starts investigating Al.
- Al fails to sell the Haganah on his refugee-flying idea.

July

- Yehuda Arazi becomes the Haganah's arms procurement chief in the United States.
- Arazi asks Al to form a fake airline to prepare to airlift weapons to the Jewish community in Palestine.
- Al sets up a Schwimmer Aviation shop in Burbank, California.
- The British block the SS *Exodus* from bringing 4,500 Holocaust survivors into Palestine.

September

- The UN committee recommends splitting Palestine between the Arabs and Jews.
- The Soviet Union champions this recommendation, which becomes known as the Partition Plan.
- Al launches Operation Yakum Purkan to create the Palestinian Jewish community's air transport command (ATC).
- Al leads a clandestine campaign to recruit pilots, crew members, and mechanics in the United States and Canada.

October

- OZ members Hank Greenspun and Willie Sosnow steal machine guns from a US Navy yard in Hawaii.
- OZ members buy C-46s and Connies from the US War Assets Administration.
- Al sets up a second Schwimmer Aviation shop in Millville, New Jersey.

November

- In the days leading up to the vote, Gromyko, the Soviets' UN representative, strongly advocates the passage of the Partition Plan.
- The United States votes for the Partition Plan.
- The United Nations passes the Partition Plan by a 33–13 vote, with 10 abstentions.

December

- The United States imposes an arms embargo on the Middle East, keeping the Palestinian Jews from acquiring desperately needed weapons.
- Hank's machine guns, as well as airplane spare parts and engines, arrive in Los Angeles.
- Pat shuts down Schwimmer Aviation.
- Al and Arazi transfer their planes to Service Airways.
- The Palestinian Jews strike a secret, large arms deal with Czechoslovakia.

1948

January

- Hank brings the stolen machine guns to Mexico.
- Golda Meyerson (later Meir) raises $50 million for the Haganah's arms procurement.

February

- Members of Congress and other American leaders challenge the US arms embargo.
- OZ makes recruiting progress in the United States and Canada.
- The OZ Burbank and Millville shops, as well as its key members, are under FBI surveillance.

March

- Al and Hank buy weapons from Mexico, opening the door to purchasing American fighter planes from the same source.
- OZ members complete picking up the C-46s and Connies that they have purchased.
- Labeling the Partition Plan "impossible to implement," the United States comes up with and advocates a UN Trusteeship that would curtail the creation of a Jewish state.
- The US State Department declares that, starting April 15, it must clear every aircraft export—from planes to parts.
- The Jews launch Operation Balak to airlift the Czech arms.
- The Jews buy ten Messerschmitt fighter planes from the Czechs.
- Pat threatens to close Service Airways.

- Al and Irvin "Swifty" Schindler come up with the idea of serving as Panama's national airline.

April
- Panama approves Al and Swifty's proposal, allowing them to transfer their thirteen planes to Lineas Aereas de Panama (LAPSA).
- The OZ/LAPSA planes leave the United States.
- The first Czech arms shipments arrive in Palestine.
- The Czechs prepare to train the OZ fighter pilots on the Messerschmitts.
- The OZ fighter pilots—who hail from the United States, South Africa, and Palestine—gather in Rome.
- Sam arrives in Panama in a Connie.
- An OZ/LAPSA C-46 crashes upon takeoff from Mexico City, killing its pilots.
- The Haganah buys twenty Noorduyn C-64 Norsemen from Germany.
- OZ members start ferrying the Canadian-made single-engine planes to Palestine.

May
- The OZ planes leave Panama for Czechoslovakia.
- The Czechs train OZ fighter pilots.
- Israel's founding father, David Ben-Gurion, declares independence.
- Five neighboring militaries invade newborn Israel.
- The Egyptians and Syrians control the skies, bombing Israeli civilian populations and military installations on a daily basis.
- OZ transport pilots Sheldon "Ike" Eichel and Norman Moonitz crash-land their C-46 in Israel.
- OZ's top fighter pilot, Canadian ace George Frederick "Buzz" Beurling, and Leonard Cohen die while test-flying a Norseman in Rome.
- OZ fighter pilot Lou Lenart leads Israel's first air attack, stopping the Egyptian advance on Tel Aviv.
- OZ fighter pilot Milton "Milt" Rubenfeld leads Israel's second air attack, blocking the Iraqi drive to split the new country in half.

June

- Modi Alon is the first Israeli Air Force (IAF) pilot to shoot down an enemy plane.
- Gideon "Giddy" Lichtman is the first IAF pilot to win a dogfight.
- The OZ members stay out of Israel's short-lived-but-scary civil war, which erupts when the Irgun, an extremist Jewish organization, brings in a ship full of French arms.
- Al buys four B-17 bombers in the United States.
- One of the B-17s is grounded in Tulsa, Oklahoma.
- Al and OZ deputy chief pilot Leo Gardner take the grounded B-17, but it never makes it to Zebra.
- The other three B-17s fly from Miami to Žatec.
- Al buys four North American Aviation P-51 Mustangs and an additional C-46.

July

- The B-17s are repaired and remilitarized in Žatec.
- On the way to Israel, they bomb Cairo, Gaza, and El Arish.

August

- The Czechs shut down Zebra.
- The Czechs sell Israel fifty-nine Spitfire fighter planes.
- The OZ members are on a roll on all fronts: airlifting weapons, bombing the enemies, and gaining control of the skies.
- The OZ members prepare the Spitfires for their flights to Israel.

September

- Al picks up two of the P-51s in Haifa.
- Three Spitfires arrive in Israel.

October

- Modi dies in a Messerschmitt crash.
- The 101 Squadron makes good use of the Spitfires.

December

- Most of the fifty-nine Spitfires arrive in Israel.
- An Egyptian newspaper, *al Musri*, exposes OZ with "Secrets of the Jewish Air Force."

1949

- The IAF Spitfires shoot down four RAF planes.
- Israel wins its first war.
- The war ends on March 10.
- The OZ leaders' trial in a federal court in Los Angeles begins.

1950

- Ten of the eleven OZ members tried are found guilty.
- Only one, Charlie Winters, serves a prison sentence.
- Charlie and the rest lose their civil rights.

Code Names

Here are the code names used by the operation members, as well as their Yishuv/Israeli partners:

Žatec, Czechoslovakia = Zebra
Tel Aviv = Tulsa
Israel = Oklahoma
United States = Detroit
Panama = Latin Detroit
Ajaccio, Corsica = Jockstrap
Nikšić, Yugoslavia = Alabama
Al Schwimmer = Ervin L. Johnson
Yehuda Arazi = Albert Miller
Aharon Remez = Roni
Hyman Shechtman = Norman
Connie = Cadillac
C-46 = Dodge
Messerschmitt = Knife
Dollars = Stephans
Rifles = Pipes
Machine guns = Machines
Bullets = Nails
SS *Kefalos* = *Dromit*

Bibliography

ACADEMIC PAPERS

Bloch, Alex. "The Fouga Airplane Project." *Israel Studies* 9, no. 2 (Summer 2004): 1–33.

Frank, Haggai, Zdeněk Klíma, and Yossi Goldstein. "The First Israeli Weapons Procurement behind the Iron Curtain: The Decisive Impact on the War of Independence." *Israel Studies* 22, no. 3 (Fall 2017): 125–52.

Karsh, Efraim. "The Collusion That Never Was: King Abdallah, the Jewish Agency and the Partition of Palestine." *Journal of Contemporary History* 34, no. 4 (October 1999): 569–85.

Nardulli, Bruce R. "Dance of Swords: U.S. Military Assistance to Saudi Arabia, 1942–1964." Dissertation, Ohio State University, 2002.

Rockaway, Robert A. "Hoodlum Hero: The Jewish Gangster as Defender of His People, 1919–1949." *American Jewish History* 82, no. 1/4 (1994): 215–35.

Slonim, Shlomo. "The 1948 American Embargo on Arms to Palestine." *Political Science Quarterly* 94, no. 3 (Autumn 1979): 495–514.

Tzahor, Zeev. "The 1949 Air Clash between the Israeli Air Force and the RAF." *Journal of Contemporary History* 28, no. 1 (January 1993): 75–101.

Ziv, Guy. "Shimon Peres and the French-Israeli Alliance, 1954–9." *Journal of Contemporary History* 45, no. 2 (April 2010): 406–29.

ARCHIVES

American Jewish Historical Society, New York
George C. Marshall Foundation
Harry S. Truman Presidential Library
Israel Government Press Office
Israeli Air Force
Machal Archives, University of Florida, Gainesville
United Nations Archives

ARTICLES

Asser, Martin. "Obstacles to Arab-Israeli Peace: Palestinian Refugees." BBC News, September 2, 2010.

"Bergson Group." *Encyclopedia of America's Response to the Holocaust.* Washington, DC: David S. Wyman Institute for Holocaust Studies.

Dvir, Boaz. "A Holocaust Survivor's German Rifle." *The Times of Israel,* May 27, 2013.

———. "The Late Lou Lenart Always Played Hard to Get." *The Times of Israel,* May 27, 2015.

———. "Why We Should Cheer World War II Operatives for Israel, but not Jonathan Pollard." *The Conversation,* September 2, 2015.

———. "World War II Veterans Offer Pearls of Wisdom." *Las Vegas Sun,* September 2, 2015.

———. "Rethinking the Notion of a Second Holocaust." *Centre Daily Times,* April 28, 2016.

Karsh, Efraim. "How Harry Truman Crossed His Own State Department to Recognize Israel in 1948." *Mosaic,* April 16, 2018.

Kugel, Herb. "Canadian Fighter Ace George Beurling: The Falcon of Malta." Warfare History Network, December 3, 2018.

Lenzner, Robert. "Al Schwimmer, an American Unsung Hero for the State of Israel." *Forbes,* June 12, 2011.

Leone, Dario. "Here's How Israel Managed to Get Three Second Hand B-17 Flying Fortress Bombers." *The Aviationist,* July 22, 2014.

Los Angeles Times [coverage of the trials of the Operation Zebra leadership], November 1949–February 1950.

Smith, Terence. "Israel Unveils the Kfir, a New Supersonic Jet Fighter." *New York Times,* April 15, 1975.

Valenta, Jiri, and Leni Friedman Valenta. "The Birth of Israel: Prague's Crucial Role." *Middle East Quarterly* (Winter 2019).

BOOKS

Avidor, Zvi, and Shlomo Aloni. *Hammers: Israel's Long-Range Heavy Bomber Arm.* Atglen, PA: Schiffer, 2010.

Barahona, Renato. *The Odyssey of the Ship with Three Names.* Reno, NV: Center for Basque Studies, 2014.

Collins, Larry, and Dominique Lapierre. *O Jerusalem!* New York: Simon & Schuster, 1988.

Levett, Gordon. *Flying under Two Flags: Ex-RAF Pilot in Israel's War of Independence.* London: Frank Cass, 1994.

Livingston, Harold. *No Trophy No Sword: An American Volunteer in the Israeli Air Force during the 1948 War of Independence.* Berlin: Edition Q, 1994.

Sacharov, Eliahu. *Out of the Limelight: Events, Operations, Missions, and Personalities in Israeli History.* Jerusalem, Israel: Gefen, 2004.

Senior, Boris. *New Heavens: My Life as a Fighter Pilot and a Founder of the Israel Air Force.* Aviation Classics. New York: Simon & Schuster, 2006.

Slater, Leonard. *The Pledge.* New York: Simon & Schuster, 1970.

Weis, Craig, and Jeffery Weis. *I Am My Brother's Keeper: American Volunteers in Israel's War for Independence 1947–1949*. Atglen, PA: Schiffer Military History, 1998.

COURT RECORDS

The United States v. Adolph W. Schwimmer, Abraham Levin, Leon Gardner, William Sosnow, Herman Greenspun, Ray Selk, J. Leonard, Sam Lewis, Service Airways. Conspiracy to Violate Neutrality Act & Export Control Law. Criminal Docket, April 6, 1949, Central District of California.

The United States v. Adolph W. Schwimmer, Ray Selk, Elynor Rudnick, Sam Lewis, Service Airways. Conspiracy to Make False Statement to the Government; False Statement: Export Control Act. Criminal Docket, April 6, 1949, Central District of California.

United States of America v. Adolph W. Schwimmer, et al. Reporter's Transcripts of Proceedings, October 25, 1949, Southern District of California, Central Division Los Angeles.

United States of America v. Adolph W. Schwimmer, et al. Reporter's Transcripts of Proceedings, February 5, 1950, Southern District of California, Central Division Los Angeles.

United States of America v. Adolph W. Schwimmer, et al. Reporter's Transcripts of Proceedings, February 9, 10, and 20, 1950, Southern District of California, Central Division Los Angeles.

DOCUMENTARY

Dvir, Boaz. *A Wing and a Prayer*. PBS, 2015.

DOCUMENTS

Al Schwimmer's pardon from President Bill Clinton, January 20, 2001.
Operation Zebra B-17 flightlog showing the bombing of Cairo, June 20, 1948.

GOVERNMENT REPORTS

FBI File No. 972912-603 on Al Schwimmer, September 19, 1949.
FBI File No. 65-15301 on Al Schwimmer, April 26–May 26, 1950.
FBI File No. 76101 on Nahum Bernstein, June 1, 1950.
Nicolas, L. B. FBI Memo on Hank Greenspun, March 31, 1952.
Thomas, Clayton. "Arms Sales in the Middle East: Trends and Analytical Perspectives for U.S. Policy." Washington, DC: Congressional Research Service, October 11, 2017.

INTERVIEWS

Brown, Sandra, Los Angeles, California, 2009–2013
Eichel, Sheldon, Pembroke Pines, Florida, 2010–2014
Frankel, Leon, Minneapolis, Minnesota, 2009–2014
Gardner, Leo, Boca Raton, Florida, 1995–1998
Goldman, Ralph, Jerusalem, Israel, 2010
Goldstein, Collie, Philadelphia, Pennsylvania, 2010
Gshur, Benny, Jerusalem, Israel, 2010
Harman, David, Jerusalem, Israel, 2010

Lenart, Lou, Los Angeles, California, 2011–2013
Lichtman, Gideon, Miami, Florida, 2008–2011
Livingston, Harold, Los Angeles, California, 2010–2018
Lowenstein, Ralph, Gainesville, Florida, 2008–2018
Marmelstein, Phil, Philadelphia, Pennsylvania, 2010
Novick, Bill, Montreal, Canada, 2010
Ribakoff, David, Orlando, Florida, 2011–2013
Ribakoff, Lawrence, Orlando, Florida, 2011–2013
Rothstein, Harold, Melbourne, Florida, and Chicago, Illinois, 2014–2016
Schwimmer, Al, Tel Aviv, Israel, 2010–2011
Schwimmer, Rina, Tel Aviv, Israel, 2010–2013
Shapiro, Danny, Haifa, Israel, 2010
Silverman, Lee, Holon, Israel, 2010
Soll, Fanya, Beverly Hills, California, 2009
Styark, Eddie, San Francisco, California, 2009
Unnamed 101 Squadron General Dynamics F-16 Fighting Falcon Pilot, Israel, 2010
Weizman, Reuma, Israel, 2010
Zdeněk, Klima, Prague and Žatec, Czech Republic, 2010–2013

WEBSITES
Jewish Virtual Library: https://www.jewishvirtuallibrary.org.
World Machal, Volunteers from Overseas in the Israel Defense Forces: http://machal.org.il.